PUBLIC FINANCE

Volume–I

S.N. Chand

Published by

ATLANTIC

PUBLISHERS & DISTRIBUTORS (P) LTD

7/22, Ansari Road, Darya Ganj, New Delhi-110002
Phones : +91-11-40775252, 40775214, 23273880, 23275880
Fax: +91-11-23285873
Web: www.atlanticbooks.com
E-mail: orders@atlanticbooks.com

Reprint 2018, 2022, 2023

Printed & bound in India by Atlantic Print Services

Preface

Centuries ago, Kalidasa, one of the greatest poets of the world, remarked, "It is only for the good of the people that the king collects taxes from them just as the sun draws moisture from the earth only to give it back a thousand fold." Since Kalidasa told so, the science of Public Finance has developed much further and its importance has grown manifold, yet what has been remarked by the poet still explains the nature and scope of Public Finance. As is clear in the verdict of the poet, the science of Public Finance studies the collection of revenue from the public and its spending for the welfare of the public.

Public Finance is simply a study of income and expenditure of governments. Although an important part of Economics, Public Finance, to some extent as a science, is older than Economics itself. Indeed, it was the forerunner of the science to which it is now subordinate, for the writing of the cameralists dealt more fully with this part of the field of political economy than with any other. In the last 15 years or so every branch of Economics has had to go through various degrees of change under the impact of Keynesian New Economics. Many foreign writers on Public Finance have realized this fact and have, therefore, attempted to recast Public Finance theory by incorporating Keynesian analysis. Indian writers, however, have, by and large, modelled their treatment of the subject on the once famous but now considerably out-of-date Dalton's Public Finance. Present edition is a dependable book covering the vast area of Public Finance. Theory, Revenue, Debt, and Expenditure— all aspects of the subject have been dealt with.

Construction of the chapters and enlisting of questions have been done after making wide analysis of the university questions and syllabi prescribed for Economics and Commerce in all the

Indian universities. Thus, this book caters to the academic needs of the postgraduate, graduate and under graduate students and is equally useful for MBA and is M.Com. courses. Besides, the aspiring candidates of various competitive examinations will find this book highly useful, informative and comprehensive. Even for the teachers and researchers, it will prove an ideal reference book. It is also beneficial for those who are in executive jobs, and those associated with policy and decision-making bodies.

Every effort has been made to make the style lucid, racy, coherent and the approach analytical. I am grateful to all those whose expert opinion and erudite scholarship have been cited or substantially reproduced in the book.

I take this opportunity to express my sincere thanks to all those persons who directly or indirectly helped me in bringing out this book. Also, I thank my family who put up with the stresses as deadlines approached and writing was taken up.

Suggestions and constructive criticisms for improvement of the book will be highly appreciated and gratefully acknowledged.

The preface of the book will not be complete without expressing a great sense of gratitude to Shri Manish Kumar Gupta, Managing Director and Shri Ashish Kumar Gupta, Executive Director of Atlantic Publishers & Distributors (P) Ltd., New Delhi, for their very kind accord and permission to publish this book of mine for the benefit of students and teachers of this subject. Further, I extend my sincere thanks to the management staff of my publishers for their help and mutual cooperation for bringing out this edition in a very short span of time.

S.N. Chand

Contents

VOLUME - II

Public Finance: An Overview

1

INTRODUCTION

Public finance is a study of the financial aspects of the government. A well-known author of the 19th century, Charles. F. Bastables, states: "Public finance deals with expenditure and income of public authorities of the state and their mutual relation as also with the financial administration and control." It is the field of 'Economics' devoted to the study of how government policy, especially tax and expenditure policy, affects the economy and the welfare of its citizens. It is one of the most exciting areas in political economy. This book develops the tools that are most useful for the economic analysis of government policies, and it illustrates their application to a variety of the most important tax and expenditure programmes. Thus, various tools of public finance can be utilised as an instrument for bringing about the desired economic and social changes in a country. So we can say that 'Economics' and 'Public Finance' are closely related with each other in various aspects.

MEANING OF PUBLIC FINANCE

In order to understand the meaning and contents of public finance in the traditional sense, it is necessary to understand the connotation of the words 'public' and 'finance'. The word 'public' is a collective term. It stands for a collection or conglomeration of individuals, *i.e.* people taken as a whole. It also implies belonging to the people. In practical usage, however, through the passage of time, the word has acquired a somewhat special meaning. A heterogeneous crowd of individuals is not always regarded as constituting a public body. What is required, is that the people should have something in common, they should possess some common characteristics and have a common interest uniting them for some specific purpose for some time. In short, the members constituting the public should form a people. It is not necessary, however, that the word 'public' is the reverse or opposite of the word 'private'.

The ordinary meaning of the term 'finance' is money resources or revenues. It does not signify the coins and notes of a country. Rather, it connotes the resources of an individual or a group of persons especially of a ruler or state, computed in terms of money. In the broader sense, the term finance also includes credit. By combining the two terms 'public' and 'finance' we derive the compound term 'public finance.'

According to the meaning of the two terms, public finance stands for the resources of a public body. Consequently, the science of public finance becomes the study of the principles underlying the acquisition and use of financial resources by the public body. This meaning of the term 'public finance' is, however, too wide and general to serve any useful purpose since what we study is not the economics of public body; we are interested in the study of the economics of the state. Consequently, it is more appropriate to call the science of public finance as the science of state finance. Strictly speaking, public finance would include the finance of a joint stock company, as also that of a college, a club or even of an anti-social organisation. Since we want to exclude the study of such institutions and organisations from our subject, we have to define the word 'public' in a narrow sense as implying the state. Thus, public finance constitutes a study of the monetary and credit resources of the state.

Economists have variously defined 'public finance' emphasising one or the other aspect of the subject following the approach to economics as the science dealing with the activity of the practical man in acquiring and applying those things that are in limited supply for the satisfaction of the external and temporal human wants.

Carl Plehn regards public finance as, "The science which deals with the activity of the statesman in obtaining and applying the material means necessary for fulfilling the proper functions to the state."

According to Charles F. Bastable, "For all states, however—whether crude or highly developed, some provisions of the kind are necessary, and therefore, the supply and application of state resources constitute the subject matter of a study which is best entitled in English as Public Finance."

According to Findlay Shirras, "Public finance is the study of the principles underlying the spending and raising of funds by public authorities. As a positive science it is concerned with facts as they exist; it investigates the intricate flux of these financial events and discovers their hidden uniformities by means of patient and systematic inquiry which we call research; and the statements of uniformity are expressed as laws."

According to Hugh Dalton, "Public finance is concerned with the income and expenditure of public authorities, and with the adjustment of the one to the other. The principles of public finance are the general principles which may be laid down with regard to these matters."

According to H.L. Lutz, "Public finance deals with the provision, custody, and disbursement of resources needed for conduct of public or government function."

Harold Groves describes it as, "A field of inquiry that treats the income and outgo of governments (federal, state, and local). In modern times, this includes four major divisions of public revenue, public expenditure, public debt, and certain problems of the fiscal system as a whole, such as fiscal administration and fiscal policy."

Thus, in whatever words one may frame the definition, it seems that there is no major difference between the various definitions since all of them state that 'public finance is a study of income and expenditure of the government at the central, state and local levels.' Government has to perform certain functions in the community in the form of supplying certain public or collective goods which individuals cannot or do not perform individually.

SCOPE OF PUBLIC FINANCE

The scope of public finance covers a full discussion of the influence of government's fiscal operations at the level of overall activity, employment, prices and growth process of the economic system as a whole.

In the words of Prof. Taylor, "Public finance deals only with the finances of the government." The finances of the government include the raising and disbursement of government funds.

According to Musgrave, the scope of public finance embraces the following three functions of the government's budgetary policy confined to the fiscal department:

(i) The stabilisation branch;

(ii) The distribution branch; and

(iii) The allocation branch.

These refer to three objectives of budget policy, *i.e.* the use of fiscal instruments:

(i) to secure adjustments in the allocation of resources;

(ii) to secure adjustments in the distribution of income and wealth; and

(iii) to secure economic stabilisation.

Viewed broadly, in public finance we should not only include the income and expenditure of the government but also the sources of income and the way of expenditure of various government corporations, public companies and quasi-Governmental ventures. Thus, this view extends the scope of the public finance to the study of various independent bodies acting under the government's direct and indirect control.

Thus, the science of public finance deals with the finances of the State. Consequently, the scope of public finance consists of the study of the collection of these funds and their allocation between the various branches of activities which are regarded as the essential duties or functions of the state. The scope of public finance may be divided into following four parts:

1. Public Debt;
2. Public Revenue;
3. Public Expenditure; and
4. Financial Administration.

(i) Public Debt

A government or public authority frequently obtains income through raising loans in order to finance the shortfall in its traditional income. The loans raised in a particular year constitute the receipts of the public authority for that year. It is an income of a capital nature while the provision of repayment of the capital sum for the year constitutes the expenditure of a capital nature. Thus, the problems related to the raising and repayment of public loans are studied under this part of public finance. The purpose for which the loan is raised, the different sources from where the loan is raised, the different methods by which the loan is raised, and the method of payment of interest and repayment of the principal amount of loan which are promised, all taken together constituting the subject matter of public debt. Here, we also examine the borrowing policy of the government and indicate the directions in which improvements could be made.

(ii) Public Revenue

In its wider sense, public revenue includes all incomes, irrespective of their source. Consequently, we may include in government or public revenue income accruing from all kinds of taxes as well as the receipts from borrowings. However, for a clear understanding, the scope of the term 'public revenue' is narrowed down by including in it only those incomes which do not carry with them the obligation of repayment on the part of the government.

We classify the various sources of public revenue in the form of taxes, fees, assessment, etc. and study the various principles and methods which should govern the raising of the public revenue. In short, we study the different canons of taxation. Taxation is the main body of this division of public finance, and we mainly analyse the problems of raising the public revenue through taxation. We also study the important problems of incidence and impact of taxation, whom the government wants to tax and who is actually taxed, etc. We also discuss the important related problems of tax evasion or tax avoidance and examine the causes of these problems and suggest remedial measures.

(iii) Public Expenditure

Public expenditure is the end and aim of the collection of state revenues. As a sub-division of public finance, under public expenditure we study the principles and problems relating to the expenditure of the public funds. We study the fundamental principles governing the flow of government funds into different spending streams and the method of incurring actual expenditure of state funds on the various items or activities. We also study the classification of public expenditure on different criteria, theoretical set-up, and the recent trends in the public expenditure. We also investigate the phenomena responsible for these recent trends. In other words, we study the changes in the pattern of public expenditure occurring over time. At times, we also discuss the normative aspect of the problem and evaluate the desirability, or otherwise, of public expenditure on the basis of certain value judgments and make suggestions for bringing improvements in the policies of the government.

(iv) Financial Administration

The scope of public finance is not confined only to the incurring of public expenditure, raising of public revenue, and public debt; we also have to examine the mechanism by which these processes are carried on. Thus, we are faced with the problem of financial organisation and administration. Under the fiscal or financial administration, we are concerned with the organisation and functioning of the government machinery responsible for performing the various financial functions of the state. The budget is the master financial plan of the government. It brings together the estimates of anticipated annual revenues and expenditures, implying the schedule of government activities to be undertaken and the means of financing these activities. Execution of the budget is another important function or task related to the financial administration. Varied statistics and estimates have to be collected, processed and prepared. The entire work starting with the procedure of the preparation of the budget, presentation of the budget before the Parliament or Assembly, passing of the budget by the Parliament, execution of the budget by the government after it has been passed by the Parliament, and evaluation of the budget, etc. constitute the subject matter of this part of public finance.

Other than the above-mentioned four constituents of public finance, there has emerged one more constituent—quite profound in its effects. It is the 'economic stabilisation'. This constituent has a wide role to play, especially, in the less-developed nations like India. The main task of this constituent is to frame and look after the implementation of various policies required for economic stabilisation.

MODERN PUBLIC FINANCE

Sometimes a question is asked in the examination as to whether public finance is positive science or normative science or both. Before giving our opinion, we will discuss both the aspects as below:

Modern public finance has two aspects:

(i) Positive aspect; and

(ii) Normative aspect.

In its *positive aspect,* the study of public finance is concerned with what are the sources of public revenue, items of public expenditure, constituents of budget, and formal as well as effective incidence of the fiscal operations.

In its *normative aspect,* norms or standards of the government's financial operations are laid down, investigated and appraised. The basic norm of modern finance is general economic welfare. On normative consideration, public finance becomes skilful art, whereas, in its positive aspect, it remains a fiscal science.

(i) Public Finance as a Positive Science

The classical economists with their faith in *laissez-faire* and market mechanism advocated minimum interference of the state in business matters. They were in favour of free market economy. They were opposed to 'feudalism', 'mercantilism' or any kind of state intervention in business matters or rather looked upon it as a positive hindrance in the way of free market economy. They argued that the way to attain greatest social advantage was to allow every individual complete freedom to follow the path of his own private gain or profit. Classical economists had full faith in market mechanism, price mechanism, profit motive, free and perfect competition. Accordingly, they believed that private sector was more efficient than the public sector. Therefore, the activities of the state in the economic field were considered as a necessary evil and were to be kept to the minimum possible scale. Hence, a small budget was considered as the best budget. In this way, the scope of public finance was limited and consequently the scope of public sector was also limited.

Public finance was mainly considered as a description of the way in which the operation of treasury would interfere with the working of the private sector of the economy and the way in which it could keep such an interference at the minimum. Under such circumstances, public finance was defined as the *revenue-expenditure process* of the government. Prof. A.R. Prast observed that the classical economists divided the subject matter of public finance into (Government) revenue, expenditure and debt aspects. Whereas Adam Smith in his book *Wealth of Nations* gave importance to expenditure, Ricardo and J.S. Mill concentrated much more on revenues. However, it was argued that the fiscal problem pure and simple should not be confused with alien consideration of social and economic policy.

As far as neoclassicists are concerned, they give very little significance to the discussion of public finance. Actually, a systematic exposition of the subject of public finance disappeared from the major works of Marshall and Edgeworth, the two great economists at the end of nineteenth century. However, a system of public finance was first made by Bastable which was exclusively devoted to public finance and was published in England in 1892. He defined public finance in a traditional way. Similarly, Prof. H. Dalton in 1922, defined public finance as, "It is concerned with income and expenditure of public authorities, and with the adjustment of one to the other."

Besides the above, some modern economists like Lutz, Carl C. Plehm, Harold Groves, Taylor, etc. defined public finance more or less in a traditional manner. For instance, according to Lutz, "Public finance deals with the provisions, custody and disbursement of resources needed for the conduct of public or government functions." Prof. Taylor defined it as "The finances of the public as an organised group under the institution of government." It, thus, deals only with the finances of the government. The finance of the government includes the raising and disbursement of government funds, public finance is concerned with the operation of the fiscal or public treasury. Hence, to the degree, that it is a science, it is a fiscal science, its policies are fiscal policies, its problems are fiscal problems.

An analysis of the above definitions clearly reveals that the public finance is a positive science. As positive science, it is concerned with what it is. It is not concerned with what it ought to be. It is concerned with explaining how public authorities collect revenue like tax, how they make public expenditure and how revenue-expenditure policies are administered. Therefore, as a positive science, public finance was not concerned with the problems such as:

(i) What criteria should be applied when one is judging the merits of the various budget policies?

(ii) What are the responses of the private sector to various fiscal measures, such as tax and expenditure changes?

(iii) What are the social, political and historical forces which have formed the shape of present fiscal institutions, and which determine the formulation of compensatory fiscal policy?

From the above study, it is evident that classical economists regarded that public finance is a positive science and it does not deal with the normative aspect of fiscal operations.

(ii) Public Finance as a Normative Science

Later on, new economists like R.A. Musgrave, J.M. Keynes, Pigou and subsequently even Dalton widened the scope of public finance by including normative science as a part of public finance. The reason being that *laissez-faire* policy failed to bring automatic adjustment between the forces of demand and supply in the economy and hence state intervention was considered necessary as a part of policy to raise the level of effective demand in the economic system. Prof. J.M. Keynes came on the scene as an economic doctor to diagnose the ailing economies and recommended the medicine of public investment on a large scale (financed by the creation of money by the government) on welfare projects in order to raise the volume of employment in the economy rather than the aggregate supply. In 1936, the influence of government fiscal operations on the overall level of economic activity and the level of employment became an integral part of the subject matter of public finance. Thus, it can be said that these economists accepted public finance as a normative science. According to Prof. A.R. Musgrave, "While operations of the public household involve money flows of receipts and expenditure, the basic problems are not related to the issues of finance. They are not concerned with money, liquidity or capital markets, rather, they are the problems of resource allocation, the distribution of income, full employment, price-level stability and growth. Therefore, we must think of our task as an investigation into the principles of public economy more precisely, into those aspects of economic policy that are used in the operations of the public budget." Thus, according to Prof. Musgrave, the object of fiscal operation is to make proper allocation of resources, the distribution of income, full-employment and price-level stability and growth.

The basic norm of modern finance is general economic welfare. On normative considerations, public finance becomes a skilful art, whereas in its positive aspect, it remains a fiscal science. Since public finance is now regarded as a normative science, the fiscal measures are used to check trade cycles, reduce unemployment, bring about proper distribution of income and wealth amongst the members of the community to promote capital accumulation and economic growth and remove regional disparities. Further, various judgments are now involved in the field of taxation, borrowing, deficit financing, public expenditure, etc.

Thus, in all, we infer that public finance is both — a positive science as well as a normative science.

NATURE OF PUBLIC FINANCE

Public finance has been held as a science which deals with the income and expenditure of the government's finance. It has been held as the "study of the principles underlying the spending and raising of funds by the public authorities." The various theories which form the basis of the collection, maintenance and expenditure of the public income, constitute the subject matter of public finance.

(i) As a Subject

Public finance embodies various theories, opinions and expressions of the experts — given for the creation of better utilities. It teaches us "How to collect taxes in the best way, How to maintain the collection economically and How to spend it properly." Although, it is based on the economic laws, even then it has much to do with the fiscal policies which influence the economic policy and economic structure of the country.

(ii) As a Process

Public finance reveals the ways adopted by a particular government while solving various financial problems before it. It reflects the volume of income, process of collection from local taxes to the central taxes, the process of classification and the way of its diversification to various channels. It also deals with the operational aspects of various financial laws passed by the legislature of the country.

(iii) As an Art

Public finance enables the concerned personnel to adopt the policies in the best possible way. It should be logical and proper according to the time. Public finance also teaches the bureaucrats and the leaders to adopt utmost economy while using the money received from the public.

PUBLIC FINANCE AND PRIVATE FINANCE

The word 'finance' is used for both — the public and the private finances. By private finance is meant the financial problems and policies of an individual economic unit (which does not form a part of state organs) as compared with those of public authorities. While some people believe that the principles of public finance are same as the principles of family budget, others believe that the principles of public finance and private finance are different from each other. Both these views are justified to some extent because of the existence of similarities and dissimilarities between the principles of public and private finances.

(i) Public Finance

Public finance is the study of the income, debt and expenditure of the government. It also includes various policies and methods employed to secure money and policies framed to pay the debt taken.

(ii) Private Finance

Private finance is the study of the income, debt and expenditure of the individual, or a private company or business venture or an association. It includes study of their own view regarding earning, expenditure and borrowing.

SIMILARITIES BETWEEN PUBLIC FINANCE AND PRIVATE FINANCE

Despite the differences in scope and nature of the public finance and private finance referred to above, given below are the similarities:

(i) Both kinds of finances are based on rationality. The individual is tempted by circumstances to act foolishly and irrationally; the government is also subject to whims and caprices in regard to its expenditure. Like the financial decisions of an individual, the decisions of government may also be unwise leading to retrogression.

(ii) Just as an individual cannot indefinitely indulge in financing his expenses with the borrowed funds, so also a government cannot for ever pursue a policy of deficit financing without taking risk of its survival. Like an individual, the government has also to repay its loans.

(iii) Like an individual or private corporation, the financial policies of the government may not be sound and may have to suffer from many loopholes. Both public and private funds may be misused, *i.e.* misappropriation of funds and may be used to serve the self-interests of few individuals.

(iv) Both the private and the public sectors are engaged in satisfying the wants of the society. The overall economic activities are divided between the two sectors and in some respects, their problems and decisions are similar.

(v) Both the private and the public sectors have limited resources at their disposal and both the sectors always endeavour to make optimum use of these resources.

(vi) Both the sectors are engaged in activities that involve large purchases, sales and other transactions. They are also engaged in production, exchange, saving, capital accumulation, investment, etc.

(vii) The basis of public as well as private finance is the same. Both seek the help of various principles of economics in determining various interrelated problems. For example, a person wants to secure maximum utility on account of minimum expenditure and government too wants to secure multiple public utility by spending the least possible amount of public money.

(viii) Limitation of resources is a problem before private as well as public finance. An individual's resources are limited upto one's earnings, past savings and ancestral property. Similarly governments' resources also depend on taxable capacity of the individual earnings of the various corporations, etc. None of the two is capable of extending its expenditure beyond their bounded limit; hence, none can afford to go to the infinity in the use of finance.

(ix) Private as well as public finance require efficient administration to look after the various acts of extravagance. In the event of the failure of an efficient administration, both might be compelled to face 'dire-consequences' in their financial field. No Individual ever wants any kind of wastage or misuse of his income, so does the government; if it is conscious to its sense of duty.

DIFFERENCES BETWEEN PUBLIC FINANCE AND PRIVATE FINANCE

(i) **Government is permanent:** The life of a public body—like the government is very much longer than that of an individual. Consequently, it tends to see more towards future. The old adage 'the king never dies' is almost a truism. The government spends its funds on long gestation projects which prove fruitful and beneficial for the society in the long run. But an individual is generally concerned with immediate gains. His life being shorter, he can wait only for a short period. Consequently, it is sometimes argued that the government spends for future while individual spends for the present.

(ii) **Power of eminent domain:** The sources of income of an individual are relatively very much limited, while those of the government are relatively wide. The government, unlike the individual, can use its power and authority. It has the power to levy taxes, to mint coins and to print currency notes. An individual can use none of these resources. In case of loans also, the credit of an individual and the scope within which he can borrow, is limited. This is not so in the case of government. Government can raise internal and external loans. It can draw upon resources of the society as a whole, even by force, if necessary. The government can take out funds from the pockets of the people for the sake of patriotism and national interest. An individual has got no such instruments under his control.

(iii) **Public finance operations are public:** In private finance, strict secrecy is maintained with regard to sources of income and expenditures. Public finance operations are, however, open to all. An individual always maintains secrecy about his accounts as he never wants that others should know his real financial position. The government, however, provides sufficient information to the public and publishes its budget in newspapers, etc. The government budget is keenly discussed in the legislature before it is passed for execution by the government.

(iv) **Compulsory character of public revenue:** The government can never do anything without income because it can always raise revenue by employing force. It can compel people to pay the taxes. An individual cannot compel any other individual to pay him money forcefully.

Furthermore, the government revenue which is raised from the people mostly by levying taxes, must be spent and consequently it should go back to the people in one form or the other. It may not, however, go back immediately and precisely to those individuals from whom it was realised through taxes. However, people as a whole receive the money back because the government does not get money for nothing and some service has to be performed in return.

(v) **Compulsory character of public debt:** It is maintained that the government can compel people to lend money. For example, during the war or periods of national emergency, the government can compel people to lend it. An individual cannot, however, compel other individuals to lend him money.

RELATIONSHIP OF PUBLIC FINANCE TO OTHER SCIENCES

Public finance has much to take and much to give to the sciences like economics, politics, history, jurisprudence, etc. As a matter of fact, public finance is a curious mixture of all these sciences as is evident from the following:

(i) Public Finance and Psychology

Public finance is also related with psychology. It deals with people and as such, most of its problems are human-problems and hence depend upon human behaviour which is the subject matter of psychology. For example, take the case of taxation on company profits. Since profits may be taken as 'rewards for risk taking,' an undue increase in the tax on company profits may adversely affect the spirit of risk taking and thereby affect investment in the companies.

(ii) Public Finance and Sociology

Social reforms which form a part of sociology, are now supposed to be the responsibility of the state and they need government finances for execution. In fact, these social reforms have enhanced the scope of public expenditure. For example, crimes are the topics which sociologists study, and a student of public finance studies the raising of revenue from criminals of one kind or the other. Taxes on inheritance, gifts, etc. may have their due effects on the social set-up of the society. In this way sociology is very much related to public finance.

(iii) Public Finance and Statistics

Public finance is closely related with statistics. The income and expenditure figures of the public finances are prepared through the assistance of statistics. Statistics is widely used in determining the rate of capital formation, taxable capacity, incidence of taxation, preparation of budget, etc. In this way, public finance is incomplete without statistics.

(iv) Public Finance and Economics

If economics is taken as a science which deals with the administration of scarce resources to satisfy human wants, public finance may be taken as that part of economics which deals with only the satisfaction of wants of the citizens of the state. Many of the problems of public finance are part of the subject matter of economics. For instance, the problems of taxation are essentially a part of economics. Taxation implies shifting of resources from private hands to the government and, therefore, the shifting of utilisation of resources by the individuals and the groups to the hands of the public authorities. Really speaking, public finance is a part of economics as economics is a wider discipline and public finance forms a part to it.

(v) Public Finance, Jurisprudence and Law

The fiscal policy of a country, in general, is always based on the principles of equity and justice. All these terms have been borrowed from jurisprudence and, in fact, are based on the foundation of legal definitions. The law of the country is the basis on which taxes are imposed and funds are allocated. There are laws which prevent improper raising of funds and their improper allocations.

(vi) Public Finance and Ethics

There is also a close relationship between public finance and ethics. Equity and justice have as much to do with ethics as they have with law and therefore, the relationship between public finance and ethics is obvious, if the fiscal policies are to be based on these principles. For instance, it is neither legal nor ethical to snatch Rs. 100 as tax from a person who earns hardly Rs. 200.

(vii) Public Finance and Politics

All social sciences are related in the sense that these deal with one or the other aspect of social life. In this manner, politics can very well be described as a sister science of public finance. British constitutional history consists mainly of the struggle between the king and the parliament for the control of the national purse. 'Taxation without representation is tyranny' was the well-known slogan which led to the independence of 13 colonies in America with the name of 'United States of America'. There is an intimate connection between voting and taxation. Much of public finance has political science aspects. According to Dr. Dalton, "Public finance is the borderline between economics and politics." In the words of Adams, "A sound policy of public finance must rest upon a thorough knowledge of political economy."

(viii) Public Finance and History

No doubt, public finance is related to history but not so closely as it is related with economics and politics. History has given shape to the nature of public finance as it has given to anything else. History puts up the lessons of the past before us in the sphere of public finance as in any other sphere. No finance policy can be formulated without keeping in view the historical developments. History provides us with facts, figures and illustrations which are essential for the formulation of any finance policy. According to Bastable, "The science of finance has another important auxiliary in history which illustrates, verifies and in some instances dates for its principle."

From the above study, it is evident that public finance is related to many of the social sciences which deal with different aspects of human behaviour.

ROLE OF PUBLIC FINANCE IN THE ECONOMIC DEVELOPMENT OF A COUNTRY

The emergence of the 'Nation-State' and their attempt for self-sufficiency, has tremendously increased the value of the study of public finance. The yoke of economic responsibility is becoming heavier day by day due to the increase in needs of the people in addition to several other problems in the modern times. Every new government's promises to secure 'social welfare' in the country further extend the importance of public finance, because the fulfilment of all these things requires money. The more money at disposal, more will be the expansion of the services for the people. All this requires keen and close analysis study of various financial policies of the government in prospective. The ancient Philosophers Plato and Aristotle attached due weight to the management of production by the 'Producing class' in the case of Plato and 'Citizens' in the case of Aristotle. But that was too crude an opinion to throw any sight on the importance of the public finance.

Particularly, economic activities of the state have increased very largely—both intensively as well as extensively. From the intensive criterion, public expenditure has become very heavy in many age-old functions of the state, such as defence and maintenance of law and order, which are now costlier than what they used to be in the past, because of modified techniques and scientific mode of operations. Public expenditure has increased extensively as the state has taken up more responsibilities like planning for development, construction of social overheads, investment in human capital, etc. With the advent of economic planning in all nations, the scope of state activity has considerably expanded. As such, every modern state is practically forced to raise large revenues every year to defray its growing expenditures. This has vast repercussions on the economic and political conditions of the community. A large part of national income goes to satisfy pubic wants and a large share of national income received by the individuals originates in the public spendings which affect the levels of employment, production and prices in the economy as a whole.

PUBLIC FINANCE IN UNDERDEVELOPED AND DEVELOPING COUNTRIES

According to R.J. Chelliah, "Public finance has a positive and significant role in the context of economic development." The importance of public finance in an underdeveloped/developing country may be summarised as under:

(i) **Problem of economic stabilisation:** A major problem of a developing country is the economic instability. After 1930s worldwide depression, it has been emphasised that public finance (revenue and expenditure process of the government) may be used to secure economic stability or to remove economic fluctuations and distortions in the economy.

(ii) **Optimum utilisation of resources:** Another major problem of developing countries is that of non-utilisation or underutilisation of the scarce and limited resources. The solution of this basic problem lies in the optimum utilisation of these available resources by means of adopting planned monetary and public finance policies. The state can direct the flow of consumption, production and distribution in the right direction by adopting balanced budget policy.

(iii) **Incentive to savings:** The main problem of developing and underdeveloped countries is that savings are very nominal which hinders their economic development. Public finance encourages the accumulation of savings.

(iv) **Increase in income:** Capital formation is not an end in itself but only a means of achieving another important end, *i.e.* increase in income. The object of public expenditure is to increase the income in underdeveloped countries so as to invest funds in such industries and in such an economical and efficient manner that least amount of money fetches the greatest possible output. The government gives subsidies and grants to industries to enable them to increase production at cheaper rates. This will lead to prosperity and development with an overall increase in the income of the masses.

(v) **Reduction in economic inequalities:** Another problem of underdeveloped or developing countries is the unequal distribution of income and wealth to the public. Public finance has an important role to play in this context. For example, the government can impose heavy taxes (such as income tax) on the richer sections of the society and spend the income so received on providing cheap food, cheap housing, employment, free medical aid, etc. for the poorer sections of the society.

(vi) **Unemployment problem:** Another major problem of an underdeveloped/developing country is the unemployment problem. Increased income may be consumed by a large mass of unemployed people. The problem of unemployment leads again to low standard of living, poverty, backwardness, ignorance and above all starvation. It is the function of public finance to provide employment opportunities. In this connection, it must be remembered that fiscal policies (public finance policies) are most effective tools to tackle the problem of unemployment.

(vii) **Capital formation:** Since development entirely depends on the rate of capital formation in the country, the first and foremost aim of public finance is to promote capital formation. Students of commerce and economics are well aware of the fact that the burning problem of an underdeveloped or developing country is the low capital formation. In the words of R. Nurkse, "For economic development, it is not the aim of public finance to bring about reduction in inequalities of incomes but its aim is to increase that proportion of the income which goes into capital formation."

(viii) **Planned economic development:** In developing countries, the productive resources are limited in quantity as well as quality. Public finance renders valuable help in the planned economic development of the country. The entire machinery of planning works through the mechanism of public finance. The principles of public finance have paramount importance in the sphere of rapid economic planning because both of these are the closely related activities of the state. For example, the government of India is raising necessary funds through taxation, etc. for formulation and implementation of its five-year plans.

SIGNIFICANCE OF FINANCIAL OPERATIONS OF THE GOVERNMENT

The financial operations of public finance can be effectively utilised to achieve various social and economic goals:

(a) Public finance can serve the interests of economic policy. Government spending can stimulate private sector, *e.g.* expenditure on industrial estates.

(b) Public finance is designed to bring about an appropriate allocation of productive resources so that national product is maximised and income distributed equitably.

(c) Public finance can be an instrument of social policy. Through fiscal operations, if national income is equitably distributed, harmony between different classes of people can be achieved.

(d) Financial operations can improve general welfare if major public spending is used for welfare projects.

(e) Government's financial operations have a unique significance in developing economies like India where public expenditure is devoted to promote capital formation and investment.

(f) Policy of taxation and public expenditure can affect the growth and pattern of production.

(g) If appropriately designed, fiscal operations can break the vicious circle of poverty in a developing economy or poverty in the midst of plenty in a developed economy.

(h) Fiscal operations can check trade cycles and lead to economic stabilisation.

STUDY-QUESTIONS

1. What do you understand by public finance? Discuss the subject matter or scope of public finance.
2. Explain the nature and scope of public finance.
3. What is the role of public finance in the economic development of a country?
4. What are the similarities and dissimilarities between public finance and private finance?
5. Trace the difference between public finance and private finance?
6. Is public finance a positive science or a normative science? Give reasons for your answer.
7. What is public finance? Discuss its relationship with other sciences.
8. Trace out the significance of financial operations of the government in modern times.
9. Bring out the importance of public finance in a developing economy.

Allocation of Resources of Public Goods

2

INTRODUCTION

The term 'public good' does not necessarily refer to a good that is provided by the government. Instead, it refers to a good (or service) that has two characteristics, regardless of whether or not the government provides it. These two characteristics are 'nonrival consumption' and 'nonexclusion'.

(i) Nonrival Consumption

A good is nonrival in consumption when with a given level of production, consumption by one person need not diminish the quantity consumed by anyone else. In other words, a number of people may simultaneously consume the same good.

(ii) Nonexclusion

The second characteristic of a public good is nonexclusion. Nonexclusion means that it is impossible, or prohibitively costly, to confine the benefits of the good (once produced) to selected persons. A person will benefit from the production of the good, regardless of whether or not he or she pays for it. Although nonrivalry and nonexclusion often occur simultaneously, there is a distinction between the two concepts. Our definition of nonrivalry said that consumption by one person need not (not does not) interfere with consumption by others; this means that although all could consume simultaneously, it may still be possible for one person to consume the good and for others not to. There are cases in which we have potential nonrival consumption but in which it is possible to prohibit consumption by some people at a moderate cost. In these cases, the goods in question are not public goods.

Television broadcasting can make the distinction between nonrivalry and nonexclusion clear. When a television programme is broadcast, any number of people (in the relevant area) can receive the signal and watch it without interfering with the reception of others. Thus, a broadcast has the nonrival characteristic of a public good. It is, however, possible to exclude selected people from viewing the program. People without television sets, for example will be unable to watch, or programmes could be scrambled so that viewers could watch a programme only after paying for a decoder. A television broadcast is, therefore, nonrival in consumption, but exclusion is possible at a moderate cost; such a good then does not have both necessary characteristics of a public good.

In many situations, nonrivalry and nonexclusion go together; then we have a public good. National defence is a good example. How could we protect you and not your neighbour? Your neighbour might be deported and thereby excluded from securing any benefits from the defence effort. Similarly, the same means could be used to exclude potential beneficiaries of the flood control project. In both cases exclusion is possible, but it involves high costs. Whether a good is nonexclusive is ultimately a matter of degree because in some cases, the cost of exclusion is higher than in others. The relevant question is whether the cost is low enough to make exclusion feasible. In the case of national defence, most people would agree that exclusion is too costly. Thus, national defence fits our definition of a public good. In contrast, most people would probably agree that exclusion is feasible with television broadcasting, so it is not a public good.

PRIVATE AND PUBLIC GOODS

In the modern economic system, the government is a very important unit having a circular flow of economic activity in relation to households and private sector firms. The private sector produces private goods and charges price on the basis of price mechanism. The government sector, on the other hand, produces public or social goods to satisfy the public or collective wants.

Public wants cannot be satisfied through the process of market mechanism because their satisfaction cannot be accounted for by price mechanism. Hence, public goods are not charged as private goods are charged.

(i) Private Goods

Private goods are those goods which are priced in the market and only those consumers are allowed to consume these goods who pay their stipulated price. To put it differently, these are the goods which are priced and the principle of exclusion applies on their use. Those who do not agree to pay their market price, or those who cannot pay for them, are excluded from the use of these good. Thus, *the ability to price a good*, *the divisibility of a good* and *the exclusion principle* are the main features of private goods.

(ii) Public Goods

Public goods are those goods which cannot be priced in the market in order to deprive those members of the society from its use or its benefits who do not pay for it. In other words, a section of the society cannot be excluded from its consumption. The term 'public good' does not necessarily refer to a good that is made available by the government. Instead, any commodity which is comprised of two features, namely *nonrival consumption* and *nonexclusion* is said to be a public good. Thus, the indivisible goods, whose benefits cannot be priced, and therefore, to which the principle of exclusion does not apply, are called *pure public goods*. On the other hand, all those goods are private goods which are completely divisible and the principle of exclusion can be applied on them.

REQUIREMENTS OF PUBLIC SECTOR

The market mechanism works efficiently only when certain conditions are fulfilled. Since most of these conditions do not prevail in this real world, the market mechanism alone, therefore, cannot, perform all economic functions. According to Musgrave, "public policy is needed to guide, correct and supplement it in certain respects." It is important to realise this fact, since it implies that the proper size of the public sector is, to a significant degree, a technical rather than an ideological issue. The following reasons can be given in favour of public sector:

(a) The public sector is needed where competition in private sector is inefficient due to decreasing cost.

(b) More generally, the contractual arrangements and exchanges needed for market operation cannot exist without the protection and enforcement of a legal structure provided by the government.

(c) The claim that the market mechanism leads to efficient resource use, is based on the condition of competitive factor and product markets. Thus, there must be no obstacles to free entry and consumers and producers must have full market knowledge. Government regulation or other measures may be needed to secure these conditions.

(d) Even if the legal structure is provided and barriers to competition removed, characteristics of certain goods are such that they cannot be provided for through the market. Problems of 'externalities' arise which lead to 'market failure' and require correction by the public sector, either by way of budgetary provisions, subsidy, or tax penalty.

(e) The market system, especially in a highly developed financial economy, does not necessarily bring high employment, price level stability and socially desired rate of economic growth.

Public sector is needed to secure these objectives. As the events of the 1980s have shown, this is the case especially in an open economy subject to international repercussions.

FUNCTIONS OF THE PUBLIC SECTOR

The public sector covers all State-owned undertakings and their activities are designed and directed either by a branch of the government itself, or by a body set up by it for common national welfare. The public sector is of vital importance to a developing economy like India. The economic performance of the public sector is wide and varied. Its major functions are:

(i) **To provide public utility services:** Most of the public utility services of mass consumption such as water supply, railways, post and telegraph, telephone exchange, electricity, etc. are controlled by the government with a view to preventing profiteering and consumer exploitation and to ensure their constant supply at reasonable rates.

(ii) **To augment and conserve natural resources:** Economic progress of a country depends on the optimal use of its natural resources. In a less developed country, there is inefficient utilisation or underutilisation of natural resources by the private sector. Thus, the public sector is obtained to tap, develop and conserve the old and new fields of natural resources such as mining, forestry, oil fields, fisheries, etc., and to channelise their output into the most desirable lines of production.

(iii) **To develop an industrial base:** To accelerate the tempo of economic development, rapid industrialisation of the country is essential. Development of basic and key industries, like the iron and steel industry, heavy machinery and tools, heavy electricals, heavy chemicals, etc. is one of its basic goals.

On account of least possibility of immediate returns on capital, involvement of huge investment, and high risks in these industries, private entrepreneurships usually avoid undertaking these ventures. Hence, it is the duty of the government to organise these industries and to construct the industrial base which will facilitate the growth of overall industry activity.

(iv) **To build social and economic overhead capital:** In an under-developed country, private investment hardly comes forward to provide for social and economic overhead capital, such as construction of roads, bridges, canals irrigation works, railways, telecommunication, electri-fication of rural areas, etc. Evidently, the state has to provide this social overhead capital which is a must for regular pace of national economic growth.

(v) **To compensate private investments:** The activities of the public sector, and the investment therein, may be designed to compensate for the gap of inadequate private sector investment in the economy. In advanced countries, public sector investment programmes are undertaken to counter cyclical fluctuations. In a poor country, public sector investment is meant to fill up the lacunae in capital formation and adequate developmental investment, caused by scarcity of capital and lack of bold entrepreneurship. In short, when private entrepreneurship is lacking, the government accepts the challenge and provides public entrepreneurship for planned economic development.

(vi) **To stimulate private sector investment:** In order to induce the private sector to undertake further investments, public sector undertakings not only create an environment through provision of economic and social overheads, basic and key industries, but may also provide financial assistance, by establishing State financial corporations, banks, etc. in the money and capital markets. For instance, fourteen major commercial banks in India were nationalised with a view to providing better channelisation of credit to the priority sector, such as small-scale industries, exports, agriculture, etc.

(vii) **To pursue egalitarian goals:** When there is a danger of the growth of private monopoly and undue concentration of economic power in a few hands, a country like India, wedded to socialism, may find an easy way out to tackle the problem by replacing private monopoly by public monopoly through extension of the public sector. Unlike private firms, public enterprises are motivated to serve the people rather than to extract huge profits. Thus, public enterprises can best serve the achievement of the egalitarian goals of preventing concentration of wealth and inequalities in income and distribution, and promoting the welfare of the masses by providing essential goods at reasonable prices. Of course, these ideals can be realised only if public enterprises are run by efficient and honest officials. Anyway, current economic philosophy advocates that a successful, planned development, and the achievement of socialism, is comparatively easy through the expansion of the public sector rather than of the private one. At least our Indian planners are fully convinced on this point. To quote the Second Five-Year Plan manifesto in this context, "The adoption of the socialistic pattern of society as the national objective as well as the need for planned and rapid development requires that all industries of basic and strategic importance, or in the nature of public utility services, should be in the public sector."

(viii) **To provide sources of funds for financing developmental plans:** When a country launches upon planning for its development, it requires huge funds to finance the planned activities. Along with the other sources of government finance like tax-revenue, etc. profits earned by the existing public enterprises can be directly used for financing other projects in the public sector. That is to say, rapid growth of public enterprises can materially contribute to increasing public savings for investment, which, in turn, will bring about further accumulation of capital and acceleration of economic growth of the country.

(ix) **To lead balanced regional and sectoral growth:** The extension of the public sector can remove the regional imbalances and lopsided development of the country. The public sector may specially concentrate more on neglected, less profitable, rural and backward regions, and thereby seek a balanced regional growth. Similarly, in the neglected or less developed sectors too, it should promote investment and a balanced sectoral growth.

The public sector in a country like India is destined to gain control of the commanding heights of the economy, to reduce income disparities, to widen and deepen the sources of public savings as a means of financing further development, to create the necessary industrial base and to accelerate the tempo of growth.

EXTERNALITIES

Sometimes in the processes of production, distribution or consumption of certain goods, there are harmful or beneficial side effects called *externalities* that are borne by people who are not directly involved in the market exchanges. These side effects of ordinary economic activities are called *external benefits* when the effects are beneficial, and external costs when they are harmful. The term *externality* stems from the fact that these effects are outside, or external to, the price system, so their impact is not determined through mutual agreement among all those affected.

Immunisation against a contagious disease is an example of a consumption activity involving external benefits. When a person is inoculated, that individual benefits directly because his or her chance of contracting the disease is reduced (this benefit is not the external benefit). The decision to be inoculated also confers benefits indirectly on others because they are less likely to catch the disease from the inoculated person; this is the external benefit. The fact that other people benefit from the individual's actions, however, will not influence that person's decision as to whether being immunized is worth the cost. What the person is concerned with is the effect on his or her own health. Thus, the benefit the inoculation generates for others is external to the person's decision.

Maintenance of a person's lawn or home may also produce external benefits for neighbours. If the neighbours well-being is improved by living in a more attractive neighbourhood, then there is an external benefit associated with the maintenence of home lawn. On a somewhat grander scale, education is often alleged to involve external benefits such as a reduction in juvenile delinquency, an improvement in the functioning of the political process, or greater social stability. External costs are also quite common, and the best examples can be found in the area of pollution. Driving an automobile or operating a factory with a smoking chimney pollutes the air that other people breathe in;

thus the operation of a car or factory imposes costs on people not directly involved in the activity. Similarly, operating a motorcycle produces a level of noise that is often irritating to those nearby, just as the noise level of a supersonic (or subsonic) aeroplane may be irritating to people living near airports. Traffic congestion is also an external cost. When a person drives during rush hour, the road becomes more congested not only for the driver, but for pedestrians as well.

NATURE OF EXTERNALITY

The nature of externality can be explained with the help of a two sector model. In this model economy is divided into two sectors—*producers* and *consumers*—there are four types of interdependence for benefits and costs respectively or positive or negative externalities and web of initiating agents and affected parties.

Table 2.1 summarises the primary characteristics of externalities as discussed in this section. There are a number of possible externality combinations:

Table 2.1: Characteristics of Externalities

Initiating economic agent	Recipient economic agent
Consumer	Consumer
or	or
Producer	Producer
Type of Externally	*Characteristics*
Positive (external economy)	A benefit or gain
	Increased profits or reduced losses to a business
	Increased utility (satisfaction, welfare) to a consumer
Negative (external diseconomy)	A cost or loss
	Reduced profits or increased losses to a business
	Disutility (Dissatisfaction, reduced welfare) to a consumer

(i) a consumption action may yield external production effects;

(ii) a production action may yield external consumption effects;

(iii) a consumption action may yield external consumption effects; and

(iv) a production action may yield external production effects.

The possible combinations increase in number and complexity when both positive externalities (gains) and negative externalities (losses) are also considered. Moreover, an action undertaken by a given economic agent—such as a producer—may exert no effects on both other producers and consumers, while action may affect both other consumers and producers.

For example, a firm manufacturing steel may acquire new blast furnaces which increase both the technical efficiency and the volume of its production. The explicit costs of acquiring this new productive capital are easily demonstrated via the price mechanism (assume an acquisition cost of $1 million). Now assume that the new blast furnaces significantly increase air pollution in the surrounding area—a result which diminishes both the profits of producers in nearby recreational industry and the welfare of residential consumers. These other producers and consumers would incur *nonmarket costs* which are excluded from the $1 million acquisition cost of the new blast furnaces. Since these are not explicit market costs which the firm must calculate when assessing its profit position, these will be to oversupply the steel and thus to create the negative externalities; to the steel firm, the scarce resource, clean air, is not priced.

Thus, externalities are elusive, though real, and potential public interest derives from their very nature. There is no self-correcting market mechanism at work, since externalities, whether positive or negative, are not measured in price values. Moreover, it is difficult to convert many externalities to control through the market.

EXTERNALITIES AND MARKET FAILURE

As we know, the existence of externalities leads to a difference between private cost and social cost. For instance, costs of pollution are not included in private cost though they are very much a part of social cost of this pollution in its cost of production but the community does have to bear the cost in some way or the other. Therefore, social cost in this case would be greater than private cost. On the other hand, when a firm trains workers enabling other firms to recruit skilled workers, it confers an external benefits on the other producers. In this case, social benefit would exceed private benefit. In the other words, externalities create a divergence between private and social costs and benefits. The market prices are thus not "truly representative" as they take into account private costs and benefits. Thus, they provide a misleading information (signals) for an optimal allocation of resources. This shows that the existence of externalities leads to market failure.

EXTERNAL COSTS AND OVERALLOCATION OF RESOURCES

To explain the impact of external costs, let us consider the pollution problem in terms of output decisions facing individual firms. Let us start by ignoring, the pollution problem, *i.e.* by ignoring the external cost. The marginal cost to the firm in this case will be equal to the marginal private cost (MPC) and the firm will compare this cost with its marginal revenue to determine the level of output that must be produced. Let us suppose that our firm is operating under perfectly competitive market conditions. In this case, the equilibrium price will be determined by the point of intersection F_1 of the supply and demand curves of the industry. As can be seen from Figure 2.1, the equilibrium price is OP_1 and at this price, Oq_1 level of output is produced by the industry. Since the firm in question is a "price taker" it merely adjusts its level of output so that its MPC is equal to this price (which, in turn, is also equal to its MR). The equilibrium level of output for the firm is Oq_1.

Let us now introduce external costs into our analysis. Let us suppose that the firm emits considerable smoke from its chimneys polluting the air in surrounding areas and creating health hazards for the people living in the vicnity of the factory. Calculation of cost must, therefore, account to this external cost as well. Therefore, instead of the marginal private cost, we require information regarding marginal social cost (MSC) which is equal to marginal private cost plus the externality costs (E), *i.e.*

MSC = MPC + E. Obviously, the new marginal cost curve will lie above the earlier marginal cost curve as the external costs in our example here are positive. The new MC curve is the MSC curve in figure B. This change at the firm level is reflected at the industry level by a shift in the industry supply curve from S_1 to S_2. The new supply curve S_2 intersects the demand curve at point F_2 which is the new equilibrium point. The output OQ_2 corresponding to this point is the optimal or the efficient output as it takes into account the externality costs, *i.e.* OQ_1 is greater than this efficient level of output. The new equilibrium price is OP_2. Corresponding to this efficient level of output, the point of equilibrium for the firm is V where MSC = Price (=MR). At this point, the firm also produces a lower level of output (Oq_2) as compared to the earlier level of equilibrium output Oq_1.

The above discussions show that since firms do not take into account the external costs while calculating their costs of production, they produce a quantity in equilibrium which is greater than the efficient or optimal level of output. We thus arrive at the following conditions:

In the case of external costs, the equilibrium level of output is greater than the efficient of optimal level indicating that

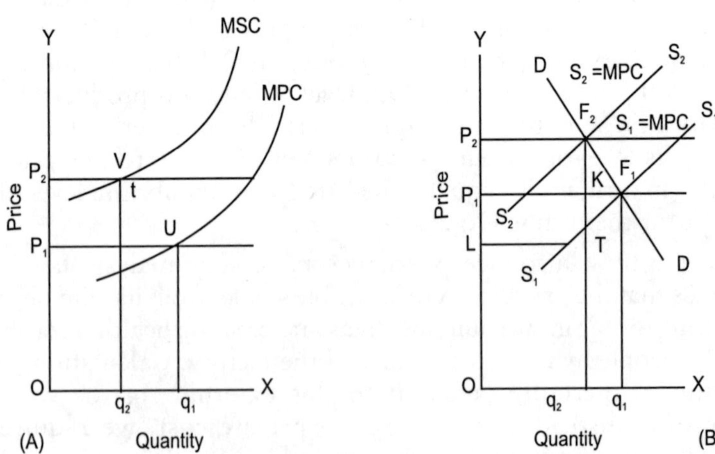

Figure 2.1: External costs and overallocation of resources

resources are over-allocated to the production of the commodity in question.

OPTIMAL AND SUBOPTIMAL INTERSECTOR ALLOCATION

An economic system must determine the mix of its resource allocation between the private and public sectors. An *actual allocation* division between the two sectors will exist at any one time. Moreover, it is possible to conceptualize the existence of an *optimal allocation mix*, known also as *social balance,* given the preference patterns and effective demand of the members of the society (more recently, the term social balance has been applied to this concept by John Kenneth Galbraith in *The Affluent Society*). The points of actual and optimal intersector allocation may or may not coincide. If they do not coincide, it can be said that intersector resource allocation is suboptimal, or alternately, that *social imbalance* or *intersector mis-allocation* exists.

The relationship between optimal and suboptimal intersector resource allocation is demonstrated in Figure 2.2. In this graph, private sector output as a percentage of total national output is measured on the horizontal axis, and public sector output as a

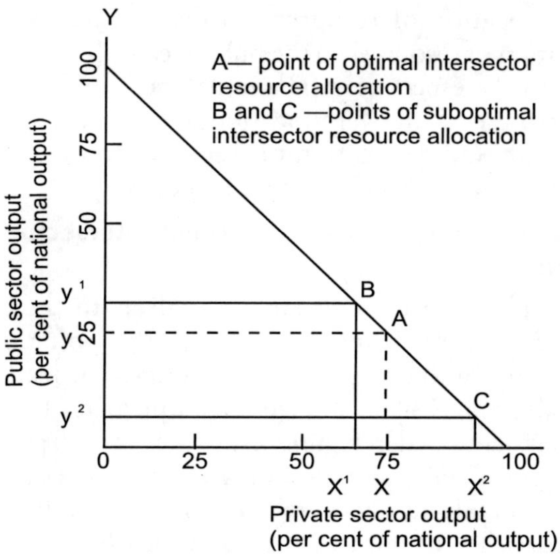

Figure 2.2: Intersector resource allocation: optimal and suboptimal points

percentage of total national output is measured on the vertical axis. It is assumed that point A represents an optimal division of national output between the private and public sectors, with the private sector controlling 75 per cent of resource allocation and the public sector controlling 25 per cent. In a concepual sense, this social balance point would thus be assumed to reflect the true preferences of the people of the society for private and public goods as made effective by the distribution of income, wealth, and political voting power among the people.

If point A represents optimal intersector allocation, and if the actual mix of resources between private and public goods in the society is also at point A, then the optimal and actual points of inter-sector resource allocation coincide and social balance is present. Given the preference patterns of the individuals of the society, no welfare improvement would result from any reallocation between private and public output. If, however, point A represents optimal intersector allocation and the actual allocation is at point B, or at point G, then suboptimal allocation or social imbalance is present. In this instance, reallocation between the two sectors is required if societal welfare is to he maximised. The imbalance gap between points A and B represents an underallocation of resources to the private sector and an overallocation of resources to the public sector by the proportions of xx^1 and yy^1, respectively. The imbalance gap between points A and C represents an overallocation of resources to the private sector and an underallocation of resources to the public sector by the proportions of xx^2 and yy^2, respectively.

The Indifference Approach to Optimal Intersector Resource Allocation

The application of indifference analysis to the concept of intersector resource allocation allows the point of optimal intersector allocation to be *logically derived,* instead of merely assumed as above. The, indifference approach to intersector allocation is developed in Figures 2.3 to 2.5. In each graph, private sector output is measured along the horizontal axis and public sector output along the vertical axis. This output may be considered either in monetary value terms or in physical unit terms, though the former is more practical.

In Figure 2.3, the *production possibility* curve of the society, designated as P, relates the marginal rates of transformation between the production of private and public goods with the scarce productive resources available to the society. That is, it shows the various combinations of private and public goods that can he produced with the full employment of the quantitatively and qualitatively limited land, labour, and capital resources available to the society at a given time. The higher the position of the production possibility curve on the graph, the greater the production potential of the society, due to the greater (quantity and/or quality of its productive resources. At point B, all of society's resources would be allocated by the private sector. At point A, all of the resources would be allocated by the public sector.

The society's production possibility curve, P, is *concave* to the origin of the graph. This reflects the fact that scarce resources cannot be substituted with equal efficiency between the production of public and private goods. Thus, in Figure 2.3, a reallocation of resources along the upper part of the P curve, as from a to b, would add more in private sector output (the distance ww^1), than is sacrificed in public sector output (the distance zz^1). This would be due to decreasing returns in the production of public goods. A movement along the lower portion of the P curve, as from c to d, however, could add more in public sector output than is sacrificed in private sector output. This would be due to decreasing returns in the production of private goods. A comparison of the distances yy^1 and xx^1, respectively, indicates this phenomenon.

The unequal trade-off between the output of private and of public goods as resources are reallocated in production between the two sectors can be explained by the following reasons. First, some economic goods, by their very nature, are produced more efficiently, with less real input costs per unit of output, by one sector than by the other. If the private sector were allocating most resources, as would be true toward the lower part of the P curve, it would likely be providing goods such as national defense. Yet, if the national defense function were transferred from federal government control to market control, production efficiency in defense would doubtless decline," with a greater loss in public sector output than what would he added in private sector output. This can be seen in Figure 2.3 toward the lower end of the P curve, with the distance y^1y representing a greater loss from the public sector not producing national defense than the value of defense production, x^1x, that would be gained with private sector production of defense. Second, but equally important, increasing costs tend to occur when too many goods are produced by one sector because the principles of diminishing returns and decreasing returns to scale come into operations. These principles of increasing cost are applied ordinarily to the analysis of private sector production, but they may also be applied validly to public sector production. Thus, toward the upper end of the P curve, the society would he incurring increasing unit costs in the production of public goods, and toward the lower end it would be incurring increasing unit costs in the production of private goods. In either situation, the reallocation of a given bloc of resources from one sector to the other would yield greatei output results in the second sector than if the same resources were retained for use in the original sector.

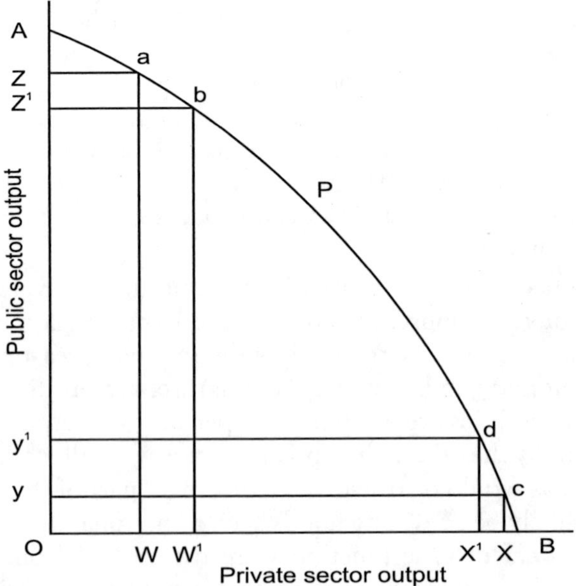

Figure 2.3: The production possibility curve

Social indifference curves

Having defined the production possibility curve for the society, the next step in the derivation of the point of optimal intersector resource allocation involves the use of *social indifference curves.* In Figure 2.4, each social indifference curve, S^1, S^2, S^3, and S^4, represents the marginal rate of substitution between private and public goods consumption by society in providing a given *level of satisfaction* (utility) along each curve. That is, each curve shows the various combinations of private and public goods which will provide a constant level of welfare to the society. Moreover, the higher the position of the social indifference curve, the greater the level of societal welfare it represents, since a greater aggregate output is being consumed.

The family of social indifference curves, only four of which are displayed in Figure 2.4 for reasons of simplicity, are importantly related to the state of market and political distribution in the society. In other words, they reflect the aggregate preferences of the individual members of the society for private and Public goods as made effective by the distribution of income

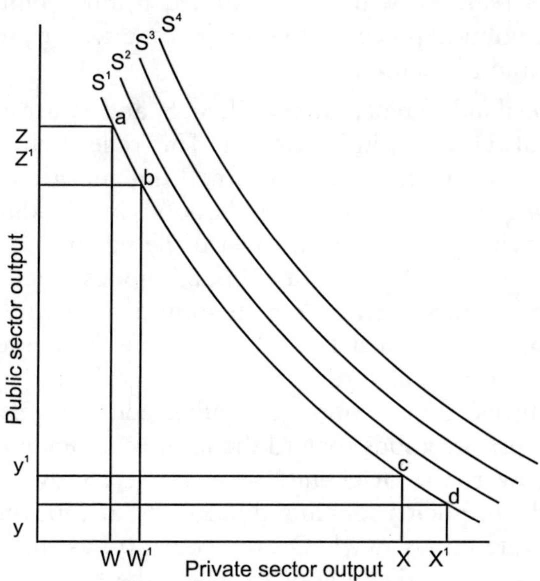

Figure 2.4: Social difference curve

and wealth in the private sector and by political representation in the public sector. Individual preferences for public and private goods are meaningless, of course, unless made effective by purchasing power in the private sector and by voting power or related political representation in the public sector. Clearly, an individual with a superior income and wealth base in the market can command a higher level of consumption than can a consumer of lesser means. Similarly, all individuals are not represented equally in the consumption of public goods. Instead, some individuals are more adequately represented than are others within the public sector by lobbies, pressure groups, and elected or appointed officials.

Thus, it is important to note that the pattern and shape of the social indifference curves do not represent mere preferences; instead, they represent the *effective* demand of the individual members of the society for private and public goods, as this demand can he made operational by the state of income, wealth, and political voting distribution in the society. The degree to which such preferences do become operational, and thus become precise allocational realities, will be determined by the ability of the market and political processes to reveal these effective preferences accurately and efficiently.

The social indifference curves, S^1, S^2, S^3 and S^4, are convex to the origin of the graph in Figure 2.4. This reflects the fact that along each curve there is a diminishing marginal *rate of substitution* between private and public goods in providing a given level of societal welfare. Thus, toward the upper end of social indifference curve S^1, the quantity of public goods that the society would he willing to sacrifice to gain additional private goods is greater than it is toward the lower end of the curve. Stated alternately, it can he said that the society is willing to give up a more than proportionate amount of public goods to get a smaller quantity of private goods toward the upper end of curve S^1, and vice versa toward the lower end. For example, a movement from a to b yields the greater loss in public goods, zz^1, for the smaller gain in private goods, ww^1. On the contrary, as the society is consuming mostly private goods toward the lower end of the curve, it would be willing to give up a less than proportionate amount of public goods to obtain a larger quantity of private goods. This is represented by a movement from c to d along curve S^1 which yields the smaller loss in public goods, yy^1, for the larger gain of private goods, xx^1, with the same overall level of societal welfare being maintained.

This declining marginal rate of substitution between the consumption of public and private goods in providing a constant level of welfare may be explained by the following reasons. First, the more *scarce* a good becomes, the greater is the tendency for its relative substitution value in relationship to another good to increase. That is, its marginal utility increases relative to the marginal utility of the other good, which now is relatively more plentiful. For example, toward the lower end of a social indifference curve such as those presented in Figure 2.4, the marginal utility of public goods would tend to be *high*. Thus, society would be willing to give up more than proportionate amount of private goods to obtain a smaller quantity of the now relatively more scarce public goods. By contrast, toward the upper end of a social indifference curve, the marginal utility per unit of public goods is *low,* as society has a relatively large supply of such goods. Thus, it would be willing to give up larger goods to obtain a smaller quantity of the now relatively more scarce private goods, while maintaining the same level of total utility. More generally, it can he said that when society's consumption approches either extreme, the marginal increments of societal welfare or satisfaction diminishes as the society consumes mostly private or mostly public goods.

A second reason for the convexity of a social indifference curve is that significant losses of both political and economic freedom are incurred as government allocation becomes dominant near the upper end of the curve. A society may well be willing to give up a more than proportionate quantity of public goods in order to attain a smaller quantity of private goods if, as a result, additional political and economic freedom can be gained. The convexity toward the lower (private sector) end of the social indifference curve, moreover, may be explained by the fact that an extreme degree of market allocation is likely to create an undesirable state of anarchy where basic law and order does not prevail. Society would thus he willing to give up a more than proportionate quantity of private goods at this point in order to ensure that the government provided law and order.

The optimal intersector allocation point

The final step in derivating the point of optimal intersector resource allocation through the indifference approach involves the placing of the societal production possibility curve and its social indifference curves on the same graph, In Figure 2.5, the relevant parts of Figures 2.3 and 2.4 are combined. Hence, the production potential of the society, as determined by its resources and technology, is brought into equilibrium with societal preferences for public and private goods, as they are made effective by the state of income, wealth, and political voting distribution. This results in optimal intersector resource allocation being established at point a in Figure 2.5, where the production possibility curve, P, is tangent to social indifference curve S^3 providing OY in public sector output and OX in private sector output. At this point, social welfare is maximised.

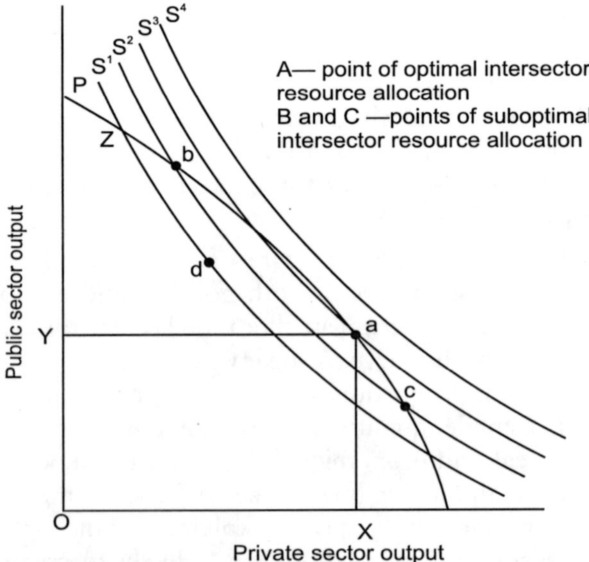

Figure 2.5: Intersector resource allocation: Optimal and suboptimal points

It should be observed that the production possibility curve, P, and social indifference curve, S^3 have the same slope at the equilibrium point. This means that the marginal *rate of* transformation in the production of private and public goods is equal to the marginal *rate of substitution* by the society in the consumption of these goods. Effective social preferences for economic goods have been brought into equilibrium with the production capabilities of the society at point a. Thus, maximum welfare from the consumption of economic goods is attained for the society. Moreover, this point of tangency, since it rests on the societal production possibility curve P, also represents a condition of *pareto optimality* which means every reallocation of resources will have been undertaken which would make one person better off without reducing the welfare of anyone else. Furthermore, it should be noted that the optimal intersector resource allocation point would be different for every different state of societal income-wealth and political-voting distribution, since the slope (but not the convexity) of the S curves would change with each state of distribution. In addition, if the state of distribution which makes social indifference curve S^3 effective corresponds to the society's preferred state of distribution, as derived from a societal ethical or value judgment, both *optimal distribution* and *optimal intersector resource* allocation are attained by the society at point a.

It is possible, of course, that the actual intersector division of resources in a society may not be at the point of optimal allocation. The deviation of actual ftom optimal allocation would result from institutional defects such as the difficulty encountered in revealing preferences for public goods in the political process and from imperfect market structure distortions in the production, and allocation of private goods in the market sector. The point of actual intersector resource allocation could be anywhere along the production possibility curve, P, or at any point inside P toward the origin of the graph. Thus, points b, c, and d in Figure 2.5 represent selected examples of points of actual allocation which deviate from the point of optimal allocation. Each reflects a condition of suboptimal *intersector resource allocation* or, in short, a condition of *social imbalance*. That is, effective societal preferences for economic goods are not being accurately revealed in the government and/or market institutions through which the allocation decisions are being made.

At point b there is an overallocation of resources to the public sector. At point c there is an overallocation of resources to the private sector. Yet, at each of these allocation points the optimal stabilization condition of *full resource* employment is present since both points rest on the production possibility curve, P, which represents full employment along its entire length. Intersector resource allocation, however is suboptimal because points b and c provide the lower level of social welfare represented by social indifference curve S^2 instead of S^3. Thus, even though points b and c represent full resource utilisation, they do not represent eflicient resource utilization. It should be observed, accordingly, that optimal stabilization is a necessary, but not a sufficient, condition for optimal intersector allocation. That is, the optimal point, a, must necessarily he on the production possibility curve, but actual allocation may also occur on the curve at suboptimal points such as b and c. Moreover, if allocation is at point d along social indifference curve S^1, the society is experiencing both social imbalance and an underemployment of productive resources (suboptimal stabilisation)—the latter because output is occurring at a point inside the production possibility curve.

THE POLITICAL INTERACTION COSTS OF DEMOCRATIC VOTING THEORY

More recent analysis by James M. Buchanan and Gordon Tullock has added further insight concerning the economic issues involved in the process of revealing individual economic preferences through a democratic political system. Figure 2.6 demonstrates some of these issues. The expected political interaction costs (discounted to present value) from collective democratic decision-making are measured on the vertical axis, while the percentage of the group required for the approval of a collective fiscal decision is measured along the horizontal axis. The political interaction costs are two-fold in nature: (1) the voter externality cost component, and (2) the decision-making cost component.

A voter externality cost, as described in the earlier chapter, refers to the cost incurred by a voter who has voted against a fiscal choice, which nonetheless has been approved by the required proportion of voters necessary to carry the decision for approval. Such an individual must abide by the collective decision even though his or her individual preferences did not opt for its approval. Assume a group of 100 voters. If the proportion of voters required to approve a collective action is only 1 per cent, then 1 of the 100 voters can oblige the remaining 99 voters to abide by a political decision which they do not approve. Quite obviously, the potential negative voter externalities incurred by the remaining 99 voters, who oppose the decision are considerable under this "dictatorship" sort of rule. However, the potential voter externalities would continually decline as the percentage required to approve a political decision increases. Ultimately, at an absolute (complete) unanimity rule of 100 per cent approval, voter externality costs would reach zero, since no voter could be bound by the collective political decision of other voters. In other words, a single voter would retain the right to vote any propposed decision. The nature of voter externity costs is representated by curve VE in Figure 2.6. A decision-making cost, in political interaction terms, refers to the bargaining cost required to reach a group political consensus or agreement. Essentially, these are real resource costs in terms of direct labour, material, and capital outlay, as well as opportunity cost considerations such as the value of time spent in bargaining. Decision-making costs may be expected to increase as the proportion of the voting group required to approve a decision becomes larger, *i.e.* under conditions requiring higher percentage approval, more effort is normally required to gain agreement. The highest cost would be expected at the point of 100 per cent approval (absolute unanimity) since the potential for strategy would reach a peak at this point. This would be true because a single voter would be capable of negating a choice which conceivably every other voter would prefer. The curve DM in Figure 2.6 represents the nature of decision-making costs. Assuming a group of 100 voters, a 1 per cent approval rule would incur little, if any, bargaining cost, since one voter (like a dictator) could approve a policy without considering the other voters. Meanwhile, approval by all 100 voters is likely to incur substantial decision-making costs, as strategy among voters would become extensive.

Curve P1 in Figure 2.6 reflects the performance of the overall political interaction costs. The curve is a summation of its two components, the voter-externality cost curve (VE)and the decision-making cost curve (DM). In this particular graph, the character of the voter externality and decision-making of cost functions, the most efficient proportion of the group required for political approval is 70 per cent. That is, this proportion yields the lowest political interaction cost per voter for a particular fiscal decision.

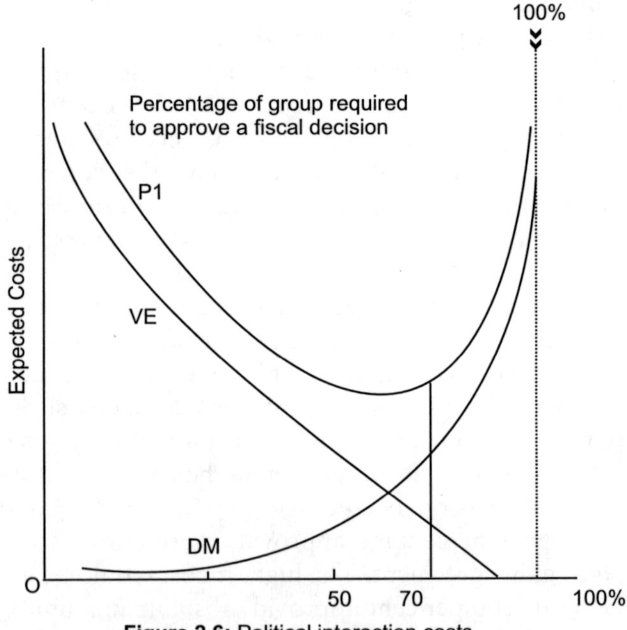

Figure 2.6: Political interaction costs

REVEALING SOCIAL REFERENCES THROUGH MAJORITY VOTING—ARROW'S IMPOSSIBILITY THEOREM

Kenneth Arrow has provided additional insight into the problems involved in making societal decisions consistent with individual preferences through group voting in a democratic political process. Although Arrow's observations pertain, in general, to the problems encountered under any democratic voting rule based on individualism, their most relevant application is to the majority voting rule which is the mainstay of Western democracies. He argues that the following conditions must be met if a collective decision reached under majority voting conditions is to accurately reveal the individual economic preferences which constitute the effective social indifference curve (the social welfare function):

(i) Social choices must be transitive (consistent). That is, a unique social ordering must exist which will yield a clear-cut winning alternative regardless of the ordering sequence in which alternative choices are voted on.

(ii) The social welfare function must be non-perverse in the sense that an alternative policy, which might otherwise have been chosen by the society, must not be rejected because any individual has changed the relative ranking of that alternative.

(iii) The rankings of the choices in the social welfare function between two alternatives must be independent of the ranking by individuals of other alternatives which are irrelevant to the choice between the two alternatives. That is, the elimination of any one alternative must not influence the ranking of the other alternatives in the social welfare function.

(iv) Voters must have free choices among all alternative policies.

(v) Social choices must not be dictatorial. That is, they must not be based solely on the preferences of one individual, independent of the choices of other individuals.

Table 2.2 A and Figure 2.7a, illustrate a situation in which majority voting violates the set of conditions necessary for consumer sovereignty to be maintained in collective democratic decision-making. Condition 1, the transitivity condition, in particular, is violated, leading to what is known as the impossibility theorem or voting paradox. Assume that three voters (A, B, and C) are selecting among three Budgetary policies (X, Y, and Z). Policy alternative X represents a decision to build three public libraries; policy Y, a decision to build two libraries, and policy Z, a decision to build one library. Since a majority of the voters (in this example, two out of three) prefer policies X to Y, Y to Z,and Z to X, the result is intentative (inconsistent) in that there is no winner. In this situation, the "sequence" in which the voting occurs, would determine the final outcome an obviously illogical result.

For example, if we first pair policy X versus policy Y, X wins since two of the three voters prefer X to Y. If we then pair policy X versus policy Z, Z wins since two of three voters prefer Z to X. Thus, a pairing sequence beginning with X versus Y results in Z as the ultimate winner. On the other hand, if we first pair policy Y versus policy Z, Y is favoured by two of three voters, but the subsequent pairing of Y and X finds X as the winner since it is preferred by two of three voters. Thus, a pairing sequence beginning with Y versus Z results in X as the ultimate winner.

Table 2.2: Example of Majority Voting: Individual Preferences for Alternative Budget Policies

(2.2A) Result: Intransitive

	Policy Alternatives		
Voter	preferences 1	preferences 2	preferences 3
A	X	Y	Z
B	X	Y	Z
C	X	Y	Z

(2.2B) Result: Transitive

	Policy Alternatives		
Voter	preferences 1	preferences 2	preferences 3
A	X	Y	Z
B	X	Y	Z
C	X	Y	Z

Finally, an initial pairing of X versus Z winning over X, but the subsequent pairing of Z versus Y finds Y winning over Z – each winning vote representing a two out of three voter preference.

Thus, a pairing sequence beginning with X versus Z results in Y as the ultimate winner. To summarize, the outcome is arbitrary since either Z, X, or Y will win depending on the ordering of the voting sequence.

A close inspection of the above paradox reveals that intransitivity occurs because one voter C prefers the two extreme policies (Z for one library and X for three libraries) over the median or intermediate alternative, voter Y for two libraries. Yet, this is an unlikely position for a voter to take, *i.e.* to prefer three libraries as a second choice instead of two libraries—which is closer to the voter's top-ranked choice of one library. When a graph is plotted, the result is the twin-peaked preference function for voter C that is demonstrated in Figure (2.7a).

Instead, if voter C behaves in a more rational manner and prefers two libraries as a second choice, the intransitivity problem disappears and the solution becomes determinate. This transitive outcome is depicted in Table 2.2B and Figure 2.7b, with the latter showing a single-peaked preference function for voter C. Now, if the first pairing is X versus Y, Y defeats X and then also defeats Z. Or, if we begin with a pairing of Y versus Z, Y wins over Z

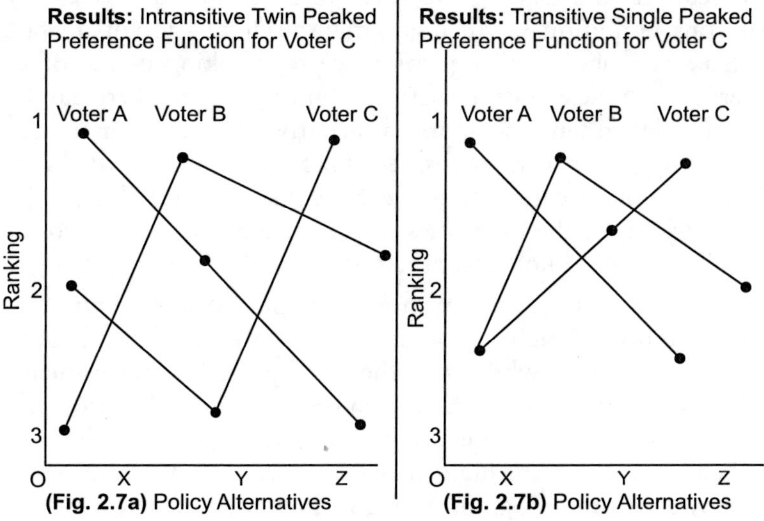

Figure 2.7: Examples of majority voting—individual preference for alternative budget policies

and also defeats X. Finally, a pairing of X versus Z finds Z the winner, but, of course Y wins over Z as observed in the previous pairing. Thus, Y is the clear-cut winner despite the ordering of the voting sequence.

It may be observed further that the three policy alternatives in the above example consist of three different quantities of the same economic good (public libraries). However, the same results would tend to hold for overall budget considerations such as budgetary size. For example, if policy X represents a large-sized budget, rational voting behaviour would result in the median policy, Y, as the winner. However, this example would hold to a lesser degree on heterogeneous policy alternatives such as would be the case if policy X represents one public library, policy Y represents one fire station, and policy Z represents one public school—all of equal cost to the tax-payer. Nevertheless, even here the median policy could be the winner as the result of voting coalitions and platforms.

Although Arrow's requirements for rational collective decision-making through majority voting are rigorous, his analysis nonetheless indicates some basic problems prevalent in democratic political decision-making. However, one condition seems unduly rigorous, condition 3, which says that the elimination of any one alternative policy shall not influence the ranking of the other alternative policies in the social welfare function. There can be no interdependencies among alternative policies. Or, stated differently, the relative intensities of preference among voters for different policies cannot be a relevant consideration. Thus, in the above example, the intensities of preferences for three, two, or one library could not affect the outcome.

Or, consider another example: One half of the community prefers improved highways and streets to solve traffic congestion in an urban area, while the other half prefers a government-subsidized mass transportation system to meet the problem. Assume the cost to be equal for both traffic congestion solutions. If those who prefer the highway solution, rank traffic congestion as a lower priority program among various alternatives than those who prefer the mass transportation system, then the particular traffic congestion solution selected (provided money is to be spent for this purpose) should be the mass transportation system; those who prefer it exhibit higher relative intensities of preference. Condition 3, however, essentially stipulates that a consideration of preference intensity is irrelevant. Arrow's approach thus tends to understate the intensity of desires among alternative policy choices. It is difficult for a system of social choice which ignores these basic preference considerations to interpret accurately individual demands expressed in the political process.

In summary, the Arrow Impossibility Theorem seems too pessimistic concerning the efficiency of the democratic political process, though it does point out some weaknesses. This pessimism stems mainly from the two points described, namely, (1) the irrational voter depicted in the twinpeaked preference function (Table 2.2A) and (Figure 2.7a) the assumption which precludes the ability of the democratic process to reveal voters' preference intensities among policy alternatives.

STUDY-QUESTIONS

1. Why is public sector required? Bring out the functions of public sector in a developing economy.
2. How do we atttain balance between private and public sectors? Explain intersectoral resources allocation with the help of Indifference Curve Approach.
3. What do you understand by the private goods and public goods? Explain the problem of free rider in the context of public goods.
4. What do you understand by the externalities? How the externalities affect allocation of resources and production of public goods?

Principle of Maximum Social Advantage

3

INTRODUCTION

The operations of public finance have a deep influence on the economic life of the community, and it should be possible to judge them by some criterion of social benefit. The best criterion for the purpose is provided by what is called by Dalton the "Principle of Maximum Social Advantage", and by Pigou the "Principle of Maximum Aggregate Welfare." Most of the operations of public finance involve transfers of purchasing power from some persons to others. Taxation causes transfers from certain individuals to public authorities, and there are transfers back from these authorities to other individuals by way of public expenditure. As a result, changes take place in the volume and pattern of the production of wealth and its distribution. What is important to consider, is whether these changes are socially advantageous? If they are, the operations are justified, otherwise not. The best system of public finance is that which secures the maximum social advantage from the operations which it conducts.

We know that the most of the expenditure is made to create social welfare which is a part of our daily need. Though, it is accepted that no further addition of goods and no profitability is aimed, yet in the absence of these services, it is not, and will never be possible for the people to undertake production. Peace and law & order are required to undertake a productive activity. Continuous fear of foreign attack and insurgency will make the productive process slow. Thus, the object of public finance is to promote the maximum social advantage, *i.e.* the maximum good of the community. At what level of the operations of public finance the maximum advantage is secured, may be theoretically considered by making use of the marginal analysis. All public expenditure, assuming that it is judiciously incurred by the government, confers some benefit on the community. However, the benefit accruing from successive small increments of public expenditure must decline with every increase in expenditure. In other words, the marginal social benefit or the marginal utility of public expenditure, like that of everything else, diminishes as the community has more of it.

On the one side, government revenue causes disutility to the people who have to part with some of their purchasing power when they make payments to the public authorities. The marginal disutility or the marginal social sacrifice of public revenue increases as the revenue becomes larger. Now, so long as the marginal utility of public expenditure exceeds the marginal disutility of public revenue, an increase in both increases the net benefit to the community. On the other hand, when the marginal utility of public expenditure is less than the marginal disutility of public revenue, a decrease in both expenditure and revenue is desirable. Therefore, the social advantage is the maximum if the marginal utility of public expenditure is equal to the marginal disutility of public revenue.

In Figure 3.1, OX represents the volume of funds available to the public authorities for expenditure on public services. These

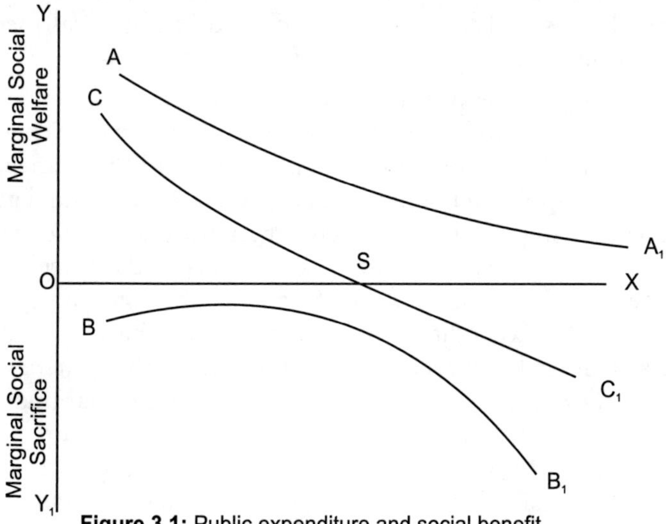

Figure 3.1: Public expenditure and social benefit

funds represent diversion of resources from private wants to public wants through taxation and hence, represent sacrifice to the community. The upper part of the figure represents the social benefit which arises from public expenditure. AA_1 is the marginal social benefit curve and it slopes downwards which indicates that the benefit to the community from additional amounts of public expenditure is declining. The lower part of the figure represents the social sacrifice which arises from taxation. BB_1 represents marginal social sacrifice of taxation. This curve slopes downwards also to show that when larger amounts of funds are levied and collected from the people by way of taxes, they would entail greater additional sacrifice to the community. Curve CC_1 may be termed as the marginal net social benefit curve and is calculated by deducting BB_1 from AA_1 (that is, sacrifice is deducted from benefit, so as to calculate net social benefit to the community). S is the optimum point, for at that point the total net social benefit is maximum (and marginal social benefit is equal to marginal social sacrifice).

This new approach to maximum welfare to the community through budget policy has definite merit since the "minimum sacrifice approach to the allocation of taxes is matched by a maximum benefit approach to the determination of public expenditures and the two are combined in a general theory of budget planning."

The aggregate satisfaction from public expenditure depends, among other factors, on the way it is distributed over various heads. The best allocation of public expenditure can also be known by applying the marginal analysis. An individual gets the highest satisfaction from a given expenditure when the marginal utility of money spent on each commodity and service is equal. In the same way, the total satisfaction to the community from a given public expenditure is the maximum where the marginal social benefit from every head is the same. When the marginal utility of expenditure on one head is less than the marginal utility from another head, the total satisfaction is increased by transferring a little money from the former head to the latter. The total satisfaction will go on increasing till the marginal utility in all heads is equal. Similarly, the total sacrifice of the public revenue depends on its distribution over various sources. The public authorities get their revenues from various tax and non-tax sources, and each source should be tapped to such an extent that it causes the least possible total disutility to the community. If the marginal disutility of revenue from one source is more than that of the revenue from another source, a little decrease in the revenue from the former and a little increase in that from the latter will reduce the total disutility to the public. The total sacrifice is the minimum when the marginal disutility of all sources of revenue is equal.

Thus, the social advantage of public finance is the maximum where the marginal utility of expenditure on all heads and the marginal disutility of revenue from all sources are equal, and the marginal utility of public expenditure is equal to the marginal disutility of public revenue. The public authorities have to enhance their expenditure over different heads and their revenues from various sources so as to realise these conditions.

DIFFICULTIES OF MEASUREMENT OF ADVANTAGE

(i) **Non-economic implications:** The principle of maximum social advantage is applied by authorities by basing their fiscal action on careful estimates of the advantages and disadvantages of any proposed measure of public finance and on comparisons of the balance of probable gain or loss to the community from various alternative proposals. Such estimates and comparisons are, however, not easy. They are difficult partly because all the possible results of a measure cannot be correctly visualised, and partly because there are innumerable economic and non-economic implications of every single measure and correct judgement often cannot be formed.

(ii) **Fiscal measures:** The long period effects of fiscal measures are difficult to foresee. How saving and productive power will be affected by such measures in the long run is difficult to judge. Therefore, the effects on social advantage cannot form a test of the goodness of policies in this respect.

(iii) **Absence of objective measurement:** The marginal analysis provides a very good theoretical explanation of how the maximum social advantage from the operations of public finance is secured, but it gives no help in the measurement of that advantage. The marginal utility of public expenditure and the marginal disutility of public revenue are concepts, the objective measurement of which is extremely difficult. The financial operations of the government involve the collection of large sums of money from taxation and other sources of revenue and the disbursement of large amounts by way of public expenditure. The effects of small additional amounts of these on the community are difficult to measure. Therefore, in practice, the public authorities are not in a position to estimate the marginal benefits and disadvantages, and the particular size of revenue and expenditure that will maximise the welfare of the community are difficult to determine.

(iv) **Effects of government policies:** Government tax and expenditure policies do not promote social advantage in every respect. A measure which is good in one way, may not be so in another way. Equity in distribution often requires measures which adversely affect production. Taxing the rich to help the poor is good for distributive justice but may discourage saving and production. On the other hand, many tax policies which promote production often increase inequalities of distribution.

(v) **Changes in conditions:** What is good under one set of conditions may not be so under another. The conditions in an economy are not static, and what might be considered as the point of maximum social advantage under some conditions may not be so under other conditions. For example, in times of war the government expenditure and revenue must increase and the increases are certainly to the advantage of the community. Public finance operations also expand in a developing economy and the expansion is socially desirable. Moreover, the size of the national income itself is determined by the financial operations of the government and the optimum in respect of public expenditure and income varies with the level of national income. What is optimum at one level of income may not be so at a higher level brought about by the fiscal measures of the government. Therefore, it is difficult to determine the point of maximum social advantage and no definite volume of government expenditure and revenue can be considered as having secured that condition.

(vi) **Effects of political and social consideration:** Furthermore, political and social considerations often put economic criteria in the background. There are various taxes, the social and political implications of which overshadow their economic effects. A considerable portion of public expenditure is incurred without regard to economic consequences.

(vii) **Effects of public finance:** The effects of public finance on social welfare should be considered with respect to the system as a whole rather than for individual measures. The effects of various kinds of taxation and public expenditure should be considered together and balanced, and conclusions drawn instead of judging each individual measure. The operations of the government, as a whole, should promote social advantage as much as possible.

OBJECTIVE CRITERIA OF MAXIMUM SOCIAL ADVANTAGE

Despite the many criticisms levelled against the concept of maximum social advantage, it must be recognised, however, that it is the avowed norm of public finance. The budgetary operation of a rational state should have the goal of maximum social advantage (or economic welfare). The practical application of the principle of maximum social advantage is to provide the basic facilities to future economic life of the individuals. The financial activity of the state has to be approved on this criterion alone.

Expenditure and improvements on under-mentioned subjects is the test of the application of the government policies. The policies are, then held as one creating maximum social advantage if the following item-subject improve:

(i) **Defence and its need:** It is neccssary for every country to secure its borders from any kind of external attack. Factories, industries, research institutes and other business activities cannot function in the absence of peace and security. To protect the nation, expenditure has to be incurred on the defence which is economically (in the strict sense) unproductive, but highly essential. It certainly increases social gains as it provides safeguards to the society.

(ii) **Improvement in the distribution of income:** A better policy which improves upon the machinery of distribution of income is far better for the society and certainly increases social gains. A policy must reduce the equality of incomes in the country if it wants to push up the social advantage. Society always benefits in the economically equal atmosphere. But, if any taxation policy does not improve upon the distribution or acts contrarily, it can never succeed in creating social advantage.

(iii) **Increase in the production of wealth:** Increase in wealth increases property. If policy increases the earnings of the labourers then it is good policy. Thus, by improving the environment of production, by eradicating unemployment, by reducing losses and by increasing production, wealth can be increased. A policy which gives encouragement to above-mentioned subjects, can be called as the creator of maximum social advantage, otherwise it is to be called a future policy.

In nutshell, it will not be out of place to mention that government is the protector of the future economic life of the individuals. Its policy must be based on broad prospects. It should be dynamic, not dumb. The future must be clearly analysed before looking for more and more social advantage for the present.

Lastly, it is for the public to peep through the deeds of the policies made by their representatives whom they have sent in the parliament and legislative assemblies to take care of their interests.

LIMITATIONS OF THE PRINCIPLE OF MAXIMUM SOCIAL ADVANTAGE

No one can deny the place which the principle of maximum social advantage acquires in the domain of State's financial activities, yet there are certain difficulties in the application of this principle. These are:

(i) **Difficult to measure the marginal utility and disutility:** It is very difficult for the state to measure the marginal utility and marginal disutility. The state is not single individual but an aggregate of individuals and groups comprising in it. A thing, constituting utility, which is useful for a person or group of a factor, may or may not be beneficial for others. Similar problems arise when one thinks to measure the disutility. Equally, the job of the state to bring an equilibrium between the marginal benefit and marginal sacrifices curves also difficult.

(ii) **Difficult to assess the capacity of the people:** It is very difficult to measure the capacity of the people of a state which they can afford to pay to the government. What people of a country afford, depends upon:

   (a) the manner in which the money is raised; and

   (b) the manner in which the money is spent.

(iii) **The terminological uses of utility, and least sacrifice is abstract:** It is difficult to find out their exact implication. How can a government come to know about an individual's likings and disliking?

In spite of the these difficulties, government must spend money so as to create the maximum social advantage causing less sacrifice as far as possible.

STUDY-QUESTIONS

1. Explain the principle of maximum social advantage. How can it be achieved? What are the difficulties in its application?
2. What are the objective criteria of maximum social advantage? Also discuss the limitations of social advantages.
3. Discuss the difficulties encountered in the measurement of social advantage.

Public Revenue

4

INTRODUCTION

The term 'public revenue' can be explained both in a narrow and a broad sense. In the broad sense, it includes all the income and receipts, irrespective of their sources and nature which the government obtains during any given period of time. In the narrow sense, it includes only those sources of income of the government which are described as 'revenue resources'. In the broad sense of the term, it includes loans which the government raises under the term 'public revenue' or more properly public income. The necessity of raising the public revenue follows from the necessity of incurring public expenditure. As the modern government has to perform several functions for the welfare of the public, and as these functions cannot be performed free of cost, they involve substantial amount of public expenditure which can be financed only through public revenue. If the government wants to provide ever-increasing welfare facilities to its citizens then an ever-increasing amount of funds raised through public revenue will be required. The government, therefore, has to think of how and from where and how much revenue should be raised from the public. The amount of public revenue to be raised is a function of the necessity of incurring public expenditure and people's ability to pay.

Public revenue is the amount of money received by the government from its different sources. Public revenue is necessary for every government in the modern times. The income of the government through all sources is called *public sources or public revenue.*

According to Dalton, however, the term 'public income' has two senses—wide and narrow. In its wider sense, it includes all the incomes or receipts which a public authority may secure during any period of time. In its narrow sense, however, it includes only those sources of income of the public authority which are ordinarily known as "revenue resources." To avoid ambiguity, thus, the former is termed as "public receipts" and the latter as "public revenue." As such, receipts from public borrowings (or public debt) and from the sale of public assets are mainly excluded from public revenue. For instance, the budget of the Government of India is classified into "revenue" and "capital." "Heads of revenue" include the heads of income under the revenue budget, whereas the heads of income under the capital budget are termed as "receipts." Thus, the term "receipts" includes sources of public income which are excluded from "revenue."

TYPES AND SOURCES OF PUBLIC REVENUE

In a modern welfare state, public revenue is of two types:

(i) Tax revenue; and

(ii) Non-tax revenue.

(i) Tax Revenue

A fund raised through the various taxes is referred to as tax revenue. Taxes are compulsory contributions imposed by the government on its citizens to meet its general expenses incurred for the common good, without any corresponding benefits to the taxpayer. As Taussig puts it, "the essence of a tax, as distinguished from other charges by government, is the absence of a direct *quid pro quo* between the tax-payer and the public authority."

(ii) Non-tax Revenue

Public income received through the administration, commercial enterprises, gifts and grants are the sources of non-tax revenue to the government. Thus, non-tax revenues include:

(a) Taxes;

(b) Commercial Revenues; and

(c) Administrative Revenues.

(a) *Taxes:* In every country, the largest part of the public revenue is raised through taxation. Taxes may be imposed on a person's income or wealth; they may be direct or indirect, and may be of different rates and nature. A tax is a compulsory charge or payment levied or imposed by a public authority on an individual or corporation. The payment of tax is made by the members of the community without any assurance given by the tax-levying authority, to provide them direct benefit for it. In other words, there is no *quid pro quo* promised by the tax-levying authority against tax to a tax-payer. There is no direct give and take relationship between a tax-payer and the tax-levying public authority.

Prof. Seligman also says that taxes are payments which cannot be postponed or avoided or ignored by those on whom that have been imposed. He writes, "Taxes are generally compulsory contributions of wealth levied upon persons, natural or corporate, to defray the expenses incurred in the common interest of all, without reference to the special benefit incurred." Taxes may be levied on income of the individuals as well the goods and commodities bought by them.

(b) *Commercial Revenues:* The revenue which government gets by selling various goods and services produced by the public undertakings is commercial revenue. It is reward of the expenditure done on the commercial undertakings. Prof. Taylor calls it the price paid by the individual for the goods produced by the government. Economists have preferred to call this kind of return as price because it is paid as the price for certain goods and services, as the prices are paid for the goods produced by the private enterprises.

(c) *Administrative Revenues:* Revenue coming from the following sources is termed as administrative revenue:

(i) Fees;

(ii) Licences;

(iii) Special assessment;
(iv) Forfeitures;
(v) Fines and penalties;
(vi) Escheats;
(vii) Gifts & grants;
(viii) Borrowings; and
(ix) Printing of currency.

Such payments to an extent depend upon the payer. They are charged irrespective of the benefits conferred upon the payer and the cost of conferring any benefit. One more characteristic of the administrative revenues is that they are the 'by-products' of the administrative function. This is why such revenues are called as 'administrative revenues'.

(i) *Fees:* Sometimes government provides certain special services to the public of the country and in payment for these services, it charges fees. Taylor states that fees are characterised by more or less free choice on the part of the payer as to whether or not he will pay more or less for direct benefit conferred upon him. The tax is also a payment made to the government and we pay taxes with the initiative that the government provides us many facilities.

(ii) *Licence fee:* A licence fee is one of the forms of fees although some people have tried to put it differently. According to Lutz, a licence fee is paid in those instances in which the government authority is invoked simply to confer a permission or a privilege rather than to perform a service of a more tangible and definite sort. Thus, when a licence fee is realised by the government, no direct service is rendered but permission is granted for doing certain things or activities.

(iii) *Special assessment:* Special assessment is an American invention which has been defined by Prof. Seligman as "a compulsory contribution levied in proportion to the special benefits derived, to defray the cost of a specific improvement to property undertaken in the public interest." It is a device for securing for the public treasury part of the unearned increment in the value of fixed property. In simple words, we can say that sometimes the government performs certain services, as a result of which the property or wealth of a particular group of persons in the community is increased. A levy in proportion to this increase in the value of wealth is known as the 'special assessment'.

Further, a special assessment resembles a price as in the case of both the payer receives a definite and direct *quid pro quo*. However, even with this similarity between price and special assessment, it differs from price in that the payment is not voluntary and does not arise out of a contract made with the public authority.

E.A.R. Seligman defined it as, "A compulsory contribution, levied in proportion to the special benefits derived, to defray the cost of specific improvement to property undertaken in the public interest."

(iv) *Forfeitures:* Forfeiture money is received by the government when some bonds and bails are granted for the appearance of a person before a court of law, but the person concerned fails to abide by the orders of the court and the bond is forfeited. The money coming by the way of forfeitures is small in proportion to the total public revenue.

(v) *Fines and penalties:* Fines and penalties are the payments made for the contravention of law. The distinction between taxes and penalties is one of motives. A public authority imposes taxes mainly to obtain revenue and imposes penalties mainly to deter people from doing contravening acts.

(vi) *Escheats:* Escheats are the money coming by the way of state acquisition of the property of an individual who dies without any heir or making a will. Governments also acquire the 'unclaimed' property of trusts, institutions, etc. This is a casual source of income and very small in amount.

(vii) *Gifts & grants:* A small portion of the revenue of the government is also derived from the gifts made by individuals, private organisations and foreign governments. This is, however, not a certain and fixed source of revenue for the government and is also out of the control of the government. Its significance as a source of public revenue has been gradually declining over the years.

(viii) *Borrowings:* Another source of public revenue—in a sense a provisional or temporary source—is the borrowing of the money. Just as individuals or firms may borrow in anticipation of other revenues, so also governments borrow funds. It is ordinarily presumed that money borrowed will eventually be repaid from other sources of revenue although in practice this may not always be the case.

Generally speaking, as a source of public revenue, taxes are better than borrowing because it is merely transferring of funds from private hands to public treasuries. There is an element of certainty in the case of a tax. However, in practice, the democratic governments are frequently afraid of taxing people because if people do not like taxes, and if a government imposes heavy taxes then it blemishes the government's image and people may throw it out of power. Therefore, as a matter of practical expediency, government prefers borrowing to taxing people beyond the limits of safety.

(ix) *Printing of currency:* Finally, the government may resort to the printing a paper money as a means of paying their bills. Governments, unlike individuals, have the power to create money and assign it legal tender qualities. However, the printing of paper money is normally avoided by pecunious governments because once this method of financing is started, it becomes difficult to stop it and it leads to inflation which may eventually bring a collapse of the government. It produces adverse psychological reactions in the form of loss of confidence in the stability of the government.

CLASSIFICATION OF PUBLIC REVENUE

The effects and incidence of various kinds of public revenue differ from each other, and in order to know this we need to classify public revenue. Further, different sources of public revenue have different relative significance which can be known only when we suitably classify the public revenue. Economists have given various classifications of public revenue. Looking from different angles, they have grouped public revenue in one manner or another. The differences of opinion in this regard are not important as they are only the different faces of the same coin viewed from different angles. Different classifications do not change the nature of public revenue. The following are the main classifications given by different economists:

1. Adam Smith's Classification

According to Adam Smith, the revenue of the government ultimately depends on the property in possession of the inhabitants of the country and the extent to which the state has control over the wealth of the country. Accordingly, Adam Smith classified public revenue into the following two categories:

(i) Revenue from public; and

(ii) Revenue from state property.

Under the revenue from public, we include all those sources which are generally known as the sources of revenue of the government from the public. Under the second category, we include those public incomes which are received from the property in possession of the state.

Adam Smith's classification does not, however, serve the purpose of modern finance since he emphasised only taxes in the former category and he could not foresee the extension of public sector and felt that the income from the second source would be fixed and limited.

2. Bastable's Classification

Like Adam Smith, Charles F. Bastable has also divided public revenue into (i) those incomes which the government receives from performing its various functions just like a private individual or corporation, and (ii) those incomes which the state derives in its capacity as 'state'.

The first category of revenue includes all the incomes which the government derives in the form of fees and prices, while the second category of revenue includes taxes and levies. Like Adam Smith's classification of public revenue, Bastable's approach is also narrow and limited.

3. Lutz's Classification

Lutz has divided public revenue under the following six heads:

(i) Commercial revenue;

(ii) Administrative revenue;

(iii) Taxation;

(iv) Public debts;

(v) Grants; and

(vi) Book-keeping revenues or transfers.

The last three, *i.e.* public debt, grants, and book-keeping revenues are not nowadays included in the category of public revenue.

4. Taylor's Classification

Taylor has classified public revenue into following four parts:

(i) *Grants-in-aid:* These are the means by which one government provides financial assistance to another, usually in the performance of a specified function in a specified manner. Education and health grants flowing from the centre to the states in the federal form of government are examples of grants-in-aid. Grants are sometimes, though very seldom, also made for general and unspecified purposes. Grants-in-aid are cost payment for the grantor government and revenue receipts for the grantee government since no obligation for reimbursement such grants is established. Gifts are voluntary contributions made by non-governmental donors generally for specified purposes. As a category of public revenue, grants and gifts are characterised by their voluntary nature and by the absence of any expectation of direct benefit for the donor.

(ii) ***Administrative revenue:*** These revenues include fees, licences, fines and special assessment, etc. They are characterised by more or less free choice on the part of the payer as to whether or not he will pay and more or less direct benefit (or penalty) conferred upon him. The amount of the assessment does not necessarily bear close relationship either to the value of the benefit. They generally arise as a by-product of the administration of a control function of the government. It is simply due to this last peculiar characteristic of these public revenues that Taylor gives them the name of Administrative Revenues.

(iii) ***Commercial revenues:*** These revenues are received in the form of prices paid to the government against produced goods and services. These include payments for postage, interest on funds borrowed from the government, tuition fees of public educational institutions, prices paid for liquor in government stores, surplus war materials, electricity distributed by public owned utilities and the like. The salient characteristic which distinguishes commercial revenues from those in other categories, is the direct receipt of a good or service in return for payment and adjustment of the amount of payment approximately to the cost of production.

(iv) ***Taxes:*** Taxes are compulsory payments made to government without expectation of any direct return or benefit to the tax-payer. Taxes are in the nature of compulsory contribution made by the tax-payers to the general funds of the government and these do not confer any specific benefits on the tax-payers, although there has been some tendency towards allocation of the benefits roughly on the basis of tax revenue.

(5) Seligman's Classification

Seligman classifies public revenue into three groups:

(i) ***Gratuitous revenue:*** All revenues such as gifts, donations and grants received by the public authorities free of cost come under gratuitous revenue. They are entirely of a voluntary nature. Further, these are very insignificant in the total revenue.

(ii) ***Contractual revenue:*** All those types of revenues which arise from the contractual relations between the public authority and the people are included in this category. Fees and prices also fall into this category. A direct *quid pro quo* is usually present in these types of revenue.

(iii) ***Compulsory revenue:*** This includes income derived by the state from administration, justice, and taxation. Taxes, fines and special assessments are regarded as compulsory revenue. These revenues express an element of state sovereignty. It is the most significant type of public revenue in modern times.

(6) Hugh Dalton's Classification

Dalton provides a very systematic, comprehensive and instructive classification of public revenue. In his opinion, there are two main sources of public revenue—taxes and prices. Taxes are paid compulsorily, whereas prices are paid voluntarily by individuals, who enter into contracts with the public authority. Thus, prices are contractual payments.

Taxes are sub-divided into:

(i) Taxes in the ordinary sense;
(ii) Attributes and indemnities;
(iii) Compulsory loans; and
(iv) Pecuniary penalties for offences.

Prices are sub-divided into:

(i) Receipts from public property passively held, such as rents received from the tenants of public lands;
(ii) Receipts from public enterprises charging competitive rates;

(iii) Fees or payments charged for rendering administrative services, such as birth and death registration fees; and

(iv) Voluntary public debt.

To these two groups must be added another group to make the classification exhaustive. Under this group, the following items are included:

(i) Receipts from public monopolies, charging higher prices;

(ii) Special assessments;

(iii) Issue of new paper money or deficit financing; and

(iv) Voluntary gifts.

(7) Ideal Classification

All the classifications have some sort of lacuna in them. The revenues, with similar characteristics and elements should be kept together, to avoid any kind of overlapping and misunderstanding.

Prof. Findlay Shirras classified, public revenue into two categories, namely:

(i) Tax revenue; and

(ii) Non-tax revenue.

(i) ***Tax Revenue:*** Tax revenue has been called with different names by different economists'. Adam Smith calls it as, "revenue from the people." Prof. Adam as "derivate revenue." Where C.F. Bastable prefers to call it as, "that taking of the revenues from the society by the power of the sovereign", Prof. Seligman calls it as 'compulsory revenue and includes, taxes, special assessments and fees.' The special assessment is defined as, "a compulsory contribution levied in proportion to the special benefits derived, to defray the cost of a specific improvement to property undertaken in the public interest."

(ii) ***Non-tax Revenue:*** This category includes the income generated from:

(a) The sale of goods and services produced by the government enterprises; it is also called as price.

(b) The payments made for the social services like education and hospital fees.

(c) The lending business of the state, and the interest earned thereon.

(d) There are some other sources which include those receipts which could not be kept under first three heads. The money received as "military receipts" and money received in the aid of superannuation, would find a place, in this category.

(8) Economic Classification

These classifications of the public revenue, in most of the cases are overlapping, though it is accepted that some of them are satisfactory. In India, the first attempt to classify the transactions was made in 1957-58, and the budget presented for the year 1957-58 was wholly based on this classification.

This proposal classified the income and expenditure of the government into the *revenue account* and the *capital account*. The revenue account embodies revenue received in the form of taxes. On the other hand, capital account is composed of:

(a) Loans from the market;

(b) Aid received from external sources; and

(c) Income from other sources, including the income from public enterprises like post and telegraph, railways, etc.

STUDY-QUESTIONS

1. Define the term public revenue? Discuss the different types of public revenue.
2. Discuss the various types and sources of public revenue.
3. What are the different classifications made by different scholars of public revenue? Explain with examples.

❖❖❖

Principles and Theories of Taxation

5

INTRODUCTION

Taxation must be levied with great care and rationality. In order to practise this rationality and care, the taxing agency must follow a certain code of conduct in the form of principles of taxation while determining the type and amount of tax. The various theories which have been developed since Adam Smith's days in order to guide the state in levying the taxes, are called the principles of taxation.

Every tax is an additional burden on the tax-payer. Thus, it becomes essential that the burden of the taxes should be divided 'fairly'. Government is responsible to provide certain facilities to the citizens, which it cannot leave on the voluntary payment of the citizens. It has to adopt a definite principle and a definite machinery to apply these principles while levying, collecting, and then utilising the money. 'A good tax system must have certain administrative qualities, including certainty, low compliance and collection costs, enforceability and acceptability.'

The system must also be fair both to promote the objective of an equitable distribution of income and to assure continued voluntary compliance by tax-payers.

THEORIES OF TAXATION

The total amount of money burden of taxation is the amount of money income transferred from the people to the government by way of various taxes. On the other hand, the total amount of direct real burden of taxation refers to the volume of goods and services transferred from tax-payers to the government or the value of money raised by the government. The total direct real burden of taxation also refers to the amount of sacrifice imposed on the community due to the transfer of money income from the tax-payers on account of the imposition of tax by the government.

We shall now explain the different criteria on which the tax proposals are generally developed and suggestions are made for the distribution of the tax burden. Firstly, according to some theories, there need not be any relationship between the taxes paid and benefits flowing from the authorities to the tax-payers. In this connection, there are two approaches:

(1) Expediency theory; and

(2) Socio-political theory.

Secondly, there is an approach which links the tax liability of the tax-payers to the state activities. It maintains that since the state is providing goods and services to the members of the society, it should charge for them. This approach simultaneously provides a justification for imposing taxation (government provides services and has a right to charge for them) and a principle for apportioning the tax burden.

1. Expediency Theory

According to this theory, in reality every tax proposal not only must pass the test of practicability, rather it must be the only consideration weighing with the authorities in choosing a tax proposal. In other words, in the choice of various tax proposals, the authorities need not consider various economic and social objectives or the effects of a tax system. In practice, however, every authority or government is pressurised by various economic, social and political factors to orient its taxation policy in certain directions. Every group of people does its best to resist a change that goes against its interests. The government, in many cases, has to adopt certain policies simply because there are pressures to that effect. Further, depending upon the changing political strength of different economic groups, the government is likely to reshape the tax structure. It is also evident that while imposing a tax, the government would be making a great mistake if it does not see the administrative feasibility, the cost of tax collection, etc.

However, to build up an entire tax system only on the consideration of expediency, must be full of pitfalls. Although in certain cases, such a tax policy may be able to yield certain good results like contributing to the equality of income distribution, or reducing the regional disparities, yet such results would be purely accidental and not the outcome of any thoughtful scheme.

2. Socio-political Theory

According to this approach, developed by the well-known German economist Adolph Wagner, it is not the expediency but final social and political objectives which should be the deciding factors. Wagner did not believe in individualistic approach to a problem. He always looked at the problem in its social and political context and made efforts to find an appropriate solution thereof. Although the society consists of individuals, it is more than the sum total of its individual members. It has an existence and entity of its own. Accordingly, a tax policy should not be designed to serve the needs of the individual members of the society. It should be used for the benefit of the society as far as it is possible.

In other words, Wagner was advocating a modern welfare approach to the entire problem of evolving and adopting a tax policy. He particularly favoured the idea of using taxation for reduction of income inequalities and to attain this purpose, he stated that all small incomes should be exempted from taxation. He maintained that private property and inheritance were there because the state was permitting them to be there. The government had the right to control the ownership of property and the right to inheritance in the interest of the society as a whole. Thus, in a modern state, taxation is generally designed to curb the economic inequalities arising out of the private right to property and inheritance.

PRINCIPLES OF TAXATION

In order to achieve the ideal of justice and equity in taxation, different economists have propounded different principles of taxation from time to time. The main principles of taxation are as follows:

(1) Physiocratic theory;
(2) Finance theory;
(3) Benefit theory;
(4) Cost of service theory;
(5) Ability to pay theory;
(6) Equity theory;
(7) Least aggregate sacrifice theory; and
(8) Principle of neutrality theory.

1. Physiocratic Theory

The physiocratic theory is the oldest and simplest theory of taxation which was propounded by earlier economists. This theory had its origin in France. This theory is based on the view that only land is capable of producing a net surplus. Thus, according to physiocrats, only agriculture is capable of yielding a net return which could add to the wealth of the country.

2. Finance Theory

The aim of the financial theory is to earn maximum revenue instead of bothering about the burden of distribution. It proceeds with the motto, "Pluck the goose with as little squealing as possible."

3. Benefit Theory

The principle of benefit requires that the burden of tax must be in proportion to the benefit received by a person from the expenditure done by the government. This principle shows the common desire that the taxes should not exceed the benefit received by the tax-payer.

The benefit principle has been criticised on the following grounds:

(1) There is no accurate measurement of the benefit conferred upon the people. How could we measure the benefit conferred upon us by the government?
(2) The benefit principle, if made applicable, puts the undesirable limitations upon the scale of government service. Whenever the government undertakes a new

plan, it has to consider first whether the benefit likely to accrue from this plan would compensate for the taxes paid by the public or not.

(3) The benefit principle cannot be applied to social services. It would be unfair to charge for beneficial services like education.

Obviously, benefit cannot be allocated among citizens with accuracy. And benefits, are to a major degree, general and the rigidity which the principle imposes upon the government also demands its rejection. Buckler has rightly remarked, "It must be concluded therefore that the benefit principle, however unsatisfactory it may be as a standard by which to apportion taxes, does leave an important influence on taxation."

According to this principle, every person should be taxed according to his ability to pay taxes. In regard to this principle Adam Smith observes, "The subjects of every state ought to contribute towards the support of the government, as nearly as possible, in proportion to their respective abilities, *i.e.* in proportion to the revenue which they respectively enjoy under the protection of the state. In the observation or neglect of this maxim consists what is called the 'equality or inequality of taxation'. By revenue, he meant the income which the person earns under the protection of the state and advocated taxing of individuals on the basis of this revenue. This indicates that Adam Smith advocated the proportional system of taxation. But this theory has been rejected for the allocation of taxes in modern times. The most classic statement of ability principle comes from the pen of J.S. Mill. He categorically rejected the benefit doctrine based on contract and protection. If taxation were to be based on protection, it would definitely lead to regressive taxation, for the poor need more protection than the rich. Besides, the protection theory was extremely inadequate to explain all the functions of the state and, therefore, a new principle of taxation would be needed. To quote Mill, "as a government ought to make no distinction of persons or classes in the strength of their claims on it, whatever sacrifices it requires of them, should be made to be as nearly as possible with the same pressure upon all, which, it must be observed, is the mode by which least sacrifice is occasioned on the whole."

Equality of taxation, therefore, as a maxim of politics, means equality of sacrifice. It means apportioning the contribution of each person towards the expense of the government so that he will feel neither more nor less inconveniences from his share of the payment than any other person experiences from his share.

4. Cost of Service Theory

Cost of service theory explains that the cost incurred by the government in providing certain services to the people must be collectively met by the people who are the ultimate receivers of the services. It was only in the nineteenth century that the classical economists narrowly interpreted the function of the state. They argued that as taxes are a premium paid for protection, the public services should be restricted to those activities that provide protection. David Ricardo, the arch-pillar of the classical economics, considered public expenditure so wasteful and useless that he completely ignored the benefit approach. The same view was taken by most continental writers.

However, towards the end of the nineteenth century, the benefits-received principle was revived by the continental writers. Taxes were regarded as a price for public works and services. The determination of tax price, in accordance with benefits received, was looked upon as a condition of efficient allocation of resources. The revenue-expenditure process became a part of the Walrasian system of general equilibrium. Prof. Mazzole argued that each consumer should pay a price (*i.e.* tax) equal to the marginal utility that he personally derived from the service provided by the government. It means that pricing of public services must differ from the pricing of goods purchased privately in the market. If public goods were sold at a single constant price, some people would find that this price exceeded the marginal utility derived by them from the consumption of these public goods. Therefore, public goods would have to be made available to different persons at different prices.

But the cost basis is also incomplete like the benefit principle. This theory has no place in the modern tax system. It has been criticised on the following grounds:

(i) It is difficult to find accurate measurement of the cost as distributed between different individuals. What cost of fighting a war should come in your share and what in mine? What part of the cost of opening of Delhi-Nainital-Lucknow air service falls on my part and what on yours? These are all indeterminate quantities.

(ii) Like the benefit principle, it also places undesirable limitations on the scale of government services.

(iii) This theory is just reverse of the accepted definition of tax. Tax has been defined as a payment which carries no direct specific *quid pro quo*. There may be some circumstances where the costs may be accurately determined. Electricity service rendered by the public utilities is one example. Here, the cost per unit electricity can be ascertained. But these payments are not actually taxes, they are prices paid for the service.

5. Ability to Pay Theory

The ability principle is the most generally accepted principle. The ability to pay approach is based on the broad assumption that those who possess income or wealth, should contribute to the support of public functions according to their relative abilities. The idea of a just and equitable taxation—the distribution of tax burdens should be just—has been associated with the earliest concept of ability to pay. According to this principle, every citizen should pay the tax to meet the cost of government expenditure according to his ability to pay. If every citizen pays the taxes according to their ability to pay, such a system of taxation would be an ideal system. Ability is the ideal ethical basis of taxation. Ability commands universal allegiance and fits in admirably with the modern conception of the state. According to Cohen, it is but a special application of the broad principles of moral solidarity.

Justification of the theory of ability to pay: The ability to pay principle has been justified on the grounds of:

(i) ***Fairness:*** It is considered fair and just to ask equal amount from each tax-payer. Every tax-payer feels psychological satisfaction in paying equal taxes. Mill says, "What could be more equitable than a situation under which each person's contribution to the support of the Government resulted in equal sacrifice for all?" Adam Smith, back in 1776, listed this on the first canon of taxation, and most people take it for granted that a fair tax system calls on the richer members of the community to pay more taxes than the poor.

(ii) ***Diminishing marginal utility of income.*** The benefit principle is held just because it is in accordance with the diminishing marginal utility of income. As income grows, the marginal utility derived from the additional unit of money decreases, and as income decreases the marginal utility of income increases. This requires that, in order to make the tax burden equal on rich and poor, the rich should be taxed more, and the poor less.

(iii) ***Interpretation of faculty.*** Income, property and wealth of a tax-payer represent the faculty. Taxes should be levied according to the faculty. Hobson went one step further and gave a new concept, 'economic surplus' which he termed as that part of the income, which is capable of bearing tax-burden. With the increase in faculty, this 'economic surplus' increases, thus inviting more burden of taxes. It also implies that the level of taxation should be more in proportion to the increase in income and wealth, as the level of 'economic surplus' is more.

HOW TO MEASURE ABILITY TO PAY

So far, economists have advanced two broad approaches for the measurement of ability to pay. They are as follows:

1. Objective Approach
2. Subjective Approach

1. Objective Approach

This theory is based on, as Seligman has put it, "faculty theory of the ability to pay." This approach considers the money-value of the taxable capacity of the tax-payers. Instead of being based on the psychological feeling, it is based on the capacity of the individuals to pay tax. Faculty theory or the objective approach of the ability to pay considers various factors, like income, property, consumption, etc. while determining a tax-payer's ability to pay. Greater the capacity, greater is the ability of the tax-payer to pay taxes.

Factors Affecting the Ability to Pay

According to the objective approach, following factors affect the ability of tax-payers:

(i) ***Income:*** Income is by far the most important determinant of a person's ability to pay taxes. Without income, how can you pay taxes? The greater the income he earns, naturally greater is his ability to pay taxes. By income, we mean the net income and not the gross income of an individual. In income we can include the property in one's possession which also earns income. A person can pay a greater amount of taxes due to potential of earning he has in the form of property. Similarly, the expectation of future income is one of the most important determinants of a person's ability to pay taxes.

(ii) ***Price level:*** The price level also affects the ability of a person to pay taxes. The higher the prices, the lower is the income on which the taxes can be paid and *vice versa*. Therefore, the prices also affect the ability of a person to pay taxes.

(iii) ***Method of taxation:*** If the taxes are so levied that they observe the canons of convenience then certainly the ability of a person to pay taxes would be greater. If the taxes are levied at the time when he receives his income, his ability to pay them, would be greater, *e.g.* deduction of income tax at source.

(iv) ***Benefits:*** Benefits accruing from the state expenditure also affect the person's ability to pay taxes. This happens in two ways. Materially, if the state provides some services free of cost or at concessional rates to its citizens, they would definitely save a part of their income and thus, enhance their ability to pay taxes. Psychologically also, the benefits which are conferred upon the public give some psychic satisfaction to the public and they feel that they have made a least sacrifice in paying tax. Their ability to pay taxes would thus increase both ways—materially and psychologically.

(v) ***Property:*** Early economists believed that property, acquired and accumulated, was the index of ability to pay. In reality, instead of being an index ability, it is a *supplementary index* of ability due to the following reasons:

(a) Though property is an important source of income, yet all properties do not produce income.

(b) The income from property does not always flow continuously.

(c) Income from property varies with the changes in place, etc.

(d) Since the property is taxed according to its capital value, and if the property does not yield any income, it would be unjust to tax the property.

Property must be considered while imposing taxes because:

(a) The person who owns property, has greater ability to pay since the possession of property increases his ability.

(b) Income received from property enables a high degree of tax-paying ability than the income received from personal services like wages and salaries.

(c) Income from inherited property (called as unearned income) increases high potentiality of ability to pay tax.

(vi) *Size of the family:* Size of the family is also a factor affecting the ability of a tax-payer to pay taxes. While imposing tax burden, the size of the family should also be considered. A larger size of family depending on a given amount of income, may have lesser ability to pay in comparison to a small size of family depending upon the same level of income. For example, a person living all alone, with the same income possesses high ability to pay than a person living with a dozen members.

(vii) *Consumption:* Amount of money spent on consumption by a person is also an index of his ability to pay taxes. Sometimes, the taxes imposed on income and property are manipulated and shifted on others. In such cases the taxes should be imposed on the consumption of the individuals. This approach was advanced by Prof. Nicholas Kaldor of Cambridge, England. He has advocated what he calls an expenditure tax, a tax on consumption. He argues that consumption rather than income, should be the proper base of taxation. It is consumption that measures the resource that an individual actually withdraws from the economy for his personal use. The part of his income not consumed, *i.e.* his savings, adds to the country's capital stock and serves to raise total productive capacity. If an individual chooses to consume more than his income (by buying on credit or drawing on his past savings) he should pay a higher tax because he is depleting the capital stock of the country. This idea is particularly attractive in underdeveloped countries where high consumption levels of the richer classes may make private capital accumulation small. An expenditure tax would discourage consumption by taxing it heavily and encourage savings by granting exemption. Such a tax could be progressive with the total amount spent by an individual on consumption.

Defects of the Objective Approach of the Ability to Pay

Certain points of defects have been raised by economists like Seligman. Some of these are as follows:

(i) Tax on property of general nature is regressive, causing more burden to the small property than the big property.

(ii) No universal technique has been devised to assess the personal property.

(iii) There is no uniform criterion developed for the assessment.

(iv) People may become dishonest by concealing their real income and property in order to escape tax burden.

In spite of the drawbacks in the ability to pay theory, it is accepted as the most satisfactory principle. It has wide acceptance.

2. The Subjective Approach

The subjective approach is based on the psychological reactions of the tax-payers to the imposition of the tax burden. What feelings come in the mind of the tax-payer after the tax-impositions is the essence of the subjective approach.

(a) *Equal Sacrifice Principle (Least Aggregate Sacrifice)*

From individual sacrifice, Pigou went to the sphere of aggregate sacrifice incurred by the whole society collectively in paying taxes and thus, advocated that the least aggregate sacrifice is the final principle of taxation. The principle is just an advancement of the ability theory and takes the sacrifice or disutility in the collective way for the whole body of tax-payers. The principle states that the taxes should be allocated in such a manner that the sacrifice, incurred by the persons paying taxes taken collectively, would be the least. The assumption, which Pigou takes for the principle that sacrifice of different individuals can be measured and summed up, is not valid. Pigou does not want to be concerned with the problem of spending revenue and the benefit accruing from public expenditure. But these benefits would affect the left by tax-payers and thus, in Prof. Adarkar's view, raising and spending of revenue should not, and cannot be studied in such isolation as Pigou advocates at the outset. Thus, the principle of sacrifice loses practical applicability.

The equity approach states that each tax-payer should be made to undergo the 'same' amount of sacrifice irrespective of his income, etc. The welfare approach states that the aggregate sacrifice of all the tax-payers should be the minimum. It means that the welfare loss due to tax to the community should be the least. However, as we shall see, the consideration of 'equal sacrifice' admits of different interpretations and one of such interpretations is linked with welfare considerations. The equity approach admits of the following three interpretations:

(a) Equal absolute sacrifice;

(b) Equal proportionate sacrifice; and

(c) Equal marginal sacrifice.

To these three interpretations, Hugh Dalton has added a fourth possible interpretation of constant inequality of incomes. This is the new element in the sacrifice theory. Dalton's interpretation states that the tax-payers should be least hurt and left as they are found. In other words, it means that the inequalities of incomes as between different tax-payers should remain the same after the payment of tax as these were before the payment of tax.

Now we shall explain the above interpretations in detail:

(a) *Equal absolute sacrifice:* It means that different tax-payers are made to sacrifice the same amount of utility by way of payment of taxes. In this case, every individual in society has to pay some tax at least and none will be exempted from contributing a share to the public revenue. If we assume identical income-marginal utility schedules for all individuals and if the marginal utility of income is constant, then it would mean that each person pays the same absolute amount of income as tax. It involves a lower rate of tax as income increases, or regressive tax rates.

(b) *Equal proportionate sacrifice:* Here also none is exempted from tax burden. In this case, each person is required to pay the same percentage of the tax. While in the case of equal absolute sacrifice, we are able to state the rules for progressive, proportional or regressive tax rates (with reference to the rate at which marginal utility falls with the increase in income), such a generalisation is not possible in this case. In this case, if the marginal utility of income is constant, then equal proportional sacrifice would call for a proportional taxation. The rationale of the proportional sacrifice doctrine is the sounding argument that persons with greater income receive much more benefit from society and thus, should bear high tax-sacrifice rather than the same amount as paid by persons with smaller incomes.

(c) ***Equal marginal sacrifice or least aggregate sacrifice:*** According to this interpretation of equity, persons should be so taxed that the total sacrifice for the society would be the minimum possible and the marginal utility of income left after tax with any person would be the same. In this principle, the emphasis is equally on the welfare of the community.

Edgeworth and Pigou advocated the equal marginal sacrifice approach not on the ground of equity, but on the ground of community welfare. According to Musgrave, "It is the ultimate principle of taxation." This principle necessarily leads to progressive taxation.

Now the problem is to select one of the above three interpretations of equity. The classical economists failed to distinguish between them clearly. Adam Smith's canon of ability can be interpreted differently. His canon states that people should contribute in proportion to their respective abilities, that is, in proportion to the revenue which they respectively enjoy. Although John Stuart Mill had advocated the equal sacrifice approach yet he did not define equality clearly. The later writers, however, clearly distinguished the three interpretations of equality of sacrifice although they did not agree on the advantages of the various interpretations. Some economists, like Cohen, preferred equal proportional sacrifice while some others, like Alfred Marshall, preferred absolute sacrifice. However, the welfare economists, like Edgeworth and Pigou rejected the concepts of absolute and proportional sacrifice on the ground that there was no logical or intuitive choice between them. They advocated equal marginal sacrifice approach on the ground of welfare. Thus, the classical writers emphasised the principle of equity and distributive justice in taxation while the modern economists have emphasised welfare. There has thus, been a shift away from equity in favour of welfare.

(b) *Equity Principle in Taxation*

Equity principle is the most important principle of taxation. It means that the burden of taxation is spread more or less uniformly among the tax-payers. This has two implications:

(a) Like people should be treated in a like manner, or those who are essentially equals, should be taxed equally.

(b) Unlike people should be treated in an unlike manner or unequals should be taxed unequally. The first implication of equity demands horizontal equity. Persons in similar circumstances should be taxed equally. For example, people with equal levels of income should be taxed at the same rate. They should sacrifice the same proportion of their incomes as tax. The principle of horizontal equity thus, demands that equals should be taxed equally. The second principle of equity is based on the principle of vertical equity. Persons in dissimilar circumstances should be treated unequally. For example persons with unequal incomes or properties should be taxed at different rates. Those with a higher level income and property should be made to pay a higher proportion of their income and property, *i.e.* a higher rate of tax be imposed on them. Thus, the principle of vertical equity demands that the unequal should be taxed unequally. However, as Paul Samuelson points out, general and abstract principles of taxation cannot resolve the fundamental political question of how much differently unequals should be treated or how we are to define equity. Nevertheless various economists have evolved different principles of taxation to establish both horizontal and vertical equity.

CRITERIA OR INDEX OF ABILITY TO PAY

If the ability to pay theory is to provide any workable criterion for the establishment and evaluation of the tax structure, suitable measures of ability or economic well-being must be developed. Here, we may discuss the following important primary criteria of the ability to pay:

1. Income as Criterion of Ability to Pay

Income is now widely accepted as an index or criterion of a person's ability to pay. A family's ability to pay depends primarily on the income received. The income figure is the amount which the family can spend on consumption goods or save. The amount of different goods, which the family is able to acquire and the total amount of saving that it can make, are the primary determinants of how well the family lives or, in other words, its level of living during the period. Accordingly, income is generally regarded as the best criterion of economic well-being and thus, of the ability to pay taxes. However, the actual level of living, which can be attained with a given money income depends in part on certain circumstances affecting the amount of income that must be spent in order to attain a given level of living which is possible with a given money income. In this regard, we have to see whether a person is married or not married. If a person is married, then the size of the family will determine the ability to pay.

(a) ***Earned or unearned income:*** Earned income is that income which is earned in the first instance from direct services while income derived from property, rent, interest, etc. is unearned income because this is earned from the already earned income. Here, the idea is that a person having unearned income possesses higher capacity to pay than a person having earned income, *e.g.* a salaried person. Earned income is taxed at a lower rate while unearned income is taxed at a higher rate.

(b) ***Windfall income:*** It is an income where no efforts are involved in earning it. This income should be taxed at a progressive rate. Such income is mostly in the nature of capital gains enjoyed by property owners.

Income is, therefore, the most reliable criterion to judge a person's ability to pay taxes. For purposes of taxation, gross income is considered unsuitable for it is composed of the cost elements. Net income is regarded as the best measure of the tax paying ability of a person because it reflects the sum of net receipts over costs. While considering income as an index of the ability to pay taxes, the classical economists recognised that the low income groups should be given a more favourable treatment. However, they did not accept the idea of progressive taxation. For example, Adam Smith advocated the complete exemption of the low and middle income groups from tax and the imposition of proportional taxation on higher income brackets. The modern economists distinguish between earned and unearned incomes. They state that taxation on earned income involves double sacrifice which is well reflected in the loss of enjoyment from the use of income and also pain of having suffered in vain, the disutility of earning such income. They favour progressive taxation on unearned incomes.

2. Personal Wealth as Criterion of Ability to Pay

A family unit's ability to pay taxes is influenced not only by the income received by it during a given period of time, but also by the amount of its accumulated wealth. In the past, wealth was considered a better index of the ability to pay than income because in addition to being a source of income, wealth provided security and insurance against risk. However, with the progress of the industrial society and the development of money economy, there was a shift from property to income as the index of the ability to pay. It is now held that wealth is unsatisfactory as a primary test of ability to pay a tax although it can provide a possible supplementary index of such ability.

3. Consumption Expenditure as Index of Ability to Pay

It has been argued by some economists that the appropriate measure of an individual's ability to pay is not his total income but the amount of income spent on consumption. This view was expressed mainly by John Stuart Mill, Irving Fisher and recently it has been expressed by Nicholas Kaldor. It is claimed that economic well-being depends upon consumption alone. Wealth accumulated yields no satisfaction until it is used for consumption purposes. The expenditure basis is also defended on the grounds of simplicity and avoidance of double taxation of income saved.

However, this index of ability to pay is also not free from criticisms. It is criticised on the ground that it favours the miser and it is difficult to make taxation progressive or even to prevent it from becoming regressive and would reduce the amount of revenue. However, in recent years expenditure tax has been imposed in countries like India complementing the personal income tax.

In the above analysis, we have discussed the three possible measures of the ability to pay without discussing which one of these three is the best measure of the ability to pay. In the light of their relative merits and demerits, we may say that the main index of the ability to pay is income while wealth and consumption can both serve as supplementary indices. In recent years, in many countries of the world direct taxation based on all the above three indices of the ability to pay has been in vogue. The main direct tax is the personal and business income tax. The supplementary or subsidiary direct taxes are estate duty and expenditure tax.

6. Equity Theory

Equity in taxation refers to fairness or justice in the distribution of the tax burden. Since taxation implies a burden or sacrifice on the part of the tax-payer, modern economists put great emphasis on justice in taxation and state that taxation should be based on the principle of equity so that direct money burden as well as real burden should be distributed in a just manner.

7. Least Aggregate Sacrifice Theory

According to Pigou, Dalton and Canon the least aggregate sacrifice is the final principle of taxation. The principle is just an advancement of the ability theory and takes the sacrifice in a collective way for the whole body of tax-payers. According to this principle, the government should devise its taxation system in such a manner that the sacrifice incurred by the persons paying taxes taken collectively would be the least. Hence, it is not essential that all the persons be subjected to taxation, but on the contrary, a minimum exemption limit should be fixed by the government.

8. Principle of Neutrality Theory

According to this principle of neutrality, tax should be levied on different persons in such a way that the economic position of the tax-payer remains neutral and the inequality of income is not affected. According to Prof. A.C. Pigou, "The function of the state is simply to realise tax and remain neutral towards reducing of inequalities of income." He has called this principle of neutrality as 'leave them as you found them'. The principle of neutrality suggests the inclusion the principles of equal sacrifice, proportional sacrifice and minimum sacrifice.

Criticisms*:* The principle of neutrality has been criticised on the following grounds:

(i) It will discourage savings.

(ii) It will reduce accumulation of capital and also investment.

(iii) It will increase the sacrifice of both the poor and the rich.

(iv) It will adversely affect the economic welfare of the society.

STUDY-QUESTIONS

1. Explain the meaning of the principles of taxation. Briefly state the various principles of taxation.
2. Briefly explain the principle of benefit theory of principle of taxation.
3. Write notes on the following:
   (a) The physiocratic theory
   (b) Financial theory
   (c) Principle of equity
   (d) Cost of service theory.
4. How can ability to pay be measured? Discuss various methods in brief.
5. Write a short note on 'principle of neutrality'.

❖❖❖

Classification of Taxation 6

INTRODUCTION

In ancient states, taxation was regarded as a minor and emergency revenue. Property, commodity, income and inheritance taxes were sometimes collected, but the small expenditures of ancient states did not require extensive system of taxation. But in modern times, in all the countries of the world, taxation is the single biggest source of public revenue. However, this is not the only factor attributing the paramount importance to the study of taxation. The study of taxation is important as we study the various theoretical and practical aspects of financial problems under the study of taxation. This is important for the government and the public as well. In a democratic political set-up, taxation, in addition to being a pure fiscal and economic problem, is also responsible for shaping the political activities of the government. All these and several other factors contribute towards the importance of the study of taxes and policy.

Tax constitutes the major source of the government's income. A tax is a liability imposed upon the tax assessees who may be individuals, groups of individuals, or other legal entities. It is a liability to pay an amount on account of the fact that the tax assessees have income of a minimum amount and from certain specified sources, or that they own certain tangible or intangible property, or that they carry on certain economic activities which have been chosen for taxation. Thus, a tax is a generalised exaction. It may be noted that a public receipt containing an element of compulsion does not automatically become a tax. In order to be a tax, the absence of a *quid pro quo* (tit for tat) is necessary.

Many economists like Seligman, Adams, Bastable, Taussig and Dalton hold the unanimous opinion that the tax is compulsory payment to the government by tax payer without any expectation of some specified return. While paying tax, the tax-payer is not entitled to force the government to give something to him in return for the sum he has paid as tax. It does not mean that the taxes are levied for some other purpose than for providing services to the tax payers. But the essence of the argument is that the tax-payer is not entitled to claim return of his taxes, though he may receive benefit of the services which the state provides by means of the taxes collected from him and many others like him. The following are the various definitions of tax given by different economists:

According to Seligman, "A tax is a compulsory payment from a person to the government to defray the expenses incurred in the common interests of all without reference to special benefits conferred."

According to Taylor, "Taxes are the compulsory payments to the Governments without expectation of the direct return in benefit to the tax-payer. We should probably say more or less compulsory payments but the degree of coercion varies with different taxes. A poll tax is paid simply because the tax-payer has reached taxable age. Income tax can be avoided by failure to reach taxable income, etc."

According to F.W. Taussig, "The essence of Tax, as distinguished from other charges by government, is the absence of a direct *quid pro quo* (tit for tat) between the tax-payer and the public authority."

According to Hugh Dalton, "A tax is a compulsory contribution imposed by public authority irrespective of the exact amount of service rendered to the tax-payer in return and not imposed as a penalty for any legal offence."

The above definitions make it clear that all the economists unanimously agree that the taxes are contributions by the tax-payer, to the state. In the opinion of R.N. Bhargava, taxes are as much compulsory as other payments like fees, etc.

From the above definitions, it becomes clear that tax is not a voluntary contribution, but it is compulsory in nature. If a person denies the tax payment orders, he may be punished by the courts and consequently may be jailed for such an offence. Tax is such a withdrawal from the people's income which reduces their purchasing power. Sometimes it is also held that tax checks production whereas public expenditure may spurt the productive process. To quote Hugh Dalton, "Whereas taxation, taken alone, may check production, public expenditure taken alone, should almost certainly increase it."

A tax is necessarily a contribution by tax-payer to the government exchequer which lubricates the administrative machinery. Being a major source of income of the government it assumes a significant place in the Budget.

FEATURES OF A TAX

The characteristics of a tax may be studied under the following heads:

(i) **Tax is a payment to the government by the people:** If payments are made by people among themselves or from government to the people, they are not taxes. This implies the taxes are imposed by authoritative institutions and under such institutions we can take here none except the government. If the Management Trust of a temple makes it compulsory for every family of a particular sect to pay a specified sum every year, it is never a tax. So, taxes are payments by public to the government only.

(ii) **Payment of taxes is compulsory:** Payment of taxes is compulsory, if the tax-payer has attained the conditions which are given in the law as the sufficient conditions for the imposition of a tax. Thus, the taxes are compulsory in a specified sense.

(iii) **Elements of sacrifice:** An element of sacrifice is there in the payment of tax in addition to the legal compulsion. We are also legally bound to pay the price of provisions which we buy. It is a mere commercial transaction and we pay the price because we have to. But in case of taxes at least in theory, a sense of sacrifice is there as the tax-payer pays the taxes for public interest.

(iv) **The aim of tax collection is public good:** It is for the benefit of the general public and for the maximum welfare of the entire community that the taxes are levied and collected. The use of taxes in the welfare of vested individual interests or for the development of a particular section in a way not agreeable to the general public, is not permissible.

(v) **The benefit received is not directly the return of tax:** Although a person may receive benefits accruing from the expenditure of the funds of which his contribution in the form of taxes constitutes a part, yet it is not intended or guaranteed by the state to give these benefits to a particular person in return for and in proportion to the payment he has made in the form of taxes.

(vi) **Tax is not the cost of the benefit:** Tax is not the cost of the benefit conferred by the government on the public. Benefits and taxes are independent of each other. Payment of taxation is, of course, designed for the conferring of benefits on general public. A tax has relation to the cost of service that a government renders to an individual.

(vii) **Taxes are paid out of income:** Taxes are paid out of income though they may be saving a part out of income.

(viii) **Taxes are paid by the persons:** Taxes are paid by the persons though they may be levied on persons or things.

To pay tax is the personal responsibility of an individual as the possessions, which he has and on which taxes are levied, cannot pay tax. It is only after the levy of a tax becomes an Act of the government that taxes are levied.

CHARACTERISTICS OF A GOOD TAX SYSTEM

Edmund Burke once remarked, "It is difficult to tax and to please as it is to love and to be wise." In a tax system, therefore, different taxes, good and bad may be combined together which tend to correct and balance one another's effects. Hence, it should be noted that a good tax system does not mean a perfect tax system which contains only the good taxes based upon the canons of taxation, fetching adequate revenues and causing no hurt to the tax-payer. A good tax system is one which has predominantly good taxes and which fulfils most of the canons of taxation; it must yield sufficient revenue, but cause minimum aggregate sacrifice to the people and minimum obstruction to incentives for production. A good tax system should possess the following characteristics:

(i) The entire structure of the tax system should have built-in flexibility, so that changes are possible according to the changing conditions of a dynamic economy. It should be possible to add or withdraw a tax without destroying the entire system and its balancing effect. A rigid tax structure is very unsatisfactory. Taxation must cope with the changing needs of the modern government. The capacity to adjust itself to the dynamic conditions of an economy is a virtue of a good tax system.

(ii) A good tax system should be a balanced one. It means there must exist not one kind of taxes but all types in the right proportion. In other words, it should not contain just progressive, regressive, or proportional taxes only, but a healthy combination of all such taxes. Similarly, it should have a balance of direct and indirect taxes.

(iii) In a good tax system, taxes are universally applicable in the sense that persons with some ability to pay are treated in the same way without any discrimination whatsoever. In the Indian tax system, however, tax is not universal as no income-tax is levied on agricultural incomes.

(iv) It should contain a predominance of good taxes satisfying most of the canons of taxation. That is to say, the taxes imposed should be more or less equitable,

convenient to pay, economical, certain, productive, flexible and simple as far as possible.

(v) It should ensure maximum social advantage. Taxation should be used to finance public services.

(vi) It should cause minimum aggregate sacrifice. In a good tax system, the allocation of taxes among tax-payers is made according to the ability to pay. It falls more heavily on the rich and less on the poor. It should be reasonably progressive so as to minimise the gap of inequality of income and wealth in the community, thereby ensuring their better distribution.

(vii) The tax system should be multiple, but too great a multiplicity is not desirable. Dalton, however, suggests that a good tax system has to be also a reasonably efficient administrative system.

(viii) Further, in a good tax system there is simplicity implying the absence of any unnecessary and avoidable complexities.

(ix) A good tax system should not hamper the development of trade and industry but instead it should help the rapid economic development of the country. Taxation is designed to mobilise the surplus resources in the economy and not deprive the private sector of its resources.

Above all, the most fundamental characteristic of a good tax system is the appreciation of the rights and problems of the tax-payer. A good tax system must contain the majority of such taxes which produce good effects on production and equitable distribution of national income and wealth. To achieve the socialistic goals of public policy, a good tax system plays a very important role. It should effectively balance the weight and burden of taxation. The weight refers to absolute sacrifice, in terms of purchasing power of real income surrendered by the tax-payer. The burden implies the relative capacity of the tax-payer to bear the tax. Thus, the tax system should contain taxes which are strictly in relation to the tax-payer's ability to pay.

THE CHARACTERISTICS OF A GOOD TAX SYSTEM IN THE CONTEXT OF INDIAN TAX STRUCTURE

A sincere effort has been made to include the good characteristics of a tax system in India. The following are the good characteristics of Indian tax structure:

(i) **Higher burden of taxes on urban areas as compared to rural areas:** Agriculture is the main source of income in rural areas and agricultural income is exempted from tax in India. Hence, there is higher burden of taxes on urban areas as compared to rural areas. Recently, Indian Taxation Enquiry Committee has admitted in its report, "the burden on urban households was distinctly higher than on the rural households in the corresponding expenditure class."

(ii) **Maximum social benefit:** While devising Indian taxation policy, Government of India keeps in mind the objective of achieving maximum social benefit. Indian taxation system is said to be used as an instrument for attaining certain social objectives, *e.g.* as a means of removing inequality of income, diverting resources for productive purposes and thereby increasing the social welfare of the community.

(iii) **Dominance of indirect taxes:** There is dominance of indirect taxes as against direct taxes in Indian tax structure. It is estimated that more than 85% of taxes are collected through indirect taxes as against only 15% revenue from direct taxes.

(iv) **Based on fundamental principles:** Indian tax structure is said to be based on fundamental principles of taxation. Almost all the principles have been included in the Indian tax structure.

(v) **Multiplicity of taxes:** The main characteristic of Indian tax structure is the multiplicity of taxes. Almost all kinds of taxes have been imposed in India, such as, income tax, wealth tax, service tax, value added tax, education cess, capital gains tax, death duty, etc.

In spite of the above good characteristics of Indian tax structure, it is subject to the following criticisms by different economists:

(i) Complexity of Indian taxation system;

(ii) Lack of uniformity in Indian taxation system;

(iii) Lack of co-ordination in Indian taxation structure;

(iv) Indian tax structure has failed to check the growing tax evasion;

(v) Indian tax structure is unbalanced and suffers from uncertainty;

(vi) Lack of built-in elasticity; and

(vii) Indian tax structure suffers from the problem of regional disparities.

CANONS OF TAXATION

Canons of taxation refer to the administrative aspects of a tax. They relate to the rate, amount, method of levy and collection of a tax. In other words, the characteristics or qualities, which a good tax should possess are described as canons of taxation. It must be noted that canons refer to the qualities of an isolated tax and not to the tax system as a whole. By canons of taxation, we mean those characteristics which a good tax system should possess. These are the qualities of a good tax and not the principles on the basis of which the taxes are levied. Very often the canons of taxation are confused with the principles of taxation. But they must be clearly distinguished so as to facilitate a clear understanding of the theory of taxation. The principles of taxation are those considerations according to which the allocation of taxes between different persons/groups is executed. These do not concern with the qualities individual taxes should possess; but they take into account the considerations relating with the entire tax policy of the State. On the other hand, the canons of taxation are not the principles which a good tax system should possess. While the canons of tax refer to the qualities of the individual tax in connection with rate, amount and methods of the levy and collection of a particular tax, the characteristics which a good tax system possess, are those considerations which the authorities should take into account in making a proper combination of all kinds of taxes – direct and indirect, simple and multiple, progressive and proportional. Thus, the canons of taxation are the qualities of a good tax while the characteristics of a good tax system are qualities of the tax system taken as a whole.

According to Adam Smith, there are four canons or maxims of taxation on the administrative side of public finance which are still recognised as classic. To him, a good tax is one which contains:

(i) Canon of Equality

Every fiscal economist, along with Adam Smith, stresses that taxation must ensure justice. The canon of equality or equity implies that the burden of taxation must be distributed equally or equitably in relation to the ability of the tax-payer. Equity or social justice demands that the rich people should bear a heavier burden of tax and the poor a lesser burden. Hence, a tax system should contain progressive tax rates based on the tax-payer's ability to pay and sacrifice.

(ii) Canon of Certainty

Adam Smith has unambiguously stated this canon and has clearly mentioned about this canon in these words: "The tax which each individual is bound to pay, ought to be certain and not arbitrary. The time of payment, the manner of payment, the quantity to be paid ought all to be clear and plain to the contributor and to every other person. The uncertainty of taxation encourages the insolence and favours the corruption of an order of men who are naturally unpopular, even where they are neither insolent nor corrupt." Adam Smith has further pointed out that even a very small degree of uncertainty is a matter of great importance than a considerable degree of inequality in taxation. If the tax is 'certain', the taxing authority cannot exploit the tax-payer in any manner. The taxpayer as well as the government both benefit if the tax satisfies the canon of certainty. This is the reason why Adam Smith assigned greater importance to the canon of certainty than to the canon of equity. He stated that "An old tax is no tax." The reason for this being so is that the tax-payers get accustomed to an old tax. Consequently, they do not feel its pinch.

(iii) Canon of Convenience

According to Adam Smith, "Every tax ought to be levied at a time or in the manner in which it is most likely to be convenient for the contributor to pay it. A tax upon the rent of land or of houses payable at the same time at which such rents are usually paid, is levied at a time when it is most likely to be convenient for the contributor to pay. Taxes upon such consumable goods as are articles of luxury, are all finally paid by the consumer and generally in a manner that is very convenient for him." This canon of taxation is important for both – the consumers and the government. The consumers feel least inconvenience in the payment of a tax and the government also comes to know the incidence of taxation and gets higher income by way of taxes as the tendency to evade taxation is reduced to a great extent.

(iv) Canon of Economy

This canon implies that the cost of tax collection should be the minimum. The tax should be such as to bring the maximum part of the collected revenue into the government treasury. In other words, the difference between what the tax-payers pay to the government and what the government receives after meeting all expenses of tax collecting should be minimum.

Some economists have expressed this canon in a different way. According to them, "If a tax produces adverse repercussions on the productive power of the country, or on its trade and industry or discourages the power of the people to save, then such a tax cannot be considered economical."

OTHER CANONS OF TAXATION

In addition to the above four canons of taxation given by Adam Smith, some other writers like Bastable, Shirras, Mrs. Urshala Hicks, etc. have added a few more canons of taxation which are as follows:

(i) Canon of Uniformity

The canon of uniformity as given by Conard and Nitty implies that there should be uniformity in the tax system. The method of imposing all taxes should be one and the same, and the determination of rates should be done keeping in view the general objectives.

(ii) Canon of Flexibility and Sufficiency

This canon of flexibility and sufficiency has been given by Shirras. This canon implies that the nature of taxes should be such that the tax can be realised without any resistance from the people and in case of imposition of new taxes, the same is not opposed. So far as sufficiency is concerned, it should provide sufficient income to the authority.

(iii) Canon of Expediency

It implies that the possibility of imposing a tax should be taken into account from different angles, *i.e.* its reaction upon tax-payers. For example, a tax on agricultural income lacks social, political and administrative expediency in India and that is why the Government of India is hesitant to levy it. This canon is of vital importance particularly in democratic countries.

(iv) Canon of Buoyancy

According to this canon, the tax revenue should have an inherent tendency to increase along with an increase in national income even if the rates and coverage of taxes are not revised.

(v) Canon of Desirability

It implies that there must be some justification for imposing a tax and this justification should be clearly understood, failing which, people may treat it as an unnecessary burden on them. This canon is of vital importance, particularly in democratic countries.

(vi) Canon of Elasticity

Taxation should be elastic in nature in the sense that more revenue is automatically fetched when income of the people rises. This means that taxation must have built-in flexibility.

(vii) Canon of Productivity

This canon was developed by the well-known classical economist Charles F. Bastable. According to him, "The principle of taxation must be based on considerations of productivity."

Taxes must be levied in order to accumulate enough money for the government to run its administration efficiently. Tax revenue must be enough to enable the government to secure enough facilities for the people. If a tax yields poor income, it cannot be considered as a productive tax. According to this canon, it is better to go in for a few productive taxes rather than to impose an unmanageable large number of unproductive taxes on the people. A large number of unproductive taxes creates problems not only for the people, but also for the government because it gets no special increase in income from them.

Further, taxation must be dynamic. It must be based on earnings and mobility of money and income in future. This implies that a detailed study should be undertaken to avoid any kind of evil influences of taxation on the various sections of the community. No tax ought to discourage the productive capacity of the individuals.

(viii) Canon of Simplicity

This canon implies that every tax should be simple so that the tax-payer can understand its implications without inviting the costly help of tax experts. If the tax is complex and complicated, the tax-payers will have to seek the assistance of tax-experts in order to understand its implications. Besides, a complicated tax also increases the chances of corruption in the country. Unfortunately, the Indian income tax does not satisfy this canon because it is beyond the understanding of the ordinary tax-payer on account of its complexities and complications. Thus, a complex system of taxation is always unjust and uneconomic.

(ix) Canon of Diversity

This canon was also developed by Bastable. It implies that diversity should exist in the tax system of a country. The reason is that if the government levies a single tax, it will become easier for the tax-payers to evade it. But if the government imposes a large variety of taxes, it will be difficult for the people to evade or avoid them. Consequently, every tax-payer will pay some tax to the government according to their ability to pay. The diversification of taxes should be practised in such a way as every section and every individual must pay something to the national exchequer.

(x) Canon of Taxation by Sismondi

The name of Sismondi will always remain alive in the history of economic thoughts. He has given the following canons of taxation:

(a) Tax should not be imposed on essential and convenient commodities.

(b) The amount of tax should be sufficient and should not lead to shifting.

(c) The tax should be imposed in such a way that the payment is made from income and not from capital.

(xi) Canon of Taxation by Mrs. Urshala Hicks

Mrs. Hicks has given the following canons of taxation:

(a) There must be uniformity and discrimination in taxation.

(b) Taxation should be utilised for development of public utility services.

(c) Taxation should be based on the capacity of paying taxes. Those who have more income, should be taxed at a higher rate.

MEANING AND DEFINITION OF DIRECT AND INDIRECT TAXES

Those taxes which are based on the receipt of income are termed direct, whereas those levied on expenditure are termed indirect, *i.e.* income tax, profits tax and capital gain taxes are, therefore, direct; customs duties, excise duties and stamp duties (based on capital expenditure) are indirect.

According to A.R. Prest, "The distinction between direct and indirect taxes is more commonly drawn by reference to the basis of assessment rather than the point of assessment." A.R. Prest has distinguished between a direct tax and an indirect tax on the basis of the income and expenditure on which a tax is imposed. This classification is, however, fraught with two difficulties. Firstly, this classification has a very simple concept of the flow of funds in the economy. According to Prest, some items are of income nature and other items are of expenditure nature as though the two categories of items are separable. This view, however, is not correct since every item is both an income and an expenditure depending on the way we look at it. In the economy, one man's income is another man's expenditure. Consequently, a tax on some person's income may also be rightly regarded as a tax on another man's expenditure. Secondly, this classification excludes those taxes which are based on the stock of capital.

Direct taxes are those taxes which cannot be shifted to others. Indirect taxes are those, which are later shifted to others though they are paid initially on whom they are imposed.

Direct taxes are imposed when the income is earned or produced, and indirect taxes are imposed when the income is spent, *i.e.* goods purchased. Prof. Antonio defines direct taxes in this manner: "Direct taxes strike a citizen's income at the moment of its production." Thus, taxes which appraise income directly, are direct taxes. Incomes which avoid or escape such direct appraisal are taxed indirectly when they are spent. Prof. Urshala Hicks of St. John College, Cambridge, uses the rod (scale of measurement) of individual calculation of tax rates and liabilities for defining taxes as direct. For her, outlay taxes or indirect taxes do not distinguish between one person and another person and their rates are common or fixed for all, irrespective of their individual differences. "For income and capital taxes each tax-payer's liability has to be separately calculated, according to his wealth and circumstances." Such taxes are treated as direct taxes in the British economy.

Direct taxes are those taxes which are paid entirely by the persons on whom they are levied or imposed. In other words, we can say that direct taxes are those which cannot be shifted on others.

John Stuart Mill has expressed his views in the following words: "A direct tax is demanded from the very persons, who, it is intended or desired should pay it. Indirect taxes are those which are demanded from one person in the expectation that he shall indemnify himself at the expense of another." Thus, if a tax is intended to be paid by the persons on whom it is imposed, it is a direct tax.

According to Prof. Hartley, "Taxes which are not legally shifted or those which are not shifted at all, are direct taxes."

According to Bastable, "Taxes which are levied on permanent recurring occasions are direct taxes."

Indirect taxes are then those which are later shifted to others though they are paid initially by those on whom they are imposed.

According to Hartley, "Taxes which are shifted quickly through commercial competition between consumers are indirect taxes."

According to Bastable, "... charges on occasional or particular events are indirect taxes."

In conclusion, it can be said that it is not easy to distinguish the direct taxes from the indirect taxes. A tax at one time is direct while at some other time it acquires the characteristic of an indirect tax and *vice versa*. It follows from the above fact that the classification of direct and indirect taxes based on the criterion of shifting of the incidence of taxation is relatively scientific and thoughtworthy.

Thus, a direct tax is that tax whose burden is borne by the person on whom it is levied. He cannot transfer the burden of the tax to some other person. In other words in the case of a direct tax, both the impact and incidence of tax fall on the same person. For example, income tax is a direct tax as its burden falls on the person who pays it to the government.

On the other hand, an indirect tax is that tax which is initially paid by one individual but the burden of which is ultimately borne by another individual. The person who pays the tax in the first instance, transfers its burden on the shoulders of another person.

In other words in the case of an indirect tax, the impact and incidence of tax fall on different persons. For example, the import duty on motor cars is paid in the first instance by the importer of cars but ultimately he transfers the burden of this duty to the purchaser in the form of a higher price. The importer includes the import duty paid by him in the price of car which is charged from the customer. Thus, all indirect taxes are borne by the buyer, although they are paid in the first instance by the traders.

Merits of Direct Taxes

(i) *Equitable:* Direct taxes such as income taxes, taxes on property, capital gains tax, etc. are progressive in their rates. Higher incomes are taxed heavily and lower incomes lightly. The principle of equity saying that broader shoulders should bear a heavier money burden of a tax, is satisfied. Direct taxes can be and are taxed according to the ability to pay off the tax-payers. Direct taxes, thus satisfy the equity principle.

(ii) *Economy:* The administrative cost of collecting these taxes is low, because the same officers who assess small incomes or properties, can assess larger incomes and properties. Moreover, the tax-payers make the payment of these taxes direct to the state and, therefore, every penny that is taken out of the pockets of the tax-payer, is deposited in the state's treasury.

(iii) *Elasticity and revenue generation:* Elasticity in direct taxes implies that more revenue is collected by the government through direct taxes automatically at higher rates. Thus, as a country is economically developed and its national income rises, government envoys a larger and larger share by way of direct taxes on rising incomes. With rising standards of living, the government also has to incur a larger expenditure in providing various amenities and services; it has to spend a larger amount on research and development and fulfil the rising expectations of the people. Thus, direct taxes help in collecting a larger revenue. They are elastic and revenue productive.

(iv) *Distributive justice:* Direct taxes are progressive. Rates of taxes increase as the level of income of persons rises. They fall heavily on the rich, take away a large part of their income by way of income and property taxes. The revenue so collected is used for providing subsidised food, clothing and housing to the poor people. The real income of the poor rises and that of rich falls. Particular mention may be made of wealth tax, inheritance taxes and death duties which reduce inequalities of income and wealth so inherent in capitalist countries. Governments frequently use direct taxes as a means for reducing glaring income and wealth inequalities in the community and through this measure, several social evils can be mitigated.

(v) *Civic consciousness:* It is said that direct taxes create civic consciousness among the tax-payers. As the tax-payer may take intelligent and keen interest in the method of public expenditure whether the revenue raised is properly utilised or not. In a democratic country this civic consciousness checks the wastage in public expenditure. A direct tax like the income tax pinches the people on whom it is imposed and the tax-payers immediately become cautious about their rights. They also see to it that the tax-income accruing to the government is not wasted on useless projects. Consequently, a direct tax creates civic consciousness.

(vi) *Absence of leakage:* Since there is direct payment of taxes by the tax payers to the government, there is no scope for any leakage. The whole amount of direct taxes, such as income taxes, property taxes and taxes on capital goods, reaches the treasury without there being any middlemen.

(vii) *Avoidance of adverse effects of direct taxes:* One of the merits of direct taxes is that their rates can be modified in time to avoid their adverse effects on willingness and ability to work, save and invest. Exemptions and concessions are given to avoid their adverse effects on production.

(viii) *Certainty of direct taxes:* Another advantage of direct taxes is that they are certain. The tax-payers know how much they have to pay and on what basis they are going to pay the tax to the government. Thus, the tax-payers can make adequate provision for the payment of tax in advance. The government can also estimate the amount of such tax which it will receive from the public and accordingly, it can prepare its development plans.

Demerits of Direct Taxes

(i) ***Uncertainty of direct taxes:*** The critics of direct taxes state that since the precise degree on needed progression cannot be estimated on account of the difficulties of measuring the ability to pay and the subjective nature of the marginal utility of income, the government would always end up with either too much or too little progression in direct taxation.

(ii) ***Unpopularity of direct taxes:*** Direct taxes are directly imposed on individuals. People have to bear both the impact and incidence of these taxes. Thus, they experience their pinch directly. Consequently, direct taxes are not as popular as indirect taxes.

(iii) ***Violation of the principle of equity:*** The burden of direct taxes falls almost exclusively on the richer sections of society while the poor sections are totally exempted from these taxes. This is unjustified and improper because the burden of state expenditure should be borne by individuals at all levels in society according to their ability to pay.

(iv) ***Large scale evasion:*** It is a fact that the people in the higher income groups do not reveal their full income. They do not hesitate to fill up false returns, concealing a considerable part of their incomes. There is large scale evasion of taxes. Commodity taxes or indirect taxes must be paid when goods are bought, but incomes can be concealed and taxes avoided illegally. It is only the honest people who suffer from direct taxation. As it is remarked, "direct taxes are a premium on honesty", black money is generated on a large scale and a parallel economy is established which is injurious to economic development. To prevent such evasion it is necessary to make the collection machinery more efficient. It is also necessary to make income tax rates mildly progressive.

In India, the income tax has been exempted upto the income of Rs. 1,00,000.

(v) *Arbitrary:* Direct taxes are found to be arbitrary because there is no logical or scientific principle to determine the degree of progression in taxation. Rates of income tax and other direct taxes are determined according to the whims of the taxing authorities. They are likely to underestimate or overestimate the taxable capacity of the people.

(vi) *Inconvenience:* These taxes are also inconvenient in nature because the tax-payer has to submit the statement of his total income along with the sources of income from which it is derived, which is generally subject to complications. Moreover, the payment of these taxes in lumpsum is not as convenient to the tax-payer as the frequent payment of small amounts of indirect taxes. Hence, these taxes are said to be inconvenient to the tax-payers.

(vii) *Lack of civic consciousness among non tax-payers:* In a poor country like India, a large mass is exempted from income tax because their incomes are very low. We can say that at present those having an income below Rs. 1,00,000/- per annum are exempted from tax. A large percentage of the total population do not feel any pinch as they do not pay any direct tax.

(viii) *Non-reliance of direct taxes in a poor country:* Since there is a small section of rich and large masses of poor people in backward countries like India, it is not possible to fully rely upon direct taxes. The revenue collection is meagre and hence, hardly sufficient to cover the huge government expenditure. Though direct taxes satisfy the important canon of equity and are progressive, a poor country has to depend heavily upon indirect taxes to collect sufficient revenues.

Merits of Indirect Taxes

(i) *Indirect taxes are convenient:* An important merit of indirect taxes is that they are less inconvenient and less burdensome than direct taxes. The tax-payers generally pay these taxes in bits, and mostly when they buy goods and services in the market. The amount of tax is included in the price of the commodity and the consumer pays the tax without experiencing its pinch. Sometimes, the consumer is not even aware of the fact that he is paying the tax in the form of the higher price of the commodity. Besides, the indirect taxes are paid by the tax-payers at a time when they have the means to pay these taxes.

(ii) ***Indirect taxes lead to social welfare:*** Indirect taxes imposed on intoxicants like wine, opium, etc. serve a great social purpose by curtailing and limiting the consumption of such harmful commodities. Curtailment of consumption of harmful goods indirectly increases social welfare.

(iii) ***Indirect taxes are justified:*** Indirect taxes are justified and equitable. They are paid by all the individuals and only when they purchase goods and services.

(iv) ***Indirect taxes help production and investment:*** Another advantage of indirect taxes is that they serve as a powerful tool in moulding the production and investment activities of the economy, *i.e.* they can guide the economy in its resource allocation. A proper structuring of indirect taxes can enable the authorities to twist the demand and supply forces in such a way as to yield desirable results by encouraging the development of high priority industries and discouraging low priority ones.

(v) ***No evasion:*** Indirect taxes are generally difficult to be evaded as they are included in the price of the commodity. A person can evade an indirect tax only when he decides not to purchase the taxed commodity. However, indirect taxes can sometimes be evaded through smuggling, maintaining false account or not taking the bill, etc.

(vi) ***Highly revenue productive in developing countries:*** Since incomes in less developed countries are low, direct taxes do not contribute much to state revenue. Since indirect taxes cover a large number of essential goods to be consumed by the masses (both rich and poor), these help in collecting a large revenue. In India, more than 85 per cent of the total tax revenue is collected from indirect taxes.

(vii) ***Rational and equitable allocation of resources:*** One major merit of indirect taxes is that they are effectively used for securing rational and equitable allocation of scarce resources of the country. By taxing luxury goods heavily, resources can be diverted for the production of essential goods which can be taxed lightly. Saving can be increased for the purpose of capital investment by taxing consumer goods so that resources are diverted from consumption goods industries to capital goods industries.

(viii) ***Educative value:*** They are paid by almost all the groups of society. Thus, they are considered as exercising a wholesome influence on people. They can thus have the educative value and raise civic sense in all the sections of society.

(ix) ***Productive:*** Indirect taxes are more productive as compared to direct taxes. Such taxes bring revenue to government from different sources and naturally the income from these is more.

Demerits of Indirect Taxes

(i) ***Indirect taxes promote economic inequality:*** Indirect taxes are generally imposed on the consumption goods. The poor people have to pay as much by way of indirect taxes on commodities as the rich people. Obviously, this is unjust and inequitable. Indirect taxes are a type of regressive taxes which promote economic inequality in society by imposing heavier burden on poorer sections of society.

(ii) ***Indirect taxes are uneconomical:*** Indirect taxes involve high costs of collecting them. Generally, the traders charge more than the actual amount of commodity tax levied by the authorities by increasing the prices of goods and services at a rate higher than the rate of tax.

(iii) ***Indirect taxes are uncertain:*** The revenue accruing to the government from indirect taxes cannot be estimated accurately. As soon as a tax is imposed on a commodity, its price rises in the market and consequently its demand falls. It cannot be said with certainty as to what extent the demand of the commodity has fallen consequently upon the imposition of the tax. Therefore, an element of uncertainty is always involved in the case of indirect taxes.

(iv) ***Indirect taxes do not create civic consciousness:*** As indirect taxes are paid only when the consumers buy the goods, they pay the amount of tax only in terms of the prices of these goods. They, therefore, do not feel an extra burden of tax. Consequently, they are not conscious about these taxes. The tax-payers generally become indifferent towards their responsibilities and fail to keep a watch on the financial irregularities committed by the authorities.

(v) ***Indirect taxes promote inflation:*** Another weakness of indirect taxes is that they feed inflationary forces. Indirect taxes begin by adding to the sale prices of the taxed goods without touching the purchasing power in the first place as in the case of direct tax (direct taxes take away a part of the purchasing power of the tax-payer which has the effect of reducing demand and prices). Consequently, in the case of indirect taxes inflationary forces are fed through an unending spiral of higher prices, higher costs, higher wages and again higher prices.

Superiority of Direct Taxes over Indirect Taxes

Some economists assert that direct taxes are superior to indirect taxes because a man's real tax burden is heavier if a good is taxed rather than taxing his income. This superiority of direct taxes over indirect taxes is stressed by Prof. Urshala Hicks and

Prof. Miss Joseph. As illustrated in the Figure 6.1. When an indirect tax is imposed on good X, the consumer's price income line becomes PS showing a rise in the price of good X, the position of consumer's equilibrium shifts from D on I^3 curve to B on I^1 showing that he will get less satisfaction than before. He buys OM^1, of X (less than before). But if the same amount of tax which is equal to AB is collected by way of income tax, the consumer's income falls. He will now be on a new price-income line P^1Q^1. The new income line (P^1Q^1) shows a fall in his income. It also shows that the price of X remains unchanged. The consumer's equilibrium is at C which is on a higher indifference curve I^2. He buys OM^2 of X which is more than OM which he could buy when an indirect tax is imposed.

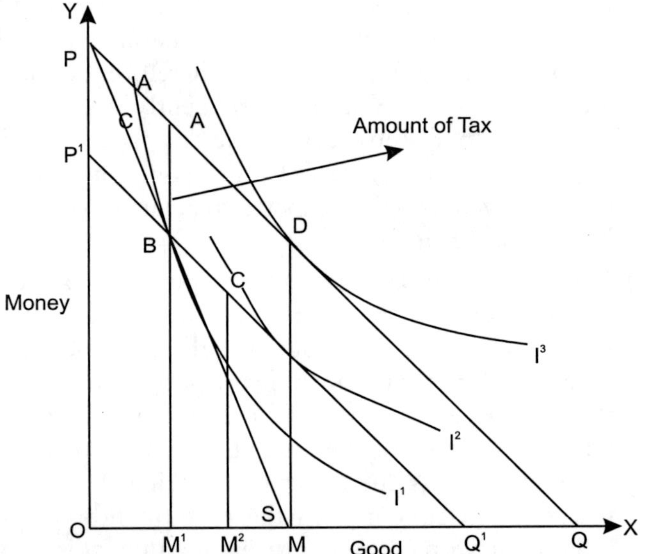

Figure 6.1: Superiority of direct taxes over indirect taxes

Thus, an indirect tax on good X will bring back the consumer on a lower indifference curve at point B from his original equilibrium D on the higher indifference curve I^3. His satisfaction level is very much reduced. But if the same amount (AB) is collected by way of a direct tax, the consumer is able to be at C on an indifference curve I^2 which is higher to I^1. Thus, it is clear that the loss of satisfaction or welfare is greater in case of indirect tax. This shows that direct taxes are superior to indirect taxes from the welfare point of view.

COMPARISON BETWEEN DIRECT AND INDIRECT TAXES

The main points of difference between direct and indirect taxes are as follows:

(i) **Transfer of burden:** The burden of direct taxes is borne by the person on whom it is levied, whereas the burden of indirect taxes is transferred from the person who pays it, to another person.

(ii) **Impact and incidence:** The indirect tax is that under which the impact and incidence are on the different persons, whereas in case of direct tax the impact and incidence are on the same person who pays the tax.

(iii) **Progressive:** Direct taxes are progressive, whereas indirect taxes are not progressive.

(iv) **Imposition:** Direct taxes are imposed on incomes, such as wages, rent, interest, property, profits, wealth, etc. whereas indirect taxes are imposed on goods and impersonal services.

(v) **Burden felt:** Direct taxes are to be paid in a lumpsum and hence their burden is felt. On the contrary, indirect taxes are hidden in prices and thus the burden on indirect taxes is not felt.

(vi) **Administrative cost:** Administrative cost of direct taxes is low, whereas the administrative cost of indirect taxes is quite high as compared to direct taxes.

(vii) **Removal of inequalities:** Direct taxes are considered as an important instrument of removing inequalities of income and wealth as they fall more heavily on the rich than the poor. The poor are usually exempted from payment of direct taxes whereas indirect taxes fall on all incomes whether rich or poor as they are generally regressive in nature. Therefore, indirect taxes are generally not suitable from the point of view of removing inequalities of income and wealth.

(viii) **Basis of assessment:** According to Prest, "Direct taxes are based on receipt of incomes, whereas indirect taxes are based on expenditure as they are imposed on expenditure."

(ix) **Basis of frequency:** According to Bastable, "Direct taxes are levied on permanent and recurring occasions whereas indirect taxes are charged on occasional and particular events."

(x) **Basis of certainty:** Direct taxes are certain, whereas indirect taxes are uncertain.

(xi) **Taxable capacity:** Direct taxes are based on taxable capacity, whereas indirect taxes are not based on taxable capacity.

CLASSIFICATION OF TAXES

The classifications have been made on different bases and naturally the results have also been different. Different bases adopted by the economists to classify taxes are the forms, nature, aims and methods of taxation. Economists have classified taxes from different angles thereby providing us a long list of different kinds of taxes. The various taxes may be classified under the following major heads:

Classification of Taxes

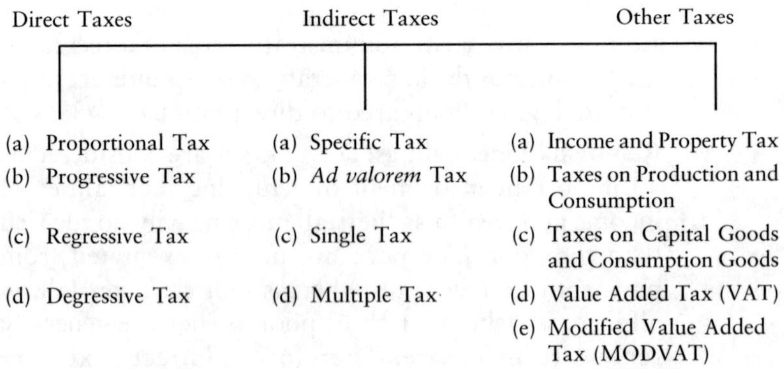

DIRECT TAXES

Direct taxes can be classified on the basis of the degree of progression or distribution of their burden on the tax-payers. According to this classification, taxes may be classified as proportional, progressive, regressive and degressive.

A tax is called progressive when, with increasing income, the tax liability not only increases in absolute terms but it also increases as a proportion of the income. If the tax liability increases in the same proportion as the increase in the tax-payer's income, then it is termed as proportional taxation. If the tax liability as a proportion of income falls with the increase in tax-payer's income, it is termed as regressive taxation. On the other hand, in the case of regressive taxation, the absolute tax liability of the tax-payer will increase. In the case of degressive taxation, there is a declining degree of progression as the tax base increases. Now, we shall discuss these taxes in detail in the following manner:

(a) Proportional Tax

In the proportional tax system, all incomes are taxed at a single uniform rate and it does not matter if the tax-payer's income is high or low. A proportional tax has the following characteristics:

(i) It is fixed and its proportion does not change with the change in tax-payer's income and wealth.

(ii) It is fixed in amount and it is never levied in varying percentages.

(iii) The tax does not alter the proportion of difference of income after the payment of tax has been made. In other words, the relative status of the individual tax-payers with respect to income and/or wealth remains unchanged after the payment of a proportional tax.

Advantages of Proportional Taxation

The following are the main arguments advanced in favour of proportional taxation:

(i) It is easy for every individual to evaluate the total amount of tax he has to pay. The tax-payers can easily and quickly calculate the amount of tax they have to pay to the government.

(ii) The proportional tax is simple and easy to understand. Even a person with an ordinary intelligence can understand its implications without any difficulty.

(iii) There is no change in the existing distribution of income and wealth in the society as a result of proportional taxation because all the tax-payers pay the tax at a single uniform rate. It is neutral with respect to income and wealth distribution and consequently it involves no structural change in the socio-economic set-up of the country.

Disadvantages of Proportional Taxation

The following are the main arguments advanced by the critics against the proportional taxation:

(i) In the case of proportional taxes, the burden of taxation falls more heavily on the poorer sections of society. The reason for this is that as the income of an individual increases, marginal utility of money for him diminishes. In other words, the marginal utility of money for the rich is lower than the marginal utility of money for the poor. If the rich and the poor are taxed at the same rate, then obviously the poorer sections of society will be making greater sacrifice than the richer section. Consequently, the proportional tax system does not satisfy the important canon of equity and justice in taxation.

(ii) This system of taxation does not reduce the inequalities of income and wealth, rather it enhances these inequalities and increases the gap between haves and have-nots.

(iii) It does not go parallel to the principle of taxable capacity.

(iv) It contributes less to the public exchequer.

(b) Progressive Tax

A progressive tax is the tax which varies with the change in the income of the individual and the rate of tax becomes gradually higher for the increasing incomes and lower for the lower incomes. It does not provide for a fixed and uniform percentage for all income levels. If the income of tax-payer increases, the rate of tax also increases and if the income decreases, the rate of tax also decreases. According to Taylor, "As taxable incomes rise under progressive taxation, the effective rate of tax rises for marginal increments of income, subject to higher tax rates." This means that the rise in tax liability is more than proportional to the rise in income. Conversely, as personal incomes fall, the effective rates of tax fall and the decrease in taxes is more than proportional to the decrease in income. A schedule of progressive tax rates is one in which the rate of tax increases as the base (income) increases. Recognising that the amount of tax paid is the result of multiplying the base by the rate in a progressive tax, the multiplier increases as the multiplicand increases. Accordingly, the amount of tax paid will increase at higher rate than the increase in the tax-base.

Advantages of Progressive Taxation

Progressive taxation has become popular in all the nations of the world today. The reasons for its universal popularity are the benefits which accrue to the community from it. The following are the important advantages of progressive taxation:

(i) *Progressive taxation is based on 'ability to pay' principle:* A very strong case for progressive tax rates exists in terms of the ability to pay and the corresponding sacrifice which taxation involves. This argument is based on the assumption that marginal utility of income is subject to reduction as income rises. Since the ability to pay increases in direct proportion to the increase in income, the rate of tax goes on increasing with every increase in the size of income.

(ii) *Progressive taxation promotes equality of income and wealth:* The distribution of income and wealth in society can be made more equitable under progressive taxation because under it the richer persons are required to pay the tax at a higher rate than the poorer persons.

(iii) *Progressive taxation is productive:* The government can increase its income substantially through progressive taxation. It can bring about a sizeable increase in its income through increases in tax rates during a period of financial crisis.

(iv) *Progressive taxation is economical:* Progressive taxation is economical in the sense that the government can bring about a sizeable increase in its income through increases in the rates of tax without any substantial increase in the cost of tax collection.

(v) *Progressive taxation is elastic:* This type of tax has the characteristic of elasticity. It is elastic in the sense that with minor changes in the tax rates substantial changes can be brought about in the income of the government.

(vi) *Social justice:* Progressive tax can be advocated on the basis of social justice also which manifests itself in the form of taxing the people according to their ability to pay. Since progressive tax rate schedules try to bring about equal marginal sacrifice on the part of the tax-payers and since through that approach the whole tax system moves towards the least aggregate sacrifice, such a tax system is just as between individual tax-payers and for the society as a whole.

Disadvantages of Progressive Taxation

The main disadvantages of progressive taxation are the following:

(i) *Non-measurability of utility:* The case for progressive tax has been disputed on the ground of non-measurability of utility. Marginal utility of net incomes of different persons cannot be measured in such a way as to permit precise comparisons between individuals. Consequently, it is impossible to discover any faultless objective standard of progression or gradation of tax rates on the basis of subjective utility.

(ii) *Progressive taxation ignores the 'benefit-received' principle:* The benefit-received theory of taxation does not favour a progressive tax rate especially when we consider the welfare activities of the government. According to this approach, the government should tax the poor people more on account of the benefits received from its welfare activities. Even if one ignores the welfare functions of the state, it becomes a point of debate whether the rich or the poor derive the maximum benefit from the state activities.

(iii) *Progressive taxation reduces capital formation in the country:* The degree of progressive taxation has an important bearing on the process of saving and capital formation in an economy. The critics of progressive taxation state that it is only the rich who can save and, therefore, if they are taxed more heavily than the poor, the saving potential will either be lost completely or reduced substantially. Consequently, the process of capital formation is adversely affected as a result of progressive taxation.

(iv) *Scope for tax evasion:* Under the system of progressive taxation, there is always a considerable scope for tax evasion and tax avoidance. The tax-payers invariably try to evade the payment of tax by presenting false statements of account before the taxing authorities and finding legal loopholes in the tax provisions.

In spite of the above defects, the system of progressive taxation is now widely recognised as desirable. The main reason for this is that under progressive taxation, it becomes possible to eliminate or reduce the glaring economic inequalities in society. This was the reason why Alfred Marshall and Arthur Cecil Pigou extended their powerful support to progressive taxation. John Maynard Keynes also laid special emphasis on progressive taxation as a means of increasing the volume of employment in society.

Progressive taxation cannot, however, be applied to all taxes. It is essential to select proper taxes, rates and exemptions so that arbitrariness which can always be levelled against any progressive tax or rate, is reduced to the minimum. The principle of progressive taxation has only limited applicability in an underdeveloped country on account of the limited scope of direct taxation. In an underdeveloped country all the finance required for development cannot be raised only through direct taxation on income and wealth and main reliance has to be placed on indirect taxation

(c) Regressive Tax

In regressive taxation, the higher the income of a tax-payer, the smaller is the proportion of his income which he contributes to the government in terms of tax. Thus, a regressive tax is just the opposite of the progressive tax. Under this system of taxation, the poorer sections of society are taxed at higher rates than the richer sections. As the income of an individual increases, the rate of tax diminishes. A schedule of regressive tax rates is one in which the rate of tax decreases as the tax base (income) increases, the multiplier decreasing with the multiplicand increasing, recognising that the tax payable is the result of multiplying the tax rate with the tax base.

Thus, in a regressive system of taxation, the tax rate falls as the tax base (income) increases. The absolute amount of tax payable may, however, increase but at a decreasing rate and it may also decrease. Since this system of taxation is not just or equitable, it has been abandoned everywhere. The *Salt Tax*, which was imposed by the British Government prior to 1947 in India, was an example of regressive taxation because its burden fell more heavily on the poorer sections of society.

Advantages of Regressive Taxation

The main merits or advantages of regressive taxation may be summarised as under:

(i) *Restricts the use of intoxicants:* Regressive taxation has been justified on the ground that it restricts the use of intoxicants in the society.

(ii) *Public interest:* From public interest of view, it is essential to impose tax on the use of goods which adversely affect the health of the individuals such as tax on wine, opium, bhang, etc. Therefore regressive tax is a must which is imposed almost in every country in public interest.

(iii) *Improvement in the economic position:* Regressive tax has been justified on the ground that it is imposed mostly on luxury items and intoxicants so as to reduce their consumption. It would increase their savings which will be used for improving the economic position of both the rich and the poor.

Disadvantages of Regressive Taxation

Regressive taxation has been criticised on the following grounds:

(i) *Non-productive and uneconomic:* Regressive system of taxation has been criticised on the ground that it is non-productive and uneconomic. Its cost exceeds the income.

(ii) *Unjust:* It is said that regressive tax is unjust on the ground that most of its burden falls on the shoulders of the poor.

(d) Degressive Tax

This tax can be called a mild progressive tax. In a degressive tax, the rate of progression does not increase in the same proportion as the income. The rate of tax increases up to a certain limit beyond which a uniform rate is charged. Thus, the degressive tax is a blend of progressive and proportional taxation. The result of this tax is that the higher income groups make less sacrifice than the lower income groups.

From the above analysis, we can conclude that a progressive system of taxation is the best system of taxation. Most advanced countries of the world, nowadays, follow this system of taxation. India is also gradually adopting the progressive system of taxation.

Advantages of Degressive Tax

The main advantages or merits of degressive tax are as follows:

(i) *Advantage of both the systems of taxation:* Degressive tax is a combination of both the systems of taxation, *i.e.* proportional and progressive. Thus, it enjoys the benefit of both the systems.

(ii) *Lower burden on the rich:* It has been justified on the ground that the burden of degressive tax is quite low on the rich. Thereby, it encourages savings, capital formation and investment which can be used for productive purposes.

Disadvantages of Degressive Tax

Degressive tax has been criticised on the following grounds:

(i) *Injustice:* Degressive tax violates the principle of justice in taxation. It ultimately increases burden on the poor.

(ii) *Less sacrifice:* The amount of sacrifice on account of degressive tax on the part of the rich is quite low, whereas, they are expected to sacrifice more.

INDIRECT TAXES

Indirect taxes may be either *ad valorem* or specific. When the tax is levied per physical unit of a good, it is called a specific tax, for example an excise duty of Rs. 500 per TV set or Rs. 5 per kg. of edible oil. Thus, a specific tax is a tax on the physical volume of goods purchased. Where a tax is levied on the value or price of a goods purchased, it is called an *ad valorem* tax. Thus, instead of per pair of shoes (specific tax), a tax is collected according to the value (price) of each pair of shoes purchased such as a sales tax of 10 per cent on the value of shoes purchased or 5 per cent tax on the price of edible oil purchased or a sales tax of 10 per cent on the aggregate value of different goods bought at a shop, etc. We can easily give some examples of different kinds of indirect taxes. Excise duties are imposed at the manufacturing stage. These duties are payable on the quantities of goods or on their value when these goods leave the factory premises. These are added to the price of the manufacturer, called ex-factory price. Sales tax is payable when the goods are bought by the customers, at the wholesale and retail stages of sale. Custom duties are of two types:

(i) *Import duties* are levied on goods imported from other countries and are payable when the goods enter the home country.

(ii) *Export duties* are payable on goods exported to foreign countries and are payable when goods leave the home country's borders. Besides there are octroi duties which are collected by local bodies. Indirect taxes are also levied on inter state movement of goods.

(a) Specific Tax

When a tax is imposed on a commodity according to its weight, size or measurement, it is called a specific tax. For instance, when the excise duty is imposed on sugar on the basis of its weight or the cloth is taxed according to its length or a tax on a picture is levied on the basis of its size, it is known as a specific tax.

The main advantage of specific tax is that it is easy to levy and more convenient to collect because it is collected either according to the weight of the commodity or according to the size of the unit of the commodity.

The main disadvantage of this tax is that it imposes a greater burden on the poor people than on the rich people. The reason is that the marginal utility of money for the rich people is lower than that for the poor people.

(b) *Ad valorem* Tax

When the tax is imposed on a commodity according to its value, it is termed as *ad valorem* tax. Whatever the weight or size of the unit of the commodity, the tax is charged according to its value. Several imported commodities are taxed not according to their weight or size, but according to their value.

The main advantage of an *ad valorem* tax is that it imposes a greater burden on the richer sections. Hence, from this point of view the *ad valorem* tax is more equitable.

The main problem with an *ad valorem* tax is that it is difficult to know the real value of the commodity at the time of imposing the tax. Generally, the traders understate the value of the commodities in their invoices in order to escape the burden of the *ad valorem* tax.

In fact, it is difficult to choose between a specific and an *ad valorem* tax. A good tax system should have both, specific as well as *ad valorem* tax according to the nature of the commodities.

(c) Single Tax

A single tax occurs in a system in which the taxes are levied only on one subject. There is only one tax which constitutes the source of public revenue.

A single tax on income can be devised with advantage. It can yield adequate revenue and avoid unfairness in the distribution of the burden of taxation by means of graduation, differentiation and other devices. There are, however, three serious objections to such a single tax. First, it would be difficult and expensive to collect, particularly in relation to small incomes. Second, it would secure no special contribution from the inheritors of wealth. Third, it would check saving more than other taxes would do.

In the case of tax on land, following are the main disadvantages of a single tax system:

(i) It would not produce adequate revenue.

(ii) It would mean a very unsatisfactory distribution of the burden of taxation. A millionaire owning no land would completely escape the burden of taxation while a poor person who had invested all his savings in the purchase of land would pay a proportionately high tax.

(d) Multiple Tax

A single tax system presented many difficulties. It proved inefficient in solving the real purpose behind a good tax system. Consequently, economists now widely acclaim the multiple tax system.

A multiple tax refers to the tax system in which taxes are levied on various items. It is absolutely against the single tax system. It can be easily seen why this must be so. A modern economy is not one or single objective economy. It tries to forge ahead simultaneously along the paths of growth, equitable distribution of income and wealth, economic stabilisation, etc. Since no single tax can be expected to help the economy on all fronts, choice for a multiple tax system becomes inevitable. Different taxes contribute to the attainment of different objectives. Thus, some taxes would help in the more equitable redistribution of income and wealth while some other taxes would help the economy in the direction of regional balanced growth. Some other taxes may still be required to provide adequate revenue for the government treasury.

Advantages of Multiple Taxation

(i) It is efficient in checking the tendencies of frequent tax evasion.

(ii) It can be made indiscriminatory and the inequality of income and wealth can be reduced.

(iii) One kind of taxation can cover up the weaknesses of the other kind of taxation.

(iv) Multiple tax system raises the income of the government.

(v) This system of taxation is more flexible than the single tax system.

Thus, a multiple tax system is generally preferable to a single tax system. However, too great multiplicity of taxes would be undesirable. A large number of taxes, howsoever small, would involve a large cost of collection. It is, therefore, best to rely on a few substantial taxes for achieving the bulk of tax revenue. Income and inheritance taxes are best to tax the rich, while indirect taxes on a few essential commodities of wide consumption, preferably on those commodities which are not necessary for health and efficiency, should be used to tax the poor.

OTHER TAXES

(a) Income and Property Tax

When the government wants to levy taxes on an individual according to his ability to pay, it is generally the income of the person that is taken as the basis of the tax. A person with greater income is taxed more heavily than a person with smaller income. The rate of tax is almost always progressive. It is the net income which is generally taxed and which is easy to calculate for a businessman but not for a professional man. In some places it is property that is taxed. It is of little significance whether the income or the property earning income is taxed so long as the rates of tax are properly adjusted. In two conditions property and income taxes are alike, firstly the incidence is the same when all kinds of capital yield income at the same rate and secondly the proportion of gross income and net income is the same in such circumstances. It is easier to adjust the burden of a tax to the ability of a person when it is assessed on income. On the other hand, it is difficult to find out the income of all kinds of property.

(b) Taxes on Production and Taxes on Consumption

Sometimes a distinction is made between taxes that fall on production and those that fall on consumption. If a tax is paid by the manufacturer of the commodity in proportion to the amount of the commodity produced, it is called a tax on production. When a tax is paid out by the consumer in the shape of higher prices, it is said to be a tax on consumption. If the tax is paid because the tax payers produces certain, commodity it is tax on production. On the other hand, if a tax payer pays the tax because he consumes a certain commodity after buying it, is called a tax on consumption. This distinction is vague. The producer may pay taxes while producing the commodity but these taxes are ultimately paid by the consumer who buys it. Taxes on production therefore, fall on consumption also. If a tax is small, it may not be shifted and may therefore fall wholly on production or consumption as the case may be. But the distinction does not hold good in case of greater amount of taxes since neither consumer nor the producer is willing to bear its burden alone.

(c) Taxes on Capital Goods and Taxes on Consumption Goods

Capital goods may be vaguely called property while consumption goods simply goods or commodities. All goods either belong to the production or consumption. If they belong to production; they are called as capital goods and if they belong to consumption, they are called as consumption goods. The government can tax either or both these kinds of goods. It is generally believed that it is better to tax consumption goods than capital goods for the latter are helpful in the production of wealth. Taxing them would be like killing the goose that lays golden eggs. In order to understand this classification, it is necessary to be clear about the distinction of capital goods and consumption goods. Indeed it is a classification of goods rather than of taxes on some sound principles of taxation. Since the distinction between the capital and consumption goods itself is not clear, the classification of the taxes on that basis is ambiguous.

(d) Value Added Tax (VAT)

The valued added tax (VAT) is of comparatively recent origin having been first adopted on a restricted scale in France in 1954. However, in a short period of time it became popular and was adopted as an instrument of tax harmonisation in the European Economic Community which was anxious to ensure that the powers of the member countries of the EEC to levy commodity taxes should be reconciled with the principle of free trade within the community.

The value added tax (VAT) belongs to the family of sales taxes. Thus, here we are required to explain the different forms of sales taxes and explain the place of VAT in them. A general sales tax is a tax on sales transactions but it is applied at only one stage of business activity. We know that a production process involves many stages from the manufacturer to the retailer before the commodity finally goes into the hands of consumers. A general sales tax may be imposed at any one of these many stages. Usually, it is collected either at the wholesale level or at the retail level.

The value added tax, as the name clearly denotes, is a tax on the value added to goods in the process of production and distribution. It means that the value added tax is imposed on the value that the business firm adds to the goods and services that it purchases from other firms. It adds value by processing or handling these purchased items with its own labour force or its machinery, building or other capital goods. It then sells the resulting product to consumers or to other firms. Thus, the difference between the sale proceeds and the cost of the materials, etc. that it has purchased from other firms is its value added, which is the tax base of the value added tax.

The Indirect Taxation Enquiry Committee, which is popularly known as L.K. Jha Committee (1976) defined value added tax as: "Value added tax in its comprehensive form is a tax on all goods and services (except export and government services), its special characteristics being that it falls on the value added at each stage from the stage of production to retail stage."

A value added tax is a tax not on the total value of the commodity being sold, it is a tax levied only on the value added to it by the last trader or manufacturer. The trader, therefore, is not liable to pay a tax on commodity's gross value, but only on the net value, *i.e.* the gross value minus the value of the commodity purchased from the other firms. In its comprehensive form, the VAT may be defined as a tax which is to be paid by all sellers of goods and services, other than those specifically exempted, on the basis of the value added by their firms. The value added is computed as the difference between the actual or presumed value of sale or output and the value of goods and services purchased from other producers and used in the production of that output. Goods usually pass through several stages of manufacture or processing before they are converted either into capital or consumer goods and sold to final buyers. At each stage of manufacture, an element of value is added and the final value of a product is the sum of all the values added in the processes of production. The VAT taxes the value added at each stage of production. It is a multi-stage tax on consumption which is collected in bits or in fractions in the chain from the point of first stage of production to the final supply to the consumer. In India the value added tax faced several problems into its implementation. They are—the constitutional problems, administrative problems, revenue considerations, and experience of developing countries. Despite the initial transitional problems and lack of clarity, the implementation of VAT has been smooth and the results are encouraging. The Empowered Committee (EC) constantly reviews the progress and tries to sort out the difficulties. The EC has advised the states to constantly interact with trade and industry to remove their apprehensions, if any, and to ensure that the benefits of VAT due to input tax credit and reduction in tax rates (wherever applicable) are passed on to the consumers. The EC is also persuading the remaining States/UTs to implement VAT at the earliest.

KINDS OF VALUE ADDED TAX

The value added tax is of the following four types:

(i) Gross product value added tax or production type value added tax: In this case, the value of the inputs purchased by a firm or manufacturer from other firms is not deducted in full, only the value of non-capital purchases is deducted. The value of capital goods, e.g. buildings, machinery, equipment, furniture, vehicle or any other asset, that will not be used up entirely within the tax year, is not deducted from the sales of the firm. Further, no depreciation can be deducted in subsequent years. In a closed economy with two factors if C is consumption, I is gross investment, W is wages, P is net profit after depreciation and D is depreciation, the aggregate base of the gross product value added tax is:

$$\text{Gross National Product} = C + I + W + P + D$$

Thus, the tax base for any firm will be just sales (minus) material (other than capital goods). This type of value added is not popular, since it militates against use of capital and retards economic growth.

(ii) Consumption type value added tax: In this case, the firm in question is allowed to deduct from the gross value of its products not only the non-capital inputs purchased from other firms, but also the capital equipment so purchased. In the absence of foreign trade, the aggregate base of this type of tax for the economy as a whole is equal to:

$$C = W + P + D - I$$

Since, $GNP = C + I + D$

$$GNP = C + I$$

W = Wages, P = Net profit after depreciation, D = Depreciation, C = Consumption, and GNP = Gross National Product.

This type of value added tax may be termed as consumption type of value added tax because the base of this tax is the aggregate consumption in the economy.

(iii) Income type value added tax: Income type value added tax allows the full value of its non-capital purchases from other firms and a depreciation of capital that occurs during the year. This approach gives us the proper net value added. The base of this tax is calculated in the given manner:

GNP = C + I + W + P + D

NNP = C + I – D = W + P

Value Added Tax (Income Type) = C + I – D = W + P

GNP = Gross National Product

NNP = Net National Product

Rest = As usual.

(iv) Wages type value added tax: The base of the wages type value added tax is obtained by deducting an amount equal to the net earnings from the firm's capital for that year. Normally, this deduction will be simply P or net profits including interest. Firm's capital for that year means net income of the firm of that year which is equal to the Gross Income of the firm (minus) the depreciation in the year. The balance left to be taxed is equal to wages paid. Thereby, this type of value added tax is called the wages type of value added tax. The tax base of this type of tax is calculated as under :

GNP = C + I = W + P + D

NNP = C + I – D = W + P

Tax base of Wages Type Value Added Tax is:

Wages = Net Income of the Firm – Net Earning of the Firm

W = C + I – D – P

W = Tax base = Value Added.

Merits of Value Added Tax (VAT)

The following are the main advantages of the VAT:

(i) A general VAT is supposed to be neutral to the forms of production and commercialisation. In the case of a turnover tax, a tax is added at each sales transaction. Consequently, a turnover tax encourages vertical integration of production so as to avoid the intermediary sales and payment of taxes and also to acquire a competitive advantage over others. A VAT, on the other hand, is neutral between these processes of integration. It, therefore, helps the economy in adopting those forms of production which are economically more suitable.

(ii) Since in the case of a VAT, the tax is divided into several parts depending on the stages of production, the possibility to evade tax by a firm is reduced.

(iii) It encourages exports of the country. In order to get a competitive edge over others, a country may refund the taxes paid on the export goods. It is easy to separate the tax from the cost of production in the cost of a value-added tax. It is not easy in the case of other types of taxes as they get mixed up with the cost of production since they are levied at the gross value of a commodity in each case. The VAT rebate has also been recognised as a legitimate practice for encouragement of country's exports by the General Agreement on Trade and Tariffs (GATT).

Demerits of Value Added Tax (VAT)

The following are the major defects of the value added tax:

(i) It is not a simple and easy tax system to adopt, especially in an underdeveloped country.

(ii) It needs an honest and efficient government tax administrative machinery to implement it. It is necessary that the country adopting this tax, should be sufficiently advanced in its financial and economic structure and the firms should be in the habit of keeping proper accounts.

(iii) Its success largely depends on the cooperation of the tax-payers because in this case, tax evasion becomes a major possibility and a common practice.

(iv) This system is highly uneconomic, especially for the smaller firms as it requires them to maintain elaborate and costly accounts.

(v) The argument that VAT induces efficiency, is an untenable argument in a shortages economy where speculative hoarding, noncompetitive price rise and similar other evil practices are quite frequent and common. In a seller's market economy, it cannot be said with certainty that producers will raise their efficiency and reduce costs and prices as a consequence of the imposition of a value added tax.

Applicability of Value Added Tax in India

Doubts are being expressed whether the habits of documentation that now exist in India are adequate or whether they can be made adequate in the near future because fulfilling this is an important prerequisite for successful implementation of value added tax in India. It is a fact that our documentation habits and systems are far from satisfactory. In fact, a regular campaign for proper maintenance of accounts and records will be a preliminary requisite for introduction of value added tax in India. Mistrust and fear seem to be very much present in assessor-assessee dealing in India. That is why, the Inquiry Committee on Indian Taxation (The Jha Committee) accepted superiority of value added tax but had hesitated in recommending it for India. It has, however, recommended its use in certain sectors only. The Special Commissioner of Commercial Taxes, Mr. S. A. Subramani, while addressing tax professionals at an executive training programme organised by the Hindustan Chamber of Commerce on 23rd December, 1994 recommended the implementation of value added tax in India on the ground that value added tax in its ideal form, would have only one rate for all items. He criticised the prevailing high levels of tax differentials between neighbouring states or Union Territories in India. He further added that value added tax would pass on certain taxation burden from the manufacturing point to the trading point.

As per the recommendations of the Jha Committee, the value added tax has been adopted to a limited number of manufacturing industries and called it 'MANVAT'. In India, it was adopted under the name 'MODVAT'.

Initial Trends in Revenue Collection from VAT

During the first seven months of VAT implementation (April-October-2005), the total revenue (provisional) for VAT implementing states showed an increase of around 14.4 per cent, which is higher than the compound annual growth rate of these States for the last 5 years. Up to January 15, 2006, VAT compensation claims for about Rs. 1,674 crore had been filed by eight States, out of which claims for Rs. 1,317 crore had been settled. Based on trends so far, the compensation liabilty for the year 2005-06 is likely to be contained within Budget Expenditure. The non-implementation of VAT by eight States/ UTs is creating complications amd may also lead to undesirable diversion of trade and business from one State to another. Further, the benefits of the VAT system like simple and uniform tax structure all over the country and achieving a common market for goods would not accrue until all the states/ UTs implement VAT. In view of this, it is imperative that the remaining eight states follow a broadly uniform pattern. There is a considerable amount of diversity in the VAT rules and procedures. The EC is looking into this issue of aligning the classification system of VAT with HS (Harmonised System of commodity description and coding).

(e) Modified Value Added Tax (MODVAT)

In India, the value added tax was applied in a modified form in 1986. It is known as, Modified Value Added Tax (MODVAT). The MODVAT scheme was inserted on 1-03-1986 as Section AA in Chapter V of the Central Excise Rules, 1944. MODVAT was announced to prevent the cascading effects of excise duty. Under the MODVAT scheme, credit of duty is allowed on inputs which are used either for producing excisable finished products or intermediate products. Thus, in a broad sense, it is levy of duty on duty. This scheme enables the manufacturer to take credit for the duty already paid on the input against the duty payable on the final product. For instance, tyres when manufactured suffer excise duty, say, to the tune of Rs. 400 and the excise duty on the final product, say motor-bike, to the tune of Rs. 4,000. The manufacturer (motor-bike) can take credit for Rs. 400 paid on the inputs (tyres) and will be liable to pay excise duty only Rs. 3,600 (Rs. 4,000 – Rs. 400 = Rs. 3,600) only. In the same way, the manufacturer (motorbike) will also be entitled to take credit on the duty paid on other inputs like gear-box, battery, electrical components and so on. The result is, that there is reduction of duty payable on the final product and the cascading effect is avoided. This system is known as 'Modified Value-added Tax or MODVAT'. It was extended to inputs for fibres and yarn in 1991 budget and only tobacco and petroleum products, textile inputs and matches were excluded from the MODVAT scheme. In 1994-95, this scheme was extended to capital goods and petroleum products.

Difference between MODVAT and VAT

As we know very well there is a lot of confusions among the readers about MODVAT and VAT. Most of us think that MODVAT and VAT both are one and the same, but this is not true. There is significant difference between MODVAT and VAT. In the case of VAT there is levy of tax only on the value added. Suppose, the value of inputs is Rs. 1,000, and by work done on the same, the value of output becomes Rs. 3,000. In such a case, the tax shall be imposed only on Rs. 2,000 which is value added, *i.e.* Rs. 3,000 – 1,000 = Rs. 2,000 only. In this way, VAT enables the deduction of the entire value of the input. On the contrary, in MODVAT, credit is given in respect of the duty already paid on inputs against the duty paid on the final product. For example, scooter when manufactured suffers excise duty to the tune of Rs. 1,400 only. However, when the scooter is ready for sale it is subject to excise duty to the tune of Rs. 4,000. In this case, the manufacturer of the scooter can take credit for the Rs. 1,400 paid on the inputs and thus, will be liable to pay excise duty only of Rs. 2,600, *i.e.* Rs. 4,000 – 1,400 = Rs. 2,600 only. Thus, VAT is far more equitable as compared to MODVAT. In other words, we can make final conclusion that Indian industrial and trade circles have not approached this MODVAT scheme.

STUDY-QUESTIONS

1. Define the meaning of tax. What are its characteristics?
2. Describe the main characteristics of a good tax system. How far are these characteristics found in the Indian tax structure?
3. Explain main characteristics of a good tax system.
4. Define canons of taxation. Explain briefly the different types of canons.

5. Discuss Adam Smith's canons of taxation.
6. Discuss the objective or aims of taxation.
7. Write short notes on the following:
   (i) VAT and MODVAT
   (ii) Direct and Indirect tax
8. Discuss the merits and demerits of direct taxes.
9. Compare and contrast direct and indirect taxes.
10. Briefly discuss the merits and demerits of indirect taxes.
11. Discuss the role of progressive taxes in an underdeveloped country.

Public Expenditure

7

INTRODUCTION

The term 'public expenditure' refers to the expenses incurred by the government for its own maintenance as also for the preservation and welfare of society and the economy as a whole. In other words, it refers to the expenses of the public authorities—central, state and local governments—for protecting the citizens and/or for promoting their economic and social welfare.

Historically, public expenditure has been continuously increasing over time in every country. Traditional thinking and philosophy have not been very encouraging to the growth of public expenditure. English economists had very little to say concerning the principles of public expenditure although they dwelt profusely on the principles of taxation.

In recent times, public expenditure has, however, increased enormously and the scope of public activities has greatly expanded. The modern state is termed as a 'welfare state'. In a welfare state, the government has a number of political, economic and social functions to perform. After the Second World War, all the countries of the world are making their best efforts to develop their economies. The government is undertaking social and economic activities on an ever-increasing scale. In a welfare state, the government first determines the size of public expenditure and then it raises its financial resources of revenue.

Public expenditure is the expenditure incurred by public authorities—central, state or local governments—either for the satisfaction of collective needs of the citizens or for promoting their economic and social welfare or for protecting the citizens and the country. Just as consumption is the end of all economic financial activities of the state, it is aimed to provide maximum socio-economic welfare of the society. It is considered to be the backbone of economic development of a country. Public expenditure is an important part of public finance. During the past few years, there has been a trend of continuous increase in public expenditure in almost all the countries of the world.

THE TRADITIONAL SCHOOL OF THOUGHT

According to Sir Henry Parenell, "Every particle of public expenditure that is incurred beyond what is a necessity absolutely required for the preservation of social order and for protecting against foreign attack is waste and an unjust and oppressive imposition on the public." The economists of the 19th century were deadly against increasing the scope of public expenditure. Dalton is surprised to see that all the English economists of that time have given such a little attention to the study of public expenditure. An American critic has even remarked: "the older English writers did not need a theory of expenditure because the theory of government which they held implied a fixed limit to government functions." In fact the notion which the economists of that period had in their mind is, that of *laissez-faire* and the political theory arising therefore that "that state is best which governs the least." They would advise the state to keep its activities to the minimum advisable, the rest of business being left at the mercy of private citizens. They would permit expenditure by the government in the matters of defence and protection and so far as the economic functions were concerned they were strong advocates of the policy of least intervention by the state; that is why, they would call 'tyranny on public' to the every coin which was spent by the state *except* in maintaining defence, peace and law & order.

THE MODERN SCHOOL OF THOUGHT

The modern school of thought which now exists in any country, consisting of modern economists is of the firm view that the state should play active role not only in safeguarding the country against foreign attack and the maintenance of law and order in the country but also in the welfare of the society. It is absolutely wrong to believe that private individuals spend money better than their government does. This is no way out. It is wrong to advocate—"let people live in their own way." Now the state is required to perform several functions over and above its traditional functions (such as defence of the country and maintenance of law and order inside the country) such as providing basic necessities like water, electricity, transport, education, establishment of basic industries in particular, social security, labour welfare, banking facilities, economic development, agricultural development, development of trade both internal and foreign, medical services, entertainment, reduction in disparities of economic and wealth, industrial development, economic stability, employment and several socio-economic measures, etc. The old *laissez-faire* policy has now become completely obsolete. Had the old traditional thinking and philosophy been practised in its entirety, public expenditure would not have grown as rapidly as it did. In reality, however, the modern state cannot ignore problems of economic growth and social justice. Now the state cannot remain a silent spectator of the mass miseries of the people.

Prof. R.A. Musgrave, a twentieth century economist, advocated public expenditure since a government is forced to do many activities such as: (i) Redistributive activities; (ii) Activities to secure a re-allocation of resources; (iii) Commercial activities, and (iv) Stabilising activities.

According to Prof. Keynes, a famous economist, pump-priming and compensatory spending were the two forms of public spending. Pump-priming was to stimulate private investment when it became deficient at the times of the recession or depression. In other words, a few doses of public spending could revive the economic system which after some time, will raise the levels of income and employment through increased private spending and was to be continued until the position of full employment was attained and maintained through the interaction of multiplier and accelerator principles and raising the levels of income, output and employment in the economy. This was really a scheme to be observed by the state during the periods of recession or depression.

From the above discussion, we conclude that today the first school of thought has now become obsolete. The popular cry is for state intervention in almost every field, government has to do many things. In spite of the fact that the public expenditure has increased considerably during the last two centuries in almost every state, and inspite of its growing role importance in national economies, the area of public expenditure even today remains unexplored.

STRUCTURE (CLASSIFICATION) OF PUBLIC EXPENDITURE

According to Schulze, "Nineteenth century fiscal writers devoted considerable space to the subject of the proper classification of governmental expenditure, but nobody agreed upon the same classification." Most of the nineteenth century economists have classified public expenditure on the basis of benefits or return whereas, others (including German and American economists) have classified public expenditure in accordance with government functions, protective, commercial and developmental.

According to Spriegal, "A structure is a detailed, systematically arranged list of all items pertaining to a particular phase of business." Structure facilitates interpretation and ease of reference to seemingly unrelated facts. A number of structure or classification of public expenditure have been made by different economists from time to time and there is little agreement between them with regard to this aspect of public finance.

Thus, the economists widely differ on the basis of structure of public expenditure. Hence, most of the economists believed that the bases of classification should not be absolute. Since different economists have classified public expenditure according to their own ideas about the suitability or importance of the base, we are giving here the main bases of classification of public expenditure:

(1) Classification on the Basis of Necessity

Prof. Mill, who has criticised Adam, divides expenditure into two parts: necessary and optional. It is difficult to justify such division of public expenditure. A private person can perhaps be considered as incurring superfluous expenditure. But it is not right to think that the state also is doing so regardless of the value of money as to spend it on superfluous items. For *optional*, he suggested that it may or may not be undertaken.

(2) Constant and Variable Expenditure

The basis of division is the nature of public expenditure—it is either for groups of people or for individuals. It is either of a type that perhaps cannot be controlled or of that which they can control:

(i) *Constant expenditure:* Constant expenditure is that amount which does not depend upon the services that are financed by it. The expenditure on defence is a clear example of this class. But there are many other expenditures that are either wholly or partly constant.

(ii) *Variable expenditure:* Variable expenditure is that which increases with every increase in the use of public services by the people for whose benefit it is incurred. Expenditure on postal service is an example of variable expenditure. It cannot be concluded that every item of public expenditure can be placed wholly under one or the other class. Such sharp distinction cannot be found in practice. For instance, a good part of the expenditure on the post office is not variable. Though more postmen have to be employed and more postal clerks are needed when a larger number of letters are written or parcels sent, yet every time there is such an increased demand for employees the government does not have to open new post offices. Nor is it necessary to employ one more postman when a few more letters are written. It is clear, therefore, that within each item of expenditure there are the elements of both constant and variable expenditure.

(3) Classification on the Basis of Benefit

German writers such as Prof. Cohen and American writers such as Prof. Plehn have classified public expenditure according to the benefit on which each class of expenditure confers. The following is Plehn's classification in brief:

(i) Expenditure which confers a common benefit, *e.g.* the expenditure on defence, education, public health and transport, etc.

(ii) Expenditure which confers a special benefit on certain people, but which should be treated as a common benefit because of the capacity of those classes, *e.g.* poor relief.

(iii) Expenditure which confers a special benefit on certain persons and at the same time is a common benefit on the remaining, *e.g.* the administration of justice.

(iv) Expenditure which confers a special benefit on some individuals, *e.g.* expenditure on state industries.

(4) Classification on the Basis of Degree of Urgency

Prof. Roscher classifies public expenditure into three groups on the basis of degree of urgency:

(i) *Necessary expenditure:* Which cannot be postponed, *e.g.* expenditure on administration.

(ii) *Useful expenditure:* Which can be postponed for a while.

(iii) *Superfluous expenditure:* Expenditure which is neither profitable nor necessary.

(5) Classification on the Basis of Income

The second classification, according to the amount of revenue obtained by the state in return for the services rendered is that by Prof. Nicholson. In many ways it is superior to that of Cohen and Plehn's classification of benefit.

(i) Expenditure without direct return of revenue, *e.g.* poor relief or in some cases even with indirect as well as direct loss, *i.e.* expenditure on war.

(ii) Expenditure without direct return, but with indirect return, *e.g.* the expenditure on education that educated persons are good tax-payers and education is conducive to increasing efficiency and productive capacity. With the result, the taxable capacity is also increased and it directly helps the state exchequer.

(iii) Expenditure with partial direct return, *e.g.* education for which fees is charged.

(iv) Expenditure with full return or even profit, *e.g.* post and telegraph, gas works, state and industries, etc.

(6) Classification on the Basis of Importance

In the nineteenth century, writers have usually classified public expenditure from the point of view of benefit conferred from the revenue received in return for services rendered. Others have classified expenditure in accordance with governmental functions. Prof. Shirras divides expenditure into primary and secondary. It is simple and apparently clear cut division.

(i) *Primary expenditure:* It is compulsive and must be incurred by the state. Expenditure on such functions can be called primary, *e.g.* the expenditure on defence, maintenance of law and order, police and justice, civil administration, payments of debts, etc.

(ii) *Secondary expenditure:* Rest of the items except those given in group one are to be categorised in this group, *e.g.* expenditure on education, public health, poor relief, unemployment, insurance, relief and social service. We do not think that a government worthy of its name can neglect the duty of educating the citizens. That some broad lines of demarcation can be drawn, cannot be disputed and, therefore, the classification of such type becomes the victim of vague terminology. In spite of this defect, the classification is a good one.

(7) Classification on the Basis of Transferability

Prof. Pigou divides public expenditure into non-transferable and transferable expenditure:

(i) *Transferable expenditure:* An expenditure is said to be transferable expenditure when it takes the form of payment of money to people either gratuitously or in purchase of existing property rights. The expenditure incurred by the government for the welfare of a certain weaker section of the community, *e.g.* unemployment insurance, old age pension, etc.

(ii) *Non-transferable expenditure:* An expenditure is called non-transferable expenditure when it is incurred to purchase current services of the resources of the nation. In this group, such expenditures are included as those on maintenance and building up of the army, navy and air-force, civil services, educational services, judiciary, post office, municipal tramway service and so on.

(8) Classification on the Basis of Grants and Purchase Price

Prof. Dalton divided public expenditure into grants and purchase price. An individual, who receives public money or money's worth, may not render in return in direct *quid pro quo* (tit for tat) to the public authority. In the former case, the public authority makes a purchase from him, in the later case it makes him a grant. This grant may exist either as money, security presumed to be derived from armaments or police. Thus, payments by a public authority to any of its employees, by way of salaries or wages, or to contractors, are purchase prices. On the other hand, payments of old age pensions, poor relief or contribution out of general revenue to scheme of health and unemployment insurance are grants.

Hugh Dalton, classified public expenditure into following three types:

(i) Progressive;

(ii) Regressive; and

(iii) Proportional.

Dalton defines these types thus: "A grant is *regressive* if the smaller the recipient's income, the smaller the proportionate addition made by the grant; *progressive* if the smaller the recipient's income, the larger the proportionate addition, *proportional* if whatever the size of recipient's income the proportionate addition is the same."

(i) *Progressive public expenditure:* If the public expenditure is incurred in such a way as to provide more and more benefit to the poor people and less benefit to the rich, it is called the *progressive expenditure*. In progressive expenditure, benefit decreases faster than the increase in income.

(a) Expenditure on the cash grants is one of the examples of progressive public expenditure. Cash grants includes following payments made by the government:

(1) Old age pension;

(2) Sickness benefits;

(3) Compensation to the unemployed persons;

(4) Scholarships, etc.

While incurring this type of expenditure, if the principle "expenditure according to ability to receive and taxation according to ability to pay" is followed, then only the maximum economic welfare may be achieved.

(b) Expenditure on the provision of free or cheap goods and services is another type of progressive expenditure. Food subsidies provided to the poor people is progressive. Such expenditure helps in narrowing the inequality gap as well as in increasing the level of welfare. Other expenditure, such as free health service narrow the area of inequality. For Dalton, "this is one road of approach to a less unequal society."

However, such grants are subject to certain limitations. If the prospect of grant causes a person to work and save less than he would otherwise have done, the effect of the grant in increasing his income will be diminished; in the opposite case its effects will be increased. So, the progressive expenditure, should not be incurred in such a way as to let the recipients feel that they are getting easy money; otherwise it might prove as a retarding factor to the economic development and growth.

(ii) *Regressive expenditure:* If the expenditure incurred by the government, creates more benefits for the rich and less benefit to the poor it is called regressive expenditure. In other words, the regressive expenditure increases with the increase in income and decreases with the decrease in the income of the individuals. This type of expenditure is not held good, since it does not help in reducing the "inequality of income", whereas "that system of public expenditure is best which has the strongest tendency to reduce the inequalities of incomes." That is why progressive expenditure is preferred.

(iii) *Proportional expenditure:* If the government uses public money in such a way as to provide the benefit in proportion to the income of the individuals, it is called *proportional expenditure.* The proportional expenditure benefits increase with the increase in income. In other words, higher the income, higher the proportional expenditure benefit, lower the income, lower the proportional expenditure benefit.

(9) Classification on the Basis of Productivity

Prof. Robinson has used a special technique of productivity for the classification of public expenditure. He classified public expenditure into two parts.

(i) *Productive expenditure:* Any state expenditure, which directly or indirectly develops natural or human resources of a nation or leads to their more economic use may be expected to increase national income by increasing national wealth. The gain due to increased expenditure is not less than the loss caused by the heavy taxation.

(ii) *Unproductive expenditure:* The public expenditure which does not result in any rise of national income, *e.g.* war expenditure.

(10) Classification on the Basis of Functions of Government

Prof. Adams has made the classification of public expenditure on the basis of functions of the Government.

(i) *Protective functions:* Expenditure incurred for the security of the citizens, to provide them justice or to counteract any external invasion, *e.g.* expenditure on military, police and courts and social diseases (jails, mental hospitals, etc.).

(ii) *Commercial functions:* Expenditure for the development of trade and commerce, *e.g.* development of means of transport and communications.

(iii) *Development functions:* Expenditure for the development of citizens and country, *e.g.* education, public recreation, prosecution of private business, public investigation, public works, etc.

THEORIES OF PUBLIC EXPENDITURE

The states had to do very little with the provision of public services, but in 20th century the concept of government changed altogether. The modern state is termed as welfare state in which the government has enormous functions to perform. For the first time, Adolph Wagner, a fiscal theorist propounded an empirical theory to the effect that government inequitably grows larger. Therefore, the various theories regarding increasing public expenditure can be classified into two parts as:

(A) General theories of public expenditure.

(B) Pure theories of public expenditure.

(A) General Theories of Public Expenditure

There are three important theories of increasing public expenditure given by:

(i) Wagner Hypothesis;

(ii) Peacock Wiseman Hypothesis; and

(ii) Colin Clark (Critical Limit) Hypothesis

(i) Wagner Hypothesis

Adolph Wagner (1835-1917) believed that a functional "cause and effect" relationship existed between the growth of an economy and the relative growth of its public sector. According to Wagner, the relative growth of the government sector was an inherent characteristic of industrialised economies. He referred not only to Great Britain, which essentially had completed her industrial revolution before Wagner's time but to nations such as the United States of America, France, Germany (in the West) and Japan (in the East) whose industrial revolutions were contemporary to Wagner's life. Wagner's hypothesis of the increasing state activity holds that as the per capita income and output increase in the industrialised nations, the public sector of these nations necessarily grows as a proportion to total economic activity.

F.S. Nitti supported Wagner's thesis and concluded with the support of empirical evidence that this "law" was not only applicable to Germany but to various governments which differed widely from each other. All kinds of governments, irrespective of their levels (central, state or local governments), intentions (peaceful or war-like) and size (territorially small or large), etc. had shown the same tendency of increasing public expenditure.

Factors Responsible for Increase in Public Expenditure

Following are the important causes responsible for this tendency:

(i) Wagner believed that social progress was the basic cause of the relative growth of government in the industrialised economies. The chain reaction circumstances described by Wagner are that social progress leads to a growth in government functions which, in turn, leads to the absolute and relative growth of governmental economic activity. Obviously, the hypothesis is secular (long term) in nature.

(ii) Wagner argued that there is a persistent tendency both towards an "extensive" and an "intensive" increase in the functions of the state. New functions are continuously being undertaken by the state while old functions are being performed more efficiently and on a larger scale.

In his attempt to validate the hypothesis, Wagner distinguished certain types of government activities or functions. According to Wagner, the most essential function of any government worth its name is that of providing the effective law and order machinery essential for the "environmental conditions" within which a market functions. Secondly, Wagner described government participation in the material production of economic goods including the provision of certain "social products" like communications, education, monetary and banking arrangements in the phase of "market failure." Moreover, Wagner believed that government corporations must produce certain economic goods requiring large fixed investment because private corporations cannot undertake such investment on a profitable basis since these industries involve heavy fixed costs.

(iii) The most important contributory factor in increasing the public expenditure in the present century is war. Expenditure on national defence generally accounts for half and at times even more than half of the total budget expenditure.

(iv) Another important factor of increasing state expenditure is the growth of population and the growing concentration of people in towns. The continuous process of urbanisation brings an expansion in the public expenditure for increased protection of life and property. With the growing population concentration, it is impossible to carry on the performance on public street, public education and other functions on small-scale. The conditions of urban life impose additional responsibilities on the government, such as the inspection of food and essential drugs, against possible adulteration, improvement in the distribution of national product, promotion of public health, slum clearance, construction and maintenance of hospitals, etc.

(v) Secular rise in prices and national income has led to significant increase in the absolute amount of public expenditure. National income in the country in the post-independence period has almost doubled and the price level has also monotonically escalated ever since. The rise in the price level has two important effects, as far as the government of a country is concerned. Firstly, the government has to pay higher prices for all the goods and services which it has to buy. Secondly, it has to find larger financial resources to meet its ever-growing expenditure. To a certain extent, the increased government expenditure is itself one of the contributory factors responsible for the rise in prices.

(vi) With the growing social acceptance of economic planning and growth as important functions of a modern welfare state the role of the public sector in community life has substantially increased and will further increase in future.

(vii) With the fast growing complexities of modern life, the police protection and welfare functions of a modern state have tremendously increased both qualitatively and quantitatively, involving continuous substantial increase in public expenditure. The present-day government is omnipotent, omnipresent and omniscient pervading all aspects of community life. Naturally, all this involves massive public expenditure.

Diagrammatical Illustration of Wagner's Hypothesis

Wagner's hypothesis of increasing governmental activity has been shown in Figure 7.1. The real per capita output of public goods has been shown on the Y-axis and the real per capita income has been shown on the X-axis.

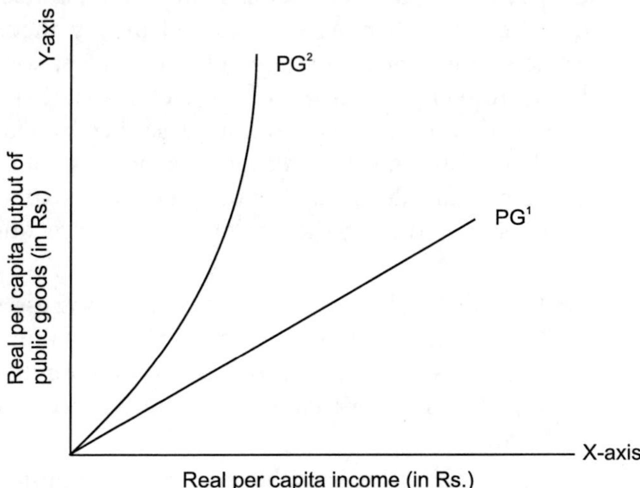

Figure 7.1: Wagner's hypothesis of increasing governmental activity

Time is an important third dimension implicit in the graph because the growth (both in the real per capita output of public goods and in the real per capita income) is realistically assumed to take place on a historical basis over an extended period of time. Line PG^1 represents a situation in which the public sector maintains a constant proportion of the total economic production of the society over time. In other words, while the real per capita income increases due to the economic development of the country, the real per capita output of the public goods remains at the same fixed proportion of the total economic activity. The constant proportions line may now be used as a reference point to the graphical presentation of Wagner's law as depicted by line PG^2. Along line PG^2, the proportion of the total resources devoted to the output of public goods is expanding over time.

Criticisms

Allan T. Peacock and Jack Wiseman have criticised Wagner's law of increasing state activities on the following grounds:

(i) Wagner's hypothesis deals with the "interdisciplinary" phenomenon although it is not essentially interdisciplinary in its analytical framework. Political science, economics, and sociology are among the several disciplines which must be involved in any theory of public sector expenditure. Such theories must consider the cultural characteristics of a society. It is, therefore, unlikely that the causal conditions described by Wagner, which are essentially of an economic nature, constitute all the primary determinants of a relatively expanding public sector during industrialisation and economic growth.

(ii) Further, although Wagner's hypothesis possesses the attribute of accumulating and partially explaining the important historical facts, its lack of a comprehensive analytical framework causes it to fall short in these explanations.

(iii) Wagner's hypothesis is based on an organic self-determining theory of the state, which is not, however, the prevailing accepted theory of state, in most western countries.

(iv) Wagner's hypothesis ignores the influence of war on government's spending activity.

(v) Wagner stresses a long-term trend of public economic activity which tends to overlook the significant "time pattern" or "process" of public expenditure growth.

(ii) Peacock-Wiseman Hypothesis

The second thesis of the growth of public expenditure was advanced by Peacock and Wiseman in their well-known study of public expenditure in the United Kingdom during the period 1890-1955. It stresses the "time pattern" of public spending trends and highlights the fact that the increase in the public expenditure does not follow any smooth and continuous trend. The increase in the public expenditure over time has occurred in jerks or step-like manner. The general approach of the hypothesis is inclusive of the following three separate, though related, concepts: (i) Displacement effect; (ii) Inspection effect; and (iii) Concentration effect.

Using the empirical data for the British economy after 1890, Peacock and Wiseman observe that the relative growth of the public sector in the United Kingdom has followed a discrete step-like pattern rather than a "continuous" growth pattern. In other words, the government's fiscal activities in the country have risen step by step to successive new plateaus during the period of almost seven decades covered by the study. Most of the absolute and relative increases (steps upward) in taxing and spending by the British Government have taken place during periods of major social disturbances which create a displacement effect by which the previous lower tax and expenditure levels are replaced by the new and higher budgetary levels. After the social disturbance has ended, however, the newly emerged levels of "tax tolerance" make the society willing to support a higher level of public expenditure since the society realises that it is capable of carrying a heavier tax burden than it previously had thought possible to bear.

Thus, when the major social disturbance ends, no strong motivation exists for the society to return to the lower pre-disturbance level of taxation. The higher government revenues are used, instead, to support a permanently higher level of public sector allocation. The following Figure 7.2, demonstrates the displacement effect. The time period (in years) has been shown on the X-axis, while the public sector revenues (mostly derived from taxes) and public expenditure as a percentage of the gross national product (GNP) have been shown on the Y-axis. The Figure 7.2, reveals that as the social disturbances cause a relative expansion of the public sector, the displacement effect which occurs helps to explain the "time pattern" by which the governmental growth took place. This displacement effect does not require that the new higher plateau of expenditure will continue with the same expenditure pattern that was created by the social disturbance. Although some of the increased government outlays (such as debt interest) are direct results of a social disturbance other expenditure items frequently involve the expansion of the government activity into new areas of economic activity. War and other social disturbances frequently force the people and their government to find solutions of important problems which previously had been neglected. This is known as the *inspection effect.*

In addition to the displacement and inspection effects, Peacock and Wiseman also describe a concentration effect. The

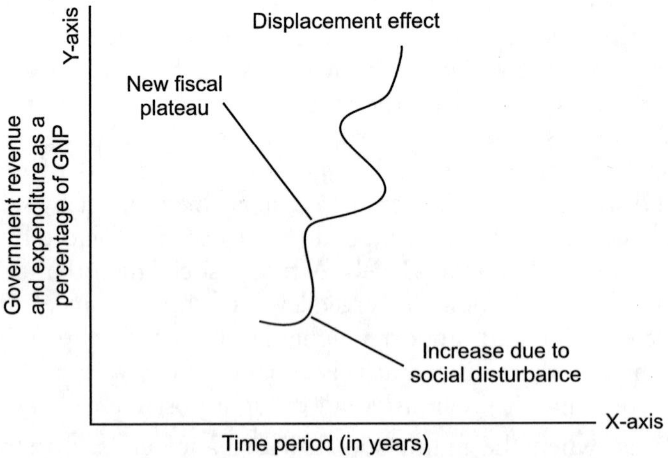

Figure 7.2: Displacement effect

concentration effect refers to the apparent tendency for the central government economic activity to become an increasing proportion of the total public sector economic activity when the society is experiencing economic growth. In brief, Peacock and Wiseman have concluded that in the United Kingdom: (i) the relative growth of the public sector has occurred in a step-like pattern (displacement effect); (ii) an "inspection" process has occurred whereby existing problems are more clearly defined with the potential solutions more carefully studied during a major disturbance; and (iii) a "concentration" process has existed whereby the central government has become a larger proportion of the aggregate public sector.

Thus, the Peacock-Wiseman approach to government spending trends is much more modest in what it purports to explain than is Wagner's hypothesis. It does not claim to be an immutable economic principle or law, it merely attempts to point out some important characteristics of the growth pattern not to isolate all the important causal variables involved in the public sector growth. Both the Wagner and the Peacock-Wiseman hypothesis, however, contribute significantly to the understanding of the process of the growth of public sector in the industrial nations.

(iii) Colin Clark (Critical Limit) Hypothesis

The third thesis of the growth of public expenditure was advanced by Colin Clark. The hypothesis was developed immediately after the Second World War. It is concerned with the tolerance level of taxation. The critical limit hypothesis concludes from the empirical data drawn from several western countries for the interwar period that inflation in the economy necessarily occurs when the share of the government sector, as measured in terms of taxes and other receipts, exceeds 25 per cent of the aggregate economic activity in the economy. The hypothesis is based on the following institutional factors:

(i) When taxes collected by the government reach the critical limit of 25 per cent ratio of the aggregate economic activity reflected in the gross national product, the community behaviour patterns change and people become less productive since incentives are harmed by the fact that increasing proportions of additional income must be paid in taxes under a progressive tax system.

(ii) People become less resistant to various inflationary means of financing the government expenditure. Thus, the loss of incentive tends to reduce the "aggregate supply" while the increased purchasing power resulting from inflationary financing techniques tends to expand government's aggregate effective demand. Inflation tends to result from this new "aggregate supply-aggregate demand equilibrium" under conditions of high employment of resources.

Colin Clark's critical limit hypothesis has received a limited following in the academic circles, although it has been well received by the business community. Empirical evidence, however, demonstrates that several countries have violated the 25 per cent critical limit during recent decades without experiencing significant inflationary trends. Moreover, it is agreed that inflation is a complex economic phenomenon characterised by multiple determinants.

(B) Pure Theories

The pure theories regarding increasing public expenditure can be further classified into four parts:

(i) Pigou's Ability to Pay Theory;

(ii) Voluntary Exchange Theory [Benefit Analysis];

(iii) Samuelson Theory; and

(iv) Johansen Theory.

(i) Pigou's Ability to Pay Theory

Prof. Pigou gave a most comprehensive treatment to ability to pay theory in the determination of optimum level of public expenditure. According to Pigou, "Goods and services which are provided by government departments and can be sold for fees so arranged as to cover cost of production pose no problem." The amount of resources which should be devoted to these purposes is determined automatically by public demand. But fees can cover neither bulk of non-transfer expenditure of government such as defence, civil administration and so forth nor transfer expenditure. So, there is no automatic machinery to determine how far expenditure shall be carried; and some other method has to be employed.

He further opines that bulk of current transfer expenditure-debt services, as pensions, old age pensions—is regulated by practically irrevocable contracts. But large parts of non-transfer expenditure are optional. The optional parts of public outlay-transfer as well as non-transfer-need to be "regulated with some reference to the burden involved in raising funds to finance them." And he propounds the principle of balance based on the concept of margin. The optimum amount of government expenditure is determined at the point at which the satisfaction obtained from the last rupee spent is equal to the satisfaction lost in respect of the last rupee. Pigou states the conditions when government expenditure could be larger as under:

(i) The greater is the aggregate income of the community, the larger will the optimum amount of the government expenditure be.

(ii) Suppose new opportunities for expenditure by government are opened up but there are no corresponding opportunities for private expenditure. In this case, the balance between marginal benefit of expenditure and marginal disutility of revenue will be struck at a higher point.

(iii) Given aggregate income and population, greater the concentration of income in the hands of a few rich persons, the higher the optimum level of public expenditure. It is for the simple reason that the tax scheme can be so framed so as to raise a given revenue with lower marginal sacrifice.

(ii) Voluntary Exchange Theory (Benefit Analysis)

Micro-economic theory analyses that price mechanism under certain conditions leads to the realisation of *pareto optimally*. Such a price mechanism does not exist for the provision of public goods and services because they are jointly consumed. Therefore, they cannot be split up and sold to individual groups. Moreover, once these goods and services are supplied, all members of the society consume them—those who pay for them as well as those who do not. In spite of these difficulties, attempts have been made to construct a theory of public expenditure based on price mechanism. The clear-cut statement of this theory was provided by Lindahl in 1919. The relevant portion of the theory is printed in the book *Classics in The Theory and Public Finance* edited by R.A. Musgrave and Allan T. Peacock. According to Lindahl, "The determination of public expenditure has connection with the distribution of the corresponding tax burden among the groups within the community. The distribution ratio for this burden will then play a role similar to that of prices in the adjustment between supply and demand in any ordinary market."

In this theory, the revenue-expenditure process, as a phenomenon of economic value and price, is arrived at in a three-fold decision.

(i) Before determining the relative distribution of tax shares between various tax-payers, a choice must be made between the satisfaction of alternative wants by private households. Let us suppose, a given sum is to be raised from the tax-payers A and B jointly. Now, if B pays a larger share of the total tax, A's curtailment of his own private outlays will be smaller (that is, A pays less tax) and vice versa.

(ii) A second choice is now required. It is between the satisfaction of alternative wants in the public sector. If more is spent on defence, less can be spent on education.

(iii) In order to determine the total revenue to be collected and spent, a third choice is to be made between the satisfaction of public wants and private wants. If public expenditures are lower, taxes will be required in smaller quantity and there will be less curtailment of private spending. However, this third decision cannot be rendered without a knowledge of the relative distribution of tax share and the expenditure allocation corresponding to varying revenue expenditures totals. The three decisions, therefore, are mutually interdependent and must be rendered jointly.

In Lindahl's theory, private economy process is followed in the public economy. Therefore, the allocation of total cost of production of two joint products X and Y is done according to the respective supply prices of the two products based on the demand prevailing for the two products respectively and not according to cost imputation. Suppose A is purchaser of X while B is the purchaser of Y. If A is willing to share only a small portion of the total cost of production of both X and Y, then B will be required to contribute a corresponding larger share. In the opposite case, when B is willing to contribute a smaller portion, A will be called upon to contribute a larger share. A's dependence on B is due to the fact that benefits derived from the supply of public services are not divisible into individual benefits. They are by all members of the community.

In the Figure 7.3, there are two tax-payers, A and B. Percentages of total contribution by A are measured along the vertical line, while the quantities of public goods which they purchase are measured on the horizontal axis. Curve aa shows the varying percentages of total costs incurred in providing these

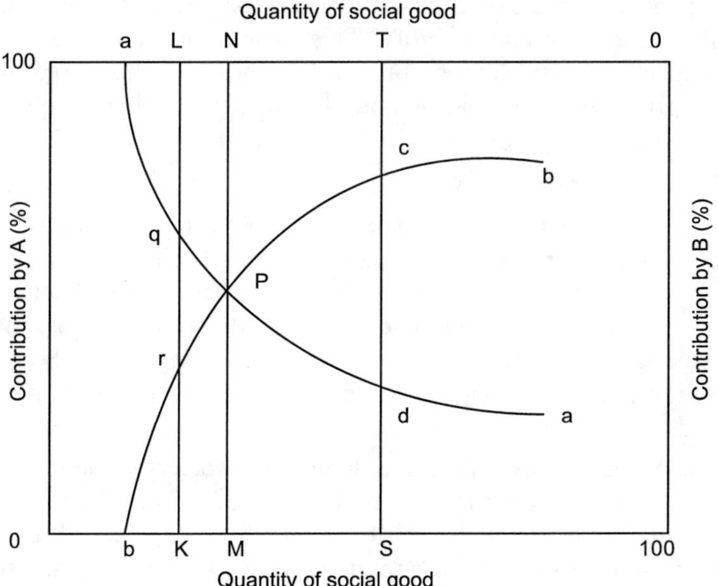

Figure 7.3: Lindahl voluntary exchange theory

goods which A is willing to contribute. Similarly, curve bb indicates the percentages of the total costs which B will be willing to share. The figure shows that the maximum amount of the public good that can be produced is OM. For this quantity, A is willing to contribute pM percentage of the total cost of production. B is willing to share the remaining portion of the total cost, that is, pN percentage. For any other amount, the total cost is either over-contributed or under-contributed. If for instance, the good is produced in OK quantity, A is willing to contribute Lq percentage of the total cost, while B shows his willingness to pay Kr percentages. Their joint contribution comes to Kq+Lr which is more than the total cost LK. In the situation, when OS quantity is produced, the entire cost of production will not be contributed by A and B together. A willing to pay only ds percentages while B is not willing to contribute more than Tc percentages. Thus, cd portion of the total cost remains uncovered.

In Figure 7.3, there are only two parties A and B. This situation is more like isolated barter or bilateral monopoly than a competitive market with many suppliers and many demanders. Lindahl has assumed that the two tax-payers possessed equal bargaining power and ability. This assumption is questionable because in a situation of bilateral monopoly, the bargaining strength of the two sides is bound to differ and then a solution like point P may not be arrived at.

(iii) Samuelson Theory

Samuelson has used market principle for providing public goods. According to him, these goods are provided collectively. These goods cannot be provided by private entrepreneurs without knowing individual preferences. In case of private goods, these preferences are reflected through the market principle. So how can the market principle be applied to the provision of public goods.

Answer to this is that in a democratic society... the ultimate justification of the governmental provision of public goods or other activities is the desire of the members of society for such goods and activities, rather than an authoritarian determination for such preferences for public goods, it may yet be assumed that such preferences are the ultimate source of justification for government activities. On this assumption, let us analyse how the market principle can be applied to the determination of the optimal provision and financing of public goods. In order to do this we take the familiar supply and demand diagram.

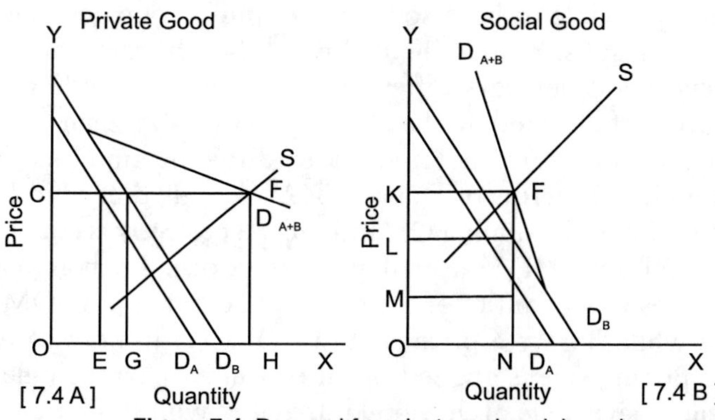

Figure 7.4: Demand for private and social goods

Figure 7.4A, shows the demand for a private good and a social good for two individuals A and B under a given distribution of income and given prices for other goods. In left side of the Figure (7.4A), D_A and D_B are demand curves for a private good X and Y. D_{A+B} is the market demand for X which is obtained by horizontal addition of D_A and D_B. S is the supply curve of X. Price of X is OC for both A and B which is determined by the intersection of market demand D_{A+B} with market supply S at the point F. Quantity purchased by A and B together is OH. A will purchase OE while B purchase OG so that OE + OG = OH.

Figure 7.4B, shows that D_A and D_B are demand schedules for A and B and D_{A+B}, which is obtained by vertical addition of D_A and D_B, and is the market demand for the social good, G. Since G is consumed in the same quantity by all tax-payer-consumers, market demand curve, S is the supply schedules of G. Equilibrium between demand for and supply of G is given at F. Consumption of G by both A and B is ON and the combined price is OK, of which OM is paid by A and OL by B so that OK = OM + OL.

It should be clear from the above that the production of a social good and its pricing are determined by the same principle which applies to the case of a private good. However, one important difference should be noted. Samuelson says that efficiency requirement in the case of private good is one in which marginal cost is incurred. Consequently, application of the same pricing principle to both social good and private goods give us different results. Each individual purchases the same amount of a social good but pays different prices for it depending on his valuation of the good. In the case of private good, each consumer pays the same price but purchases different amounts of this commodity. In terms of Figure (7.4A), marginal benefit derived by A and B in consuming OE and OG respectively is equal to the marginal cost HF, (case of private good). Each individual consumes ON quantity of the social good but A pays OM price for it while B pays a price equal to OL. Yet in both cases, the same pricing rule is applied. Each consumer pays a single price for successive units of the good purchased while the price equals the marginal benefit that the purchaser derives. This analysis presents the efficient provision of private and social goods and it was done by comparing a market for private good with a pseudo-market for social goods. Each market was viewed in separate partial-equilibrium setting assuming that the demand for public goods would be revealed.

Difference between Samuelson and Musgrave Approaches

Musgrave says that Samuelson's solution pertaining to the optimum level of public goods determined according to tax-payer consumer's preference is not operational. The benefits from those goods are available to all. So consumers will not reveal their preference by bidding in the market; they will rather act as free-riders. Samuleson's solution of this problem is based on the assumption that consumer's preferences are known. Thus, the central problem, *i.e.* knowing consumer's preferences for social goods is left without a solution.

Hence, the most immediate problem is to analyse the process by which individuals may be induced to reveal their preferences. In the real world, there is no omniscient planner to whom the individual preference are revealed. This is not an operational approach. Therefore, a political process must be used. It is done for two purposes:

(i) To obtain revelation of preferences, that is, individuals must tell the government what public goods should be provided; and

(ii) The government must be furnished with the fiscal resources needed to pay for these goods. This is done by a voting process. The task is to devise a voting system which is effective in securing preference revelation and an efficient system of tax-expenditures determination. It is the voting process that helps to reveal the pseudo-demand schedules of Samuelson determine the budget size and apply the tax-price. Musgrave says that this is the best that we can do, keeping in mind that the voting process by its very nature cannot bring about a perfect result. Individual preferences are not homogeneous. It, therefore, precludes unanimity because some voters will always remain dissatisfied. But some systems of voting give better results than others. One task, therefore, is to find the best approximation.

Musgrave brings in the question of distributions as well. He says that voting on the provision of social goods and meeting their costs through taxes proceed on the assumption of a given distribution of income which may not be correct one. This raises another problem and it is the determination of the optimal state of distribution. It is a different issue of social choice but a more difficult one than the determination of social value.

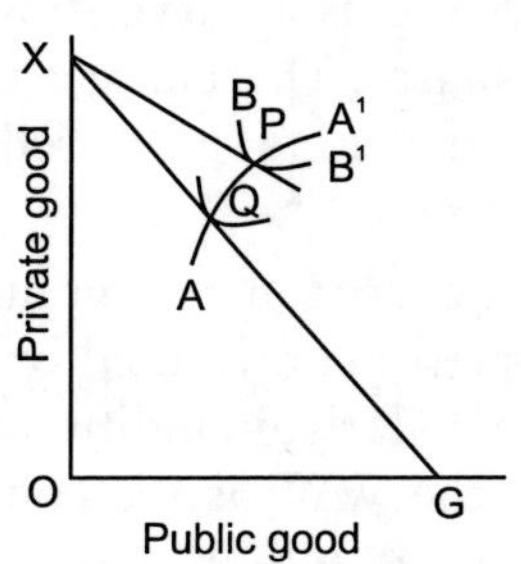

Figure 7.5: Preference with regard to private good and public good

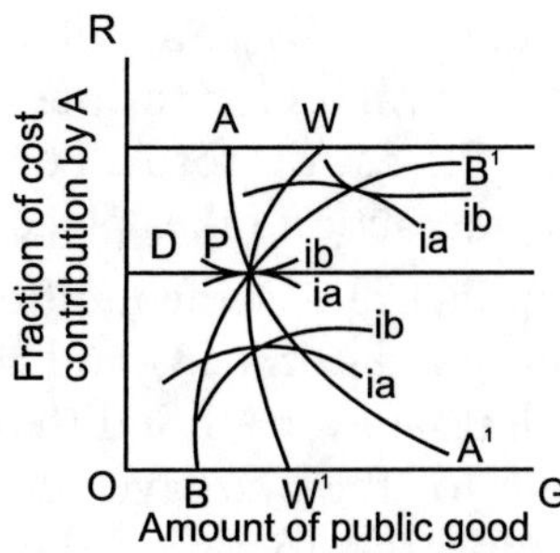

Figure 7.6: Combinations of public good output cost share

(4) Johansen's Theory

Samuelson's pure theory of public expenditure solves two problems under assumptions of given preferences and distribution of income. These are divisions of total output between public good and private good and division of the total supply of private goods between two consumers A and B. All these solutions are *pareto optimal* because any departure from them involves a loss to either A and B. The optimum of all such optimals is then decided on the basis of a social utility function as a part of the general problem of welfare maximisation.

According to Musgrave, "This formulation meets the test of theoretical rigour and sweeping elegance and ranks among the great contribution to the theory of welfare economics as applied to public finance." Even then, Samuelson's theory does not satisfy those who intend to apply fiscal theory to partial problems and specific issues. From the implementation point of view, it is far from satisfactory. Moreover, Johansen has tried to remove some of these difficulties. This fact is illustrated with the help of Figure 7.5.

Thus, Johansen assumed that there is a fraction of the total cost of producing public good G which is borne by the tax-payer A. The share borne by B is ib. He considers the case of A and examines his preferences with regard to a private good X and a public good G. In the Figure 7.5, two budget lines are drawn correspondingly to two different values of G, steeper the budget line higher is the value of G represents best preference for A. The two points P as in Figure 7.6 are points of this kind and a curve AA^1 obtained by pairs all such points is a curve showing most preferred values for various cost shares. This curve is redrawn in Figure 7.5 as AA^1 for A. For B a smaller curve is labelled as BB^1; their interaction takes place at point P.

In Figure 7.6, the indifference curves show combinations of public good output G and cost shares contributed by A among which tax-payer A is indifferent. Similarly, in indifference curves drawn for the tax-payer B. The line WW^1 is the contact curve showing the locus of the points at which the two sets of indifference curves are tangent. Only at point P, we find the most preferred position because it lies on AA^1, BB^1, ia and ib. For Johansen, this P point is only one of the many *pareto optimal* solutions. It is so because P is the only one of the several points on the contract curve WW^1.

REASONS FOR THE GROWTH OF PUBLIC EXPENDITURE

Public expenditure has increased manifold in the recent past and it continues to be on increasing trend in almost all countries of the world. The end of the *laissez-faire* policy has contributed much to his fact in the recent period. C.C. Plehn has rightly agreed: "Public expenditure grows because, and as, public activities increase. This increase is both extensive and intensive. Government in every branch—central, intermediate and local—are constantly assuming new work or duties and are constantly performing the older functions and in turn, newer ones also, on an ever larger scale." Therefore, statistics of public expenditure by modern welfare governments demonstrate such persistent increase, so that Adolph Wagner's law of increasing expansion of state activities proved empirically. Let us examine the reasons responsible for inducing increased volume of expenditure as under:

(i) **Welfare States:** In the modern times, states are the welfare states. Their aim is to promote the economic, political and social life of the people. It is the moral duty of the state to improve the living standard of the general public. To achieve this aim, the state has to undertake many welfare functions like education, public health, etc. This is true in all types of governments, either capitalistic or communist. States intervention is increasing through legislative and administrative measures to enhance production and improving distribution system. The state satisfies many wants of the society collectively which were earlier satisfied individually. Keynes and others are of the opinion that state must intervene in the economic system of the country to secure stabilisation in advanced countries and pace of rate of growth in underdeveloped countries. The new functions are social insurance, unemployment reliefs, cheap medical facilities, old age pensions, housing facilities, etc. The state has come to reduce the social inequalities in the society. Especially, in underdeveloped countries such as India, the state expenditure is rising very fast.

The welfare aspect of government activity is described by Wagner as the pressure for social progress. In terms of Wagner's hypothesis, the pressure of social reform may be regarded as the root cause of the relative growth of the public expenditure in modern times. In short, these functions have necessitated the adoption of the strategy of planned economic development which involves huge amount of expenditure.

(ii) **To meet the defence needs:** Due to rapid growth of science and technology in the sphere of nuclear weapons, there is a grave threat of foreign attacks. The political situation all over the world is uncertain and insecure. If one country strengthens its defence forces, the other countries are forced to take similar steps in their self-defence in anticipation. The manufacture of modern nuclear weapons, training and planning of the army is a very costly affair. The technique of war is a changing phenomenon and with the change of technique of war, new weapons have to be purchased for army. It increases the burden of public expenditure.

In India, the defence expenditure has been increased manifold since Chinese aggression in 1962 and war with Pakistan in 1965 and 1971 respectively. Furthermore, the defence expenditure also includes the maintenance of Army, Air Force, Navy, development of military art and practice. Obviously, this has led to a huge increase in public expenditure.

(iii) **Development of agriculture:** In developing countries like India, the development of agriculture is the key factor to the progress of the economy. The government has come to know the effect of agriculture on the industrial sector. The interrelationship between agriculture and non-agriculture sector is vital to the development of both the sectors.

The expansion of agricultural sector provides stimulus to industrialisation. On the other hand, industrial sector also helps to supply modern tools and implements to it which, in turn, are responsible for the rise in agriculture productivity. The governments are spending huge amounts for the development of the agricultural sector. For this purpose the government is providing loans, subsidised fertilizers and pesticides on minimum prices are given for its betterment. They also spend a lot of money on agricultural research and conservation programs.

(iv) **Urbanisation:** The spread of urbanisation is another factor for the relative growth of public expenditure in the modern times. There has been increased tendency of expenditure on civil administration with the rise of population in these areas. Expenses on water supply, electricity, transportation, maintenance of roads, educational institutions, traffic controls, public health, etc. have increased tremendously in these days. Hence, increase in expenditure on civic amenities has led upward increase in public expenditure.

(v) **Democratic and socialistic structure of the government:** The growth of democracy and socialism everywhere in the world has been responsible for the increase of public expenditure to a greater extent. A democratic form of government is more expensive that the other forms of government. For instance, democracy in India has become a costly affair, *i.e.* expenditure on election, by-election and administrative set-up is increasing. The ruling party has to persuade the public opinion in their favour by making excessive expenditures on new policies. Furthermore, they have to fulfil their promises made in the manifesto at the time of election. Similarly, there is a gradual shift of thinking from capitalism to socialism with the result that state governments have to shoulder larger responsibilities to perform social activities. Public sector and nationalisation are equally responsible to push the public expenses to a larger extent.

(vi) **Rural development schemes:** The government has to spend huge amounts for the development of rural folk in developing countries like India, where majority of population lives in villages. It has to undertake schemes like community development projects and other social measures. In India, many such schemes have been introduced to eradicate poverty. They are IRDP, DPAP, NREGS, TRYSEM, SGSY, PMGSY, etc. Undoubtedly, they have raised the expenditure of the government multifold.

(vii) **Industrial development:** After worldwide depression (1929-30), government took active participation to promote industrial development. Actually, it brought a happier life, higher standard of living, increased efficiency and raised the production of all commodities to a sufficient level. In addition to it, government also took measures to control monopolies and to provide consumer goods and services at reduced cost. This led naturally to a greater share for public expenditures.

(viii) **Rising population:** The growth of population is also responsible for increase in the public expenditure as the government needs money to perform various functions efficiently. In fact, rising population is a grave threat to the development of poor countries like India. The state bears additional responsibility of solving problems such as food, unemployment, housing and sanitation, etc. The government has also to check the growth of the population. So it has to spend huge amounts for promoting the family planning programmes every year to persuade people to have smaller families.

(ix) **Growth of transport and communication:** The growth of transport and communication is another factor which has contributed to increase in the expenditure. With its expansion, the state has to spend to maintain quick and efficient transport system. Government is supposed to run these services at no profit no loss basis. The government in backward and underdeveloped countries has to make huge investments for the development of railways, roads and communication to cater the needs of the general public.

(x) **To check the cyclical fluctuations:** As we know, fiscal policy has been recognised as a controlling measure during cyclical fluctuations. Thus, the government has to spend a huge amount in the period of depression or recession. In a developed economy, the policy is designed to maintain full employment. In a less developed economy, the theory of functional finance requires the growth of public expenditure to attain full employment.

(xi) **Adoption of planning:** In the modern world, all popular governments have adopted an economic planning in one form or the other for the development of the country. In a developing country when public sector is expanding its role, the public expenditure shows an increasing trend. In India, the development expenditure in 1951-52 was Rs. 375 crores. It rose to Rs. 84,000 crore during 1980-85, *i.e.* 53 per cent of the total outlay. The Indian Government has marked Rs. 4,27,656 crore for the public sector development in 2004-05.

(xii) **Increasing price level:** Another factor which has contributed to the rise in public expenditure, is the rise of price level all over the world since Second World War. Rise in the price level has two important effects on the government: (a) the government has to pay higher prices for all goods and services which it has to buy; and (b) it has to find larger financial resources to meet its growing expenditure.

(xiii) **Increase in national income:** The increase in national income is also responsible for raising the public expenditure as it leads to economic development of a country. As a result, public revenue increases by the method of taxation which, in turn, stimulates public expenditure.

(xiv) **Expansion of traditional functions:** In ancient times, the state had only limited functions of justice, internal security and external security. But with the passage of time, there has been tremendous expansion of these functions. Now states are welfare states. For instance, in India, there has been an increase in session courts, high courts, police network consisting of sophisticated technology even computers and nuclear weapons for army for external safety resulting in increase in the expansion of these functions by the state.

(xv) **Social progress:** With the motto of socialistic pattern of society, the state has undertaken a lot of new functions like the upliftment of scheduled castes, scheduled tribes, development of tribal areas, backward classes and economically weaker sections of the society. The government has set up Scheduled Caste Welfare Corporation, Backward Classes Development Board and other similar organisations for the welfare of these sections. The government grants interest-free loans, subsidised ration and other facilities resulting in social progress to remove disparities between the rich and poor class.

(xvi) **Defective administration:** Generally, there are extravagances and wastages in administration as these unnecessarily create multiplicity of work in government offices. As a result, there is huge increase in the public expenditure to meet these expenses.

COMPARISON BETWEEN PUBLIC AND PRIVATE EXPENDITURE

Similarities

The following are the similarities between public expenditure and private expenditure:

(i) **Similarity as to flexibility**: In both the public expenditure and the private expenditure the element of flexibility is common. Both—the public expenditure and the private expenditure can be increased or decreased. However, they differ in degree, *i.e.* private expenditure cannot be increased to the same extent as public expenditure.

(ii) **Similarity as to application of economic laws:** There is similarity between public and private expenditure as to application of economic laws. The economic laws are equally applicable in both cases, *i.e.* public expenditure and private expenditure.

(iii) **Similarity as to control on wastage:** Both try to maximise returns with the minimum possible expenditure.

(iv) **Policy as to income and expenditure:** Both—public expenditure and private expenditure—usually follow the same policy as to income and expenditure.

Dissimilarities

There are some vital differences between public and private expenditure which may be stated as under:

(i) **Difference as to dependence:** Public expenditure is not dependent directly on the state revenues, whereas, the private expenditure is directly dependent on one's own income.

(ii) **Difference as to control:** In case of private expenditure, control exists in the hands of those individuals who actually incur the expenditure. On the contrary, the control is varied in case of public expenditure such as departmental control, assembly/parliament control and audit control.

(iii) **Difference as to compulsion:** The private sector is not guided by the principle of compulsion. For instance, it is up to the public sector to incur expenditure on a particular project or not, such as compulsory education up to degree and postgraduate level. On the contrary, the private sector is bound to incur expenditure on the maintenance of a certain level of standard of living.

(iv) **Difference as to elasticity:** Elasticity exists in case of private expenditure, whereas elasticity does not exist in case of public expenditure.

(v) **Difference as to economy:** Greater emphasis is placed on economy in case of public expenditure as against private expenditure. An individual tries to gain maximum utility out of his expenditure, whereas the public expenditure does not have such an objective.

(vi) **Difference as to working:** The scope of working of private expenditure is limited, *i.e.* to man himself and his own family, whereas the scope of working of public expenditure is quite wide.

(vii) **Difference as to effects:** The effect of private expenditure is limited; whereas the effect of public expenditure is wide and far reaching.

(viii) **Difference as to motive:** The motive of public expenditure is the welfare of the public; whereas the motive of private expenditure is purely personal welfare. Further:

(a) the scope of public welfare is wide, whereas the scope of private welfare is limited; and

(b) the object of public expenditure is of long-term nature, whereas the object of private expenditure is of short-term nature.

(ix) **Difference as to influence or consideration:** Public expenditure is influenced by various political, motivated and social aspects whereas, there is no such consideration or influence in case of private expenditure.

(x) **Difference as to adjustment of income and expenditure:** Private expenditure is always adjusted according to income, whereas in case of public expenditure, the government collects revenues according to expenditure to be incurred. In other words, in case of private expenditure we follow the principle of income first and expenditure next or "cut your coat according to cloth." On the contrary, in case of public expenditure we follow the principle of expenditure first and income (revenue) next.

IMPORTANCE OF PUBLIC EXPENDITURE

Earlier, the state used to act as a passive spectator and the countries were left to the free working of the economic forces. It was Prof. J.M. Keynes in the twentieth century, who realised that state interference is necessary to keep the economy of a country in a stable equilibrium and the road leading to the destination of full employment. At a time when there was worldwide depression (1929-30), the economies of the world were facing the acute problems of overproduction and mass unemployment, private investment was showing a chronic deficiency, the emphasis was shifted from private spending to public spending. The doses of public spending served to uplift the economic system of the world through the interaction of multiplier principle, from the cruel hands of worldwide depression. The role of public expenditure may be studied under the following heads:

(i) Economic-social welfare in a country depends on the amount of public expenditure incurred on them. Economic and social welfare programmes like labour welfare, child welfare, women welfare, welfare of physically and mentally handicapped persons, welfare of scheduled castes, scheduled tribes, backward classes and backward areas, welfare of economically and socially weaker sections of the society, etc.—all these require huge public expenditure.

(ii) It is now unanimously agreed that public expenditure plays a positive role, especially, problems of underdeveloped countries are of such a magnitude that they cannot be left at the mercy of the old *laissez-faire* policy. Private sector cannot undertake the development projects, where a large amount of risk and capital investment is involved. The only available solution lies in the rapid increase of public expenditure.

(iii) Today, great emphasis is being given in almost all countries of the world to the reduction of disparities of income and wealth. Public expenditure has a vital importance in the attainment of this vital objective. Programmes for the upliftment of the poor and backward classes may be undertaken by adopting a suitable policy of public expenditure.

(iv) Economic stability of a country depends on the public expenditure. In case of depression, heavy public expenditure is incurred for increasing investment, capital formation and employment and also for saving the economy from adverse effects of depression. On the contrary, in case of boom period public expenditure is incurred in such a way as to increase production and control the rising price level.

(v) Public expenditure plays a crucial role in the economic development and planning. The success of economic planning depends on the public expenditure because:

(a) Economic planning itself requires heavy public expenditure;

(b) For the success of economic planning proper allocation of public expenditure is to be done on different items such as roads, transport, irrigation, electricity and power, industries and agriculture;

(c) The government is required to establish and manage the working of several government undertakings;

(d) Speedy capital formation is to be undertaken;

(e) Balanced economic development requires heavy public expenditure. Planned development programmes cannot be undertaken without increasing public expenditure.

(vi) Formerly, the activities of the state were limited, *i.e.* internal administration, maintenance of peace, law and order, judiciary and defence of the countries. Nowadays, the state is required to perform several functions over and above the basic functions such as education, providing basic necessities like water and electricity, transport, establishment of basic industries in particular, labour welfare, banking including issue of currency, agriculture development, socio-economic welfare, medical services, assistance to industries and trade, entertainment, etc. All these require huge amount of investment for public expenditure.

LIMITATIONS OF PUBLIC EXPENDITURE

Theoretically speaking, only those expenditures of the state are considered suitable which can provide maximum social benefit to the society. The state should keep certain points in mind while planning and incurring public expenditure such as expenditure on providing safety and security, expenditure on socio-economic welfare activities, expenditure on building the country, expenditure on administration, and expenditure on the development of industry, trade and commerce, etc.

According to Alfred Benchier, "No definite percentage of income can be named as the proper limit for the cost of the government since such a limit must depend on the desires and needs of a community, or the effects of government spending and the revenues supporting the spending, the willingness of the population to be taxed, existing burden of taxation, the resources and the population of a community, the distribution of wealth and income, the state of economic development and other variables."

The amount of public expenditure in a country is influenced by several factors, such as:

(i) Economics and social status of the public;
(ii) Stage of economic development of the country, *i.e.* undeveloped, developing or developed;
(iii) Political alertness of the people about their rights, duties and powers;
(iv) Size and quality of the population;
(v) Dependence of the public on the state;
(vi) Taxable capacity of the public;
(vii) Standard of living of the masses;
(viii) Needs and requirements of the residents;
(ix) Availability of the economic and natural resources; and finally
(x) Moral and education background of the public, etc.

ECONOMIC EFFECTS OF PUBLIC EXPENDITURE

The ultimate effects of public expenditure in the form of greater production and more equitable distribution of wealth are always expected to be present, if the expenditure is incurred after considerable thought and utmost nationality. While a sound tax system is that which exerts the least bad effect on production, a sound expenditure policy is one which aims at encouraging production to the greatest possible extent. Public expenditure is not 'expenditure' in the sense of a private individual where the money spent leaves the person who spends a considerable part of his income. But the spent money always remains within the economy, it generally does not flow out of it. The only effect which is exerted by public expenditure is to alter the direction of flow of income and redistribution of income and wealth. It thus, encourages production which is not encouraged at all or encouraged only insufficiently while left in the hands of the private individuals. On the other hand, it helps in raising the incomes of hard-pressed sections of the people and consequently bringing out more equality in the levels of living of the different classes of the society. Effects of public expenditure on the economy of any country can be studied under the following heads:

(1) Effects of Public Expenditure on Consumption.

(2) Effects of Public Expenditure on Distribution.

(3) Effects of Public Expenditure on Production and Employment.

(4) Miscellaneous Effects of Public Expenditure.

(1) Effects of Public Expenditure on Consumption

On account of public expenditure, the size of consumption tends to increase in the economy. Since public expenditure tends to redistribute the income in favour of the poor people and their marginal propensity to consume being high, the overall impact of public expenditure leads to an increase in the consumption of the economy. Many social goods are provided to the community for consumption, *e.g.* expenditure on public parks, playgrounds, museums, libraries, etc. and public expenditure provides valuable services, *e.g.* free medical care, education, etc. so that the real income of beneficiaries improves their capacity to consume and saving also improves.

Apart from the above, we know that public expenditure has proved to be a powerful tool for bringing economic stability in the economy, particularly during the days of depression in a capitalistic economy. Keynes came as an economic doctor on the scene and recommended that public expenditure could work as a compensatory mechanism to bring the economy on the road leading to full employment. In an underdeveloped economy, public expenditure could be a powerful tool in the hands of planners and policy makers to act as a catalyst in the process of economic development by raising the rate of capital formation in the economy and providing social goods and social services to the community as a whole, particularly to the lowest section of the society. The basic infrastructure facilities required for economic development can be provided with the help of public expenditure.

(2) Effects of Public Expenditure on Distribution

Public expenditure has its effects not only on production but it is also a most powerful weapon in the hands of the government to bring out an equitable distribution of wealth. For bringing out an equitable and justified distribution of wealth, the government uses not only its taxation policy, but public expenditure can also help to a great extent in this direction. While formulating its expenditure policy, the government has to take into account as to which of the groups are being specially benefited by it. Greater bulk of expenditure on the welfare of the rich strata would bring greater inequalities in income and standards of living. On the contrary, if the greater bulk of the public expenditure is incurred in such activities which specially benefit the poorer sections of the society, it will bring about a more equal distribution of wealth in the society. Provision for free medical care, free education, family planning etc. goes a long way in improving the real income of the masses. Public expenditure redistributes taxed income from the rich in favour of the poor strata of the society. Public expenditure by its nature may be progressive or regressive. An expenditure which yields greater benefits to the poor is regarded as progressive. Old age pension, free education to economically weaker sections, subsidies to essential goods of mass consumption, etc. are progressive expenditure. Progressive public expenditure only reduces inequalities of income distribution. A regressive expenditure which confers larger benefits to the richer sections, *e.g.* provision of subsidised milk in rich localities or subsidies on luxury goods, etc. tends to widen the gap of inequalities. As Dalton puts, "That system of public expenditure is best which has the strongest tendency to reduce the inequalities of income." Obviously, it is the progressive public expenditure system.

It is a debatable issue whether personal incomes should be distributed more equally or not. Economists like Lutz are of the opinion that it is possible but an undesirable aim because much unproductive expenditure is involved in fulfilling this aim. Of course, in the preliminary stages of economic development the problem is as to what to be distributed rather how it should be distributed. But even in these stages a particular section of the society cannot be sacrificed at the cost of development.

Humanitarian nations may not be the immediate concerns of an economist but he cannot do anything without them. Even those who do not believe in complete equality of incomes, believe that the existing inequalities should be reduced. But what is to be aimed is reductions in inequalities in early stages of development and after the economy has attained a certain level of developments, attempt must be made towards complete equality.

(3) Effects of Public Expenditure on Production and Employment

Public expenditure acts on the level of production and productivity directly. An increase in public expenditure affects the following, which in consequence affect the general level of production in the economy:

(i) Effects on willingness to work, save and invest;

(ii) Effects on capacity to work, save and invest; and

(iii) Effects on diversification of resources:

  (a) between different uses; and

  (b) regions or localities.

(i) *Effect on willingness to work, save and invest:* Expenditure on the following 'heads' by the government reduces the willingness to work and save of a person. These are:

  (a) Old-age pension;

  (b) Insurance against sickness;

  (c) Insurance against unemployment; and

  (d) Provident Fund benefit, etc.

When an individual is in receipt of above such payments, he becomes careless and does not resort to hardwork and saving for the future. Finding his future, secure an individual does not worry about anything for his future.

Again, if the government frames its fiscal policy so as to restrict the savings of the individuals from earning any income in future, it is bound to reduce the propensity to save. Here, finding the future of savings insecure, he will not further save and invest.

On the other hand, if a person feels that his savings and investments will earn for him in future and he will get reward for more work, his willingness to work, save and invest would go up. He will feel his future secure, and thus work more, save more and invest more. Thus, the willingness of the people to work, save and invest depends upon the same way as the government spends public money.

(ii) ***Effects on capacity to work save and invest:*** Public expenditure, if incurred on the following can increase the capacity of a worker to work, save and invest:

(a) Expenditure on education;

(b) Expenditure on public health, sanitation and provision of health service;

(c) Cheap housing facilities;

(d) Cheaper means of transportation and communication; and

(e) Public entertainment.

There are certain types of expenditure, like—the expenditure for increasing the wages and salaries of the working people—which may help in increasing their ability to work. Expenditure for supplying cheaper goods, and other essential commodities, may increase their purchasing power, standard of living, efficiency, and also their propensity to save.

On the contrary, if a large amount is spent on social functions like—manufacturing of alcoholic goods and other intoxicants, injurious to health—it may bring down the working efficiency and ethical standard of the people as a whole. Heavy expenditure on hotels, bars, cinema houses, etc. is bound to bring the efficiency at a low-level; whereas the expenditure for schools, technical training institution, roads, railways, dams, etc. may increase the level of productivity in the country.

(iii) ***Effects on diversification of resources:*** Public expenditure can be diverted from private to public use in many ways which has far reaching effects on the utilisation of resources as between alternative uses. The major areas of diversion of resources are as follows:

(a) *Diversion of resources to unproductive areas:* There is the diversion of public expenditure to a number of unproductive areas such as expenditure on armaments and armed forces, on police and on civil administration, etc. Such an expenditure is often called *economic waste.* This type of expenditure ought to have been incurred on the social security and welfare of the society. In our opinion, it is not a wastage. For example, expenditure on armaments and armed forces is a must as it reduces the danger of foreign invasion and reduces huge economic loss which would have resulted in the event of a war. Similarly, expenditure on police and civil administration is also essential for the maintenance of law and order inside the country.

(b) *Diversion of resources to providing infrastructure:* There is also the diversion of resources from the private to public use by incurring expenditure on providing infrastructure, such as roads, railways, irrigation projects, water and electricity, etc. This diversion is a must in all types of economies, *i.e.* developed, developing and even undeveloped.

(c) *Diversion of resources to social security and welfare activities:* Diversion of resources is also essential for conducting social security and welfare activities such as encouragement to research and inventions, promotion of education, training, public health, sanitation, social security schemes, old-age pensions, etc. Fiscal theorists, however, argue that the government should actually curtail such expenditure on many of these measures. On the contrary, most of the theorists agree with that "in order to bring about the distribution of the community's resources between different uses, which will give the best results, balancing without bias the present and the future is desirable."

(iv) ***Diversion of resources for reducing regional disparities:*** Diversion of resources from the private to public is essential for reducing regional disparities. For example, Rajasthan, Bihar and Eastern Uttar Pradesh in particular are considered to be the most undeveloped and backward areas in our country. Public expenditure can be effectively used for reducing regional disparities by means of establishing labour-intensive and subsidised industries, providing basic facilities like—water, electricity, cheap finance, technical know-how, spread of technical education, cheap loans and advances and developing employment opportunities, etc.

(v) ***Diversion of resources for economic growth and maintenance of economic stability:*** Diversion of resources from private to public are essential for rapid economic growth and the maintenance of economic stability, full employment and price stability. Public expenditure can help private investment and production through measures which reduce cost of production, push up demand or remove particular shortages and bottlenecks. Creation and maintenance of social overheads would lead to an all-round reduction in cost of production and improvement in efficiency. This, therefore, increases profitability and production. Also social overheads bring different regions and sectors of an economy in close contact and thereby stimulate economic growth. Increase in the volume of public investment may provide more employment opportunities. Emphasis on the development of small-scale and cottage-industries may also give a big relief on the employment front.

Dalton concluded on the effects of public expenditure on production and employment as, "whereas taxation taken alone, may check production, public expenditure, taken alone, should almost certainly increase it." Dalton was of the firm opinion that public expenditure will always increase production provided that it is carried on wisely.

(4) Miscellaneous Effects of Public Expenditure

(i) ***Effect of public expenditure on economic stability:*** It is an admitted fact that public expenditure has proved to be a powerful tool for bringing about economic stability in country. It is an excellent instrument for regulating and controlling volume of employment in a country. The government should make a substantial increase in public expenditure at a time of depression, because this will help bring about an automatic increase in the volume of employment. On the contrary, the government brings about a substantial reduction in its expenditure at a time of boom (inflation), because this helps to save the economy from the adverse effects of inflation. Inflation is a condition when investment exceeds savings. In this situation the aim of the government should be to have a surplus budget, *i.e.* the government spends less than its revenue. The funds acquired by means of a surplus budget may be used to provide additional capital to those sectors of economy which experience shortage of capital so that the total productive capacity of the economy may increase. The rising price-level may also be checked by increasing the production of goods and services leading to control of inflation.

(ii) ***Effect of public expenditure on economic growth:*** There is a close relationship between public expenditure and economic growth. According to John Adler, "a rising proportion of additional output should be developed to capital formation, so that the economic growth of an undeveloped country may be speeded up." For this purpose, twofold change in the government budget is required. Firstly, the government budget should be raised so that a rising proportion of the additional output may be available for development purposes. Secondly, a rising proportion of government revenues should be used to finance expenditure on development. The basic infrastructure facilities required for economic development can be provided with the help of public expenditure. In this way, public expenditure has a significant role to play in the process of economic growth.

(iii) ***Effects of public expenditure on employment:*** Unemployment is the burning problem in underdeveloped countries, developing countries and now even in developed countries of the world. Public expenditure can play a vital role in influencing the level of employment in an economy. According to Prof. J.M. Keynes, "The government should step up its expenditure on public works such as roads, buildings, canals at the time of depression and unemployment. This will add the volume of employment in the economy."

On the contrary, the government should cut down its expenditure to deal with the problem of the shortage of human resources in a country.

BAD EFFECTS OF INCREASE IN PUBLIC EXPENDITURE

According of Prof. J.K. Mehta, "Public expenditure is a double-edged weapon. It can do much good to the community, but if it is unwisely made, it can do much harm." The bad or adverse effects or dangers involved in the increase of public expenditure are as follows:

(i) **Unnecessary assistance to industries and business:** If the government gives protection and provides financial assistance to those industries and businesses which have lost their shape and do not occupy any importance in the economic development of the country, then it is mere wastage of public resources. It will lead to development of those industries and businesses which hinder the path of economic development and thereby the country is likely to go for the worse.

(ii) **Excessive expenditure on defence:** If the government incurs excessive expenditure on defence, it will adversely affect the development of the poor and backward community of the country. Pakistan is glaring example of the same. From moral and human point of view also, excessive expenditure incurred on defence is treated as uneconomic and unnecessary. It will also affect the security and peace of the entire region.

(iii) **Tendency of gaining political influence:** Nowadays, the concept of public expenditure is being applied by ministers in particular for gaining political influence and sound vote bank. Huge amount of public expenditure is being incurred by both—central and state ministers in their respective areas just to gain political influence at the cost of other backward areas of the country/state.

It leads to severe criticisms and dissatisfaction amongst the masses. It is also one of the major factors of political instability in the country.

(iv) **Advantage to a particular community:** Sometimes public expenditure is incurred just to give advantage to a particular community or class over and above the other communities. It will lead to division of the society in two clear-cut classes leading to class conflicts, feelings of superiority and inferiority and more movements, unrest, strikes, dharnas, etc. As a matter of fact, the peace of the entire country is badly hurt and disturbed.

(v) **Rapid increase in taxation:** In order to meet the rising public expenditure, government imposes new taxes every year leading to heavy incidence of taxation on the community. If it is not enough, then the government takes the shelter of deficit financing which leads to rapid inflation. The service class and poor classes in particular are adversely affected. In case of India too, deficit financing is increasing every year leading to inflationary tendency along with a general rise in price level every year.

(vi) **Fear of minority political parties:** Political parties led by minority groups are always fearful of the increase of public expenditure on the ground that the political party or parties in power will use the public expenditure in fulfilling their own political interests. However, this view is not true in case of India where minority is leading the majority.

(vii) **Dominance of public sector reduces the authority of private sector:** While citing the dangers of increase in public expenditure, capitalists argue that it reduces the authority of private sector which is the backbone of capitalist economy.

However, in the modern economy, the above criticism does not stand true as the interference of the government is increasing in all types of economies whether socialist economy, capitalist economy or mixed economy.

STUDY-QUESTIONS

1. What is meant by public expenditure? Discuss the scope of public expenditure. Explain the causes of increase in public expenditure.
2. Distinguish between public and private expenditure.
3. Explain the classification of public expenditure.
4. Discuss the importance and limitation of public expenditure.
5. Discuss the economic effects of public expenditure.
6. What do you mean by progressive, proportional and regressive expenditure? Discuss their role.
7. Write short notes on the following:
   (a) Progressive expenditure
   (b) Proportional expenditure
   (c) Regressive expenditure.

Trends of Public Expenditure in India

8

INTRODUCTION

Public expenditure regulates the economic activities and helps to attain the long-run and short-run objectives of economic development. This is the reason that there is continuous upward trend in both revenue and expenditure of the Indian Government. In this way, it accelerates the pace of modernisation, especially in backward and developing economies. Thus, German economist Wagner's concept of increasing activities is reflected in the growth of public expenditure.

CLASSIFICATION OF PUBLIC EXPENDITURE

Here, we must remember that revenue and capital account expenditure, both collectively are known as 'economic classification of the budget'. Revenue and capital expenditure can be further classified in the 'economic functional classification of the budget'. It means a more detailed break-up of revenue and capital expenditure. In a sense, functional classification of public expenditure aggregates budget data in a particular period to show the share of public expenditure devoted to each sector. This data is more significant for policy formulation, review and implementation of various development schemes.

Broadly, public expenditure can be classified into two parts:

1. **Expenditure on Revenue Account**
   (a) Developmental expenditure; and
   (b) Non-developmental expenditure.

2. **Expenditure on Capital Account**
   (a) Developmental expenditure; and
   (b) Non-developmental expenditure.

1. Expenditure on Revenue Account

This revenue expenditure is incurred for the normal running of government departments and services, interest charges on debt, etc. Broadly, such expenditure does not result in the creation of assets. All assets given to state governments are also considered as revenue expenditures. Generally, major heads of revenue, expenditure are being shown in the budget of the central government as defence services, civil services, grants-in-aid, interest payments, tax collection and economic services.

(i) *Economic services:* It includes the expenditure on department of commerce, shipping and transport, irrigation, energy, chemicals and fertilizers, company affairs and electronics, industry and agriculture sectors, etc. The total outlay for economic services was Rs. 4,06,859 crore in 2003-2004.

(ii) *Collection of taxation:* Taxes also play a prominent role in the revenue of any government. In 1997-98, expenditure on the collection of taxes amounted to Rs. 5,293 crore, Rs. 5,692 crore in 1998-99, Rs. 6,570 crore in 2000-01 and it further increased to Rs. 8,915 crore in 2003-04.

(iii) *Grants-in-aid to states:* The state expenditure has also continuously been on upward side to meet the plan expenditures and other welfare schemes. In 1950-51, it was just Rs. 61 crore which increased to Rs. 1,04,972 crore in 1990-91. In 1995-96, it stood at Rs. 1,85,232 crore and further increased to Rs. 4,87,163 crore in 2003-04.

(iv) *Interest payments:* It includes expenditure on the payment of interest on the outstanding debt. In 1995-96, interest payment amounted to Rs. 58,944 crore. It was Rs. 78,639 crore in 1997-98, Rs. 90,188 crore in 1998-99, Rs. 1,07,289 in 1999-2000 and Rs. 1,24,356 crore in 2000-01. In the budget of 2005-06, it stood at

Rs. 1,30,032 crore. Now, it is estimated to be Rs. 1,39,823 crore for 2006-07.

(v) *Civil services:* It includes expenditure on Parliament administration, justice, election and on the office of Comptroller and Auditor General of India. Besides these expenditures, expenditures on secretariat and attached offices of ministries of education and social welfare, health and family welfare, information and broadcasting, labour and employment and department of atomic energy, culture, science and technology and aerospace, etc. are also included.

(vi) *Defence expenditure:* Popularly, there are three major defence services Army, Navy and Air Force. The charge on revenue account is as a result of maintenance of these forces on salaries, dearness and other allowances, pensions and retirement benefits provided to defence personnel. During 1996-97, it was to the extent of Rs. 29,505 crore. It rose to Rs. 35,278 crore in 1997-98. In 1998-99, defence outlay was Rs. 39,897 crore, Rs. 47,071 crore in 1999-2000 and Rs. 49,622 crore in 2000-2001. It was further increased to Rs. 77,000 crore in 2004-05. It stood to Rs. 81,700 crore in the budget of 2005-06. Now, it is to be estimated to Rs. 89,000 crore for 2006-07.

(a) *Developmental Expenditure*

It refers to expenditure on heads like education, art, culture, medical, family welfare, public health, labour, employment, scientific services and other community services, etc. Developmental expenditure also consists expenditure on economic services such as agriculture and allied services, industries, minerals, foreign trade and export promotion, water and power development, transport and communication, etc. Similarly, grants-in-aid to states and union territories for development activities are also included in developmental expenditure on revenue account. The developmental expenditure in 1990-91 was Rs. 1,05,922 crore which further increased to Rs. 3,17,464 crore in 2000-01. It rose to Rs. 4,27,656 crore in 2004-05.

(b) *Non-developmental Expenditure*

It includes expenditure on audit, collection of taxes and duties, currency, coinage and mint. Besides, payments on administrative services like police, external affairs and other administrative services, pensions, other retirement benefits, grants to states and union territories are also accounted in non-developmental expenditure on revenue account.

2. Expenditure on Capital Account

The expenditure on capital account is financed out of the capital receipts like, market loans and borrowing by the government from domestic as well as foreign resources. Therefore, capital account expenditure consists of all those expenditures used for the acquisition of assets like land, buildings, machinery equipment as investment in shares, etc. and loans and advances of state governments by the central government. It also includes government companies, corporations and other institutions for their developmental activities. Capital account expenditure as provided in the budget of the Government of India, has been illustrated as under:

(i) ***Economic services:*** Capital expenditure on economic services are of the kind of foreign trade and other allied services like, irrigation, animal husbandry, dairy, fishery development, industrial and mineral development, atomic energy, mining and metallurgical industries, water and power development, transport and communication, etc.

(ii) ***Defence services:*** This head consists of central government expenditure on capital as on Army, Navy and Air Force. It includes capital expenditures on the construction of non-residential buildings, ordinance factories, machine tools and other equipments, etc.

(iii) ***Social services:*** Social services are helpful to raise the efficiency and productivity of human resources. They are also useful from the viewpoint of raising the standard of living of common masses. Therefore, they include the expenditure on the services like, education, health, art, culture, family planning, sanitation, water supply, housing, urban development, social security, welfare activities and scientific development, etc.

(iv) ***General services:*** This head refers the expenditure on currency, coinage and mint. It also includes expenditures on fiscal services like India's contribution to international monetary fund and other international financial institutions. Furthermore, it consists, capital expenditures on public works and expenditure on non-residential buildings.

(v) ***Loans and advances to states and union territories:*** Generally, states and union territories face acute shortages of funds to meet the requirement of development activities in the region. Therefore, central government provides them loans and assistance to undertake such developmental activities.

(a) *Developmental Expenditure*

The main items under developmental expenditure are on social community services, economic services, loans to states and union territories for developmental projects and public enterprises.

(b) *Non-developmental Expenditure*

It consists of the expenditures on defence, state trading schemes, currency, mint, security and printing press, etc.

Table 8.1: Overall View of Revenue, Capital and Total Expenditure

(Rs. in Crore)

Year	Revenue	Capital	Total
1997-98	1,80,335	51,718	2,32,053
1998-99	2,16,461	62,879	2,79,340
1999-00	2,49,078	48,975	2,98,053
2000-01	2,77,839	47,753	3,25,592
2001-02	3,01,468	60,842	3,62,310
2002-03	3,39,627	74,535	4,14,162
2003-04	3,62,887	1,11,368	4,74,255
2004-05	3,85,493	92,366	4,77,829

Source: Economic Survey 2004-05.

Table 8.2: Developmental and Non-Developmental Expenditure of the Central, State Governments and Union Territories

(Rs. in Crore)

Year	Developmental	Non-developmental	Total
1996-97	2,02,640	1,67,857	3,70,497
1997-98	2,28,119	1,94,631	4,22,750
1998-99	2,58,930	2,45,336	5,04,266
1999-00	2,91,435	2,80,181	5,71,616
2000-01	3,17,464	2,98,194	6,15,658
2001-02	3,42,234	3,38,675	6,80,909
2003-04	4,06,859	3,86,499	7,93,358
2004-05	4,27,656	4,22,166	8,49,822

Source: Economic Survey 2004-05.

TRENDS OF PUBLIC EXPENDITURE

The expenditure trends both—developmental and non-developmental, largely depend on the stage of economic development, outlook of the government, ability of the government and prevailing economic conditions in the country. Till 1947, India was under British rule and foreign government took no lead to prepare any comprehensive developmental programmes to pull the country out of vicious circle of poverty and imperfections. Second World War also affected the public expenditure of the government to a great extent. The partition too had similar effects. With the advent of independence, economic policy underwent a radical change. The government undertook positive steps to bring the economic and social changes in the country. The introduction of planning led to increasingly large expenditure on various development schemes, both—by the centre and state governments. It has completed Tenth Five-Year Plan and Eleventh Five-Year Plan has been started since 1st April 2007. Therefore, expenditure trends during these years have been summarised below:

1. Defence Expenditure

India's defence expenditure was Rs. 82 crore in 1921 which rose to Rs. 45 crore in 1934-35. In 1938-39, the amount stood at

Rs. 46.18 crore and it continued increasing till 1944-45 as it touched the colossal figure of Rs. 395.49 crore during Second World War. In 1929, A.J. Toynbee stated his views saying that, "In a list of 41 nations, India stood first with 45.29 per cent of her expenditure on defence. The percentage in USA and UK was about 16.09 and 19.05 per cent respectively in the same year." The basic reason of huge expenditure on defence was that India was dependent on Britain. In order to keep India away from internal uprising and to check nationalistic movement, foreign government had to maintain army in the country. As a result, a large amount of British officers were paid very high salaries.

In 1991-92, outlay on defence on revenue account was Rs. 11,467 crore which in 1995-96 increased to Rs. 18,841 crore. It stood at Rs. 37,278 crore in 2000-2001 and further Rs. 42,041 crore in 2001-02. On the other hand, total expenditure of revenue account was Rs. 926 crore in 1960-61 against Rs. 346 crore in 1950-51. This is about more than eight times. This amount rose to Rs. 73,516 crore in 1990-91. It increased to Rs. 1,39,816 crore in 1995-96 and Rs. 2,77,838 crore in 2000-2001. During 2001-02, it rose to Rs. 3,01,478 crore. In 2002-2003, 2003-04 and 2004-05 it was Rs. 3,39,628 crore, Rs. 3,62,887 crore and Rs. 3,85,493 crore respectively.

2. Trends in Developmental and Non-developmental Expenditure

Developmental expenditure was Rs. 53,380 crore in 1985-86, whereas it was around Rs. 208 crore on the eve of independence, *i.e.* 1950-51. Further, in 1990-91, it amounted to Rs. 1,05,922 crore which rose to Rs. 1,89,050 crore in 1995-96. In 1997-98, it was Rs. 2,28,119 crore which was registered at Rs. 4,27,656 crore in 2004-2005. As far as non-developmental expenditure is concerned it was Rs. 12,491 crore in 1980-81 against Rs. 320 crore in 1950-51. It was further expected to rise at Rs. 4,22,166 crore in 2004-05.

Table 8.3: Developmental Expenditure

(Rs. in Crore)

Year	Total
1990-91	1,05,922
1997-98	2,39,386
1999-00	2,99,997
2000-01	3,17,464
2001-02	3,42,234
2003-04	4,06,859
2004-05	4,27,656

Source: Economic Survey 2004-05

Table 8.4: Non-developmental Expenditure

(Rs. in Crore)

Year	Total
1996-97	1,67,857
1997-98	1,94,631
1998-99	2,45,336
1999-00	2,69,403
2000-01	3,12,275
2001-02	3,38,675
2003-04	3,86,499
2004-05	4,22,166

Source: Economic Survey 2004-05

3. Grants and Loans to State Governments and Union Territories

The government provides assistance in terms of grants-in-aid and loans to the state and union territories. The advances and loans to states and union territories changed to capital account while grants-in-aid to states and union territories changed to revenue account. In 1988-89, total grants and loans were estimated to be Rs. 6,064 crore which further increased to Rs. 7,664 crore in 1990-91. However, in 1991-92, expenditure and loans were recorded to be Rs. 8,797 crore which in 1993-94 increased to Rs. 10,121 crore. In 2001-02, it rose to Rs. 44,702 crore and further increased to Rs. 49,771 in 2002-03. It is noteworthy that grants-in-aid loans from central government to different states and union territories has also increased with the passage of time.

4. Social and Community Services

This type of expenditure helps to raise the standard of living efficiency of the labour and productivity of human resources. The expenditure on those services is increasing rapidly as our government is democratic and committed to establish welfare state. In 1995-96, expenditure on social and development services was Rs. 20,848 crore which increased to Rs. 25,209 crore in 1996-97, Rs. 24,250 in 1997-98, Rs. 54,803 crore in 2002-03 and further increased to Rs. 62,909 in 2003-2004.

5. Economic Services

The expenditure on economic services includes agriculture and allied services, industries, minerals, water, power development, foreign services, etc. which leads to an increase in national income gradually. During 1996-97, it increased to Rs. 1,579 crore and further increased to Rs. 1,104 crore in 1997-98. In 1999-2000, it stood at Rs. 2,579 crore which was reduced to Rs. 1,914 crore in 2000-01. During 2001-2002 was increased to Rs. 2,349 crore. In 2002-03, it was Rs. 3,320 crore and further increased to Rs. 3,814 crore in 2003-04.

6. Debt Servicing Charges

Indian government has incurred debt from internal resources at massive scale for various developmental projects in the country from time to time. As a result, a large amount of interest has to be paid annually. Therefore, it includes expenditure on the payment of interest with outstanding loans and appropriations made every year for repayment or redemption of debt. Since 1992-93, debt resources charges have considerably reduced to Rs. 18,082.40 crore. This was followed by Rs. 15,589 crore in 1993-94 and further to Rs. 15,124 crore in 1996-97 respectively. In 2000-2001, it further rose to Rs. 24,739 crore. In 2003-04 it was Rs. 27,397 crore.

7. Administrative Expenditure

The expenditure on administration was recorded to be Rs. 7,040 crore for the year of 1990-91. It rose to the tune of

Rs. 9,834 crore in 1992-93 and Rs. 1,19,670 crore in 1994-95 which again in 1995-96 increased to Rs. 13,619 crore, Rs. 16,457 crore in 1996-97 and Rs. 18,719 crore in 1997-98. During 1998-99, it was registered at Rs. 24,403 crore. It further increased to Rs. 30,547 crore in 1999-2000. It was further increased to Rs. 35,809 crore, 40,714 crore, 43,981 crore, and 48,711 crore in 2000-01, 2001-02, 2002-03 and 2003-04 respectively.

TRENDS IN RECEIPTS

Trends in receipts largely depend upon the economic set-up and economic policies of the country. Since the dawn of independence, the government has adopted the economic policy aiming at social welfare with economic justice. However, receipts of the government can be categorised under two heads as:

(a) Revenue receipts; and

(b) Capital receipts.

During the period of 1990-91 to 2004-05, revenue receipts of the central government have increased more than five times, *i.e.* from Rs. 54,954 crore to Rs. 3,09,322 crore. It further increased to Rs. 3,51,200 crore in the budget of 2005-06. Of these, the major contribution made by tax revenue which was Rs. 42,978 crore in 1998-99, which rose to Rs. 1,36,658 crore in 2000-01. It further increased to Rs. 1,86,982 crore in 2003-04. Again, it rose to Rs. 2,33,906 (B.E.) and 2,24,857 (R.E.) crore in the budget of 2004-05. In the budget of 2005-06, it was Rs. 2,73,466 crore.

The contribution by non-tax revenue is also considerable. In 1990-91, it contributed Rs. 11,976 crore which rose to Rs. 38,214 crore in 1997-98. During 2000-01, it increased to Rs. 55,947 crore and further to Rs. 67,774 crore in 2001-02. Again it rose to Rs. 72290 crore, Rs. 76,896 crore, Rs. 80,330 crore, and Rs. 77,734 crore for the years 2002-03, 2003-04, 2004-05 and 2005-06 respectively.

Regarding capital receipt, it was Rs. 83,345 crore in 1997-98. against Rs. 31,971 crore in 1990-91. However, it stood at Rs. 1,93,261 crore in 2004-05 which is expected to be Rs. 1,63,144 crore in 2005-06. Our other sources of capital receipts include small savings, compulsory deposits, reserve funds, etc. and its combined receipts have increased manifold over the years.

During 2000-2001, repayment of loans was almost double. Total expenditure on repayment of loans and advances was estimated at Rs. 26,802 crore in 2004-05 against Rs. 31,691 crore in 2003-04. It was Rs. 19,514 crore in the budget of 2005-06.

The overall primary deficit was Rs. 16,108 crore in 1990-91 which rose to Rs. 33,495 crore in 2001-02. In the budget of 2002-03, it was Rs. 27,268 crore, but in the year 2003-04 it was Rs. (–816) crore. This is due to the fact that with the progress of planning and industrialisation, our import requirements of various kinds outstripped our exports, necessitating large scale of external loans and grants. In the budget of 2004-05, it was estimated Rs. 7,907(B.E.) and 1,435 crore. Further it rose to Rs. 17,199 crore for the budget of 2005-06.

CONTROLLING METHODS OF PUBLIC EXPENDITURE

Public expenditure in India has been increasing rapidly during recent years. This is so because of the ambitious plans of economic development but it is the end of the hour to have control and checks to ensure that public funds are not wasted but used in a most judicious manner for the benefit of the society as a whole. Over time, various measures have been devised to keep the expenditure on administration at low level with efficiency avoiding wastage as far as possible. Now let us consider the methods of control over it referring to the practice at the behest of central government:

1. Annual Budget

The first stage of control over public expenditure is the preparation of annual budget itself. It is an elaborate exercise which consists of:

(i) To recognise the economic, political and social policies and amounts involved therein;

(ii) To provide legislature with relevant information of policies and amounts involved therein;

(iii) To get the sanction and authority from the legislature to raise the said revenues and spendings;

(iv) To systematise the plans to raise and spend with necessary rules and regulations; and

(v) To provide a subsequent means for auditing and scrutiny of the factual implementation of the financial plans.

2. Fixation of Responsibility

The overall responsibility lies with the Ministry of Finance. There are general instructions that public funds should be spent with utmost care, prudence and propriety to avoid wastage, etc. A whole system of rules and regulations has been made to ensure that no official is able to misuse or misappropriate the fund. No amount can be spent without the proper sanction from the appropriate authority. There is no permission to divert the resources from one authorised purpose to another.

3. Auditing

The Auditor General of India audits the government accounts and prepares audit reports. The accounts are audited in respect to their proper maintenance, observance of all rules and regulations from time to time.

4. Control of Parliament

Parliament has been empowered to inquire into any particular item of expenditure or a deal, etc. which the government entered into. There are two committees: (i) public accounts committee, (ii) estimates committee to look into certain aspects of public expenditure regularly.

5. Secrecy of Budget Proposals

Another method of control is that all budget proposals and estimates are kept top secret. But this view has been criticised as budget proposals should be made public as it would provide a chance to debate and express the viewpoint because budget represents the collective view of the society.

RECOMMENDATIONS OF EXPENDITURE REFORMS COMMISSION (ERC)

The centre has set up an Expenditure Reforms Commission(ERC) in February 2000 as part of the Union Budget proposals to look into ways and means of reducing wasteful government expenditure. The Commission is headed by the former Finance Secretary, Mr. K.P. Geethakrishnan. Other Members of Commission are Mr. V.S. Jafa, Former Financial Adviser, Ministry of Defence. Mr. Kirit Parekh, well-known economist, Mr. C.M. Vasudev, Secretary (Expenditure), Mr. J.S. Mathur, Additional Secretary in the Finance Ministry as member secretary. The Commission had expressed its intentions to concentrate on the problems of subsidies for starters and then go on to right-sizing. Thus, the Commission was set up to suggest ways and means for reducing the functions, activities and administrative structure of the government.

Expenditure Reforms Commission (ERC) has submitted three reports so far for downsizing six ministries and departments. The first report submitted on July 10, 2000, dealt with food subsidy. The report contains a road map for restructuring of the Public Distribution System (PDS), reduction of Food Corporation of India's carrying costs and restructuring of the Minimum Support Price (MSP) to the farmers.

The second report, submitted on September 20, 2000 is in four parts dealing with: (i) Rationalising fertilizer subsidy; (ii) Optimising government staff strength; (iii) Rationalisation of the functions, activities and structures in the Ministry of coal; and (iv) Rationalisation of the functions, activities and structures of the Ministry of Information and Broadcasting.

The recommendation of the first report regarding modification of economic cost of wheat and rice has been implemented. The second report which is in four parts, is under examination of the concerned ministers or departments.

The ERC has submitted its third report, which is exclusively dealing with the crucial Department of Economic Affairs (DEA) for the rationalisation of its structure.

EXPENDITURE REFORMS COMMISSION ON FERTILIZER SUBSIDY

The Expenditure Reforms Commission (ERC) set up in February 2000, reviewed all non-developmental government expenditure including subsidies on fertilizers, food, etc. The following recommendations were made with regard to urea:

(i) **Phased Decontrol:** Replacement of existing Retention Price-cum-Subsidy Scheme (RPS) by Group Based Concession Scheme. A four stage programme for dismantling the control system, leading at the commencement of fourth stage, to a fully decontrolled urea industry which can compete with import, albeit with a small level of protection and a feed stock cost differential compensation to Naphtha/Liquified Natural Gas (LNG) based units to ensure self sufficiency.

(ii) **First Phase; February 1, 2001 to March 31, 2002:** The existing Retention Price-cum-Subsidy Scheme (RPS) for urea units should be replaced by group-based concession scheme. The existing urea units may be classified into five groups with the rate concession being determined on the basis of averaging of retention prices as on April 1, 2000 of the respective group, rounding off the averages to the lower of Rs. 100 in each group. While working out the rates of concession for units, based on Naphtha, Fuel Oil/ Light Sulphur Heavy Stock (FO/ LShS) and mixed feed stocks, the commission has worked out the concession rates on the association that these units will either import their feed stocks requirements or procure these from domestic resources if the latter are willing to sell these at import parity price.

(iii) **Second Phase; April 1, 2002 to March 31, 2005:** From April 1, 2002, the rates of concession payable to the groups are reduced taking into account the reduction in capital related charges besides the expected progress in improving energy efficiency in the case of three non gas based groups of units.

(iv) **Third Phase; April 1, 2005 to March 31, 2006:** From April 1, 2005, all non-gas based plants are to examine the feasibility of modernisation and switching over to LNG. For plants that do not switch over to LNG as feed stock, only the level of concession that the unit would have been entitled to if it had switched over to LNG would be allowed. However, ERC has also stated (in para 53) that in order to achieve the self-sufficiency in urea production, new plants based on FO/LSHS, etc. may also be permitted and provided with feedstock differential cost.

(v) **Fourth Phase; For April 1, 2006:** The industry is fully decontrolled.

(vi) **7 per cent annual increase in MRP:** The commission recommends 7 per cent increase in the price of urea in real terms every year from April 1, 2006, a level at which the industry can be freed from all controls and be required to compete with imports, with variable levy ensuring availability of such imports at the farm gate at Rs. 7,000 per tonne of ureas.

(vii) **Dual price scheme and employment guarantee scheme:** For protecting small and marginal farmers against the price rise of urea, the commission has suggested introduction of dual pricing scheme through tradable coupons and expansion of employment guarantee.

(viii) **Action taken on ERC's recommendations:** The department of fertilizers has discussed the recommendations of ERC with the concerned ministries/ departments and the state governments. Fertilizer industry as well as many of the state governments have expressed serious apprehensions over some of the recommendations of the ERC, particularly those pertaining of 7 per cent annual increase in farm gate prices of urea, replacement of existing RPS by a group-based concession scheme based on averaging of retention prices, dual pricing scheme, etc.

Government expects to finalise the new pricing policy for ureas after examining all the relevant aspects and the views of the fertilizer and state governments on ERC's recommendations.

ROLE OF PUBLIC EXPENDITURE IN UNDERDEVELOPED COUNTRIES

According to Ragnar Nurkse, "They are in the grip of vicious circle of poverty." He further says that the most significant cause of economic backwardness is the existence of the vicious circle of poverty in a poor country because they lack sufficient resources for promoting development. Under these adverse circumstances, public expenditure works effectively and regulates economies activities. Inevitably, the role of public expenditure becomes requisite in such economies. In fact, the theory of public expenditure in a backward country is the theory of investment. Therefore, investment expenditure programmes should be planned in such a manner which may help to achieve the long-term and short-term objectives of economic development. Keeping these arguments in view, the role of public expenditure can easily be discussed as:

1. Long-term Objectives

The aim of long-term objectives of public expenditure is not to attain maximum increase in output over a short period but to have more rapid rate of output in the long-run. Therefore, it aims at:

(i) *Basic and key goods industries:* In view of long-term perspective, it follows a policy to establish basic and key capital goods industries which may impart a momentum to the development and create sufficient saving for future investment. This would, in turn, reduce the dependence of underdeveloped countries on foreign countries in respect of equipments and machinery.

(ii) *Social overheads:* Public expenditure, in underdeveloped countries, makes efforts to infrastructures like, railways, roads, dams, shipping, telephones, banking facilities, educational institutions and health facilities, etc. These social overheads are considered the basic foundations of economic growth.

(iii) *Self-sustained growth:* Another positive role of public expenditure in underdeveloped countries is to generate self-sufficient and self-sustained growth. This is only possible after bringing about structural changes in the economy. This requires a big push in the economy which is not possible in the absence of public expenditure. Therefore, public expenditure assumes this responsibility to push the economy to reach the stage of self-generating growth.

2. Short-term Objectives

Investment expenditure in a country should not neglect the immediate needs of the economy during the course of preparing long-term development strategies on the basis of perspective planning. Investment needs, otherwise neglected have serious repercussions on the country. For the smooth working, there are three fundamental factors as:

(i) Improvement in the productivity of agriculture sector;

(ii) Supply of essential consumer goods to curb inflationary tendencies in the economy; and

(iii) Creation of employment opportunities to absorb surplus population and to avoid unnecessary wastage of human power.

It is obvious, public expenditure in an underdeveloped country should play dual role. In other words, it should prepare for structural change and fulfilling the immediate needs of the economy by making proper allocation of existing resources.

MAJOR RECOMMENDATIONS OF EXPENDITURE REFORMS COMMISSION (ERC)

1. Food Subsidy

With a view to reducing subsidy on food, ERC has suggested a series of measures which among others include:

(i) Efforts to ensure that quantities allocated for Below the Poverty Line (BPL) population reach them at the prices at which the Government of India releases. To this end, state governments would need to identify BPL population in a transparent manner.

(ii) In those states where the total distribution under the Public Distribution System (PDS) is in excess of the quantities earmarked for BPL population and at prices at or below the price at which the sales are to be made to the BPL population, the Government of India could provide the subsidy amounts directly to the state governments, leaving it to them to procure the foodgrains required for the BPL population.

(iii) A National Food Security buffer stock of 10 million tonnes—4 million tonnes of wheat and 6 million tonnes of rice—should be maintained at all times.

(iv) The cost of buffer stocks held in excess of the above requirement should be treated as "producer's subsidy" and action taken to phase it out over the next three years through: (a) moderating the increase in minimum support prices; (b) moving towards procurement of single (common) variety of paddy/rice, as in the case of wheat. Besides, through a suitable adjustment in the pricing mechanism, reduce procurement of paddy and increase procurement of rice through a levy system; and (c) encouraging state governments and private sector to enter procurement, trade and export of foodgrains through an assurance of continuity of policy over the next 15 years. The objective of the procurement policy should be to maintain a food security buffer of 10 million tonnes and availability of 21 million tonnes per annum for distribution through the PDS. Thus, the total average stocks to be maintained for distribution and buffer stock should not be more than 17 million tonnes or so compared to a likely level of 24 million tonnes in the current year.

Every effort should be made to minimise FCI's overheads as between distribution and buffer stocks needs to be modified to ensure that the consumers, particularly those below poverty line are not made to pay for the cost attributable to excess stocks of FCI's inefficiencies.

2. Rationalising Fertilizer Subsidies

The Retention Price-cum-Subsidy Scheme (RPS) has led to the development of a large domestic industry and near self-sufficiency. However, the unit-wise RPS in a cost plus scheme. It results in high cost fertilizers, excess payments to industry and provides no incentives to be cost-efficient. Besides, fertilizer subsidies have grown over the years. The package suggested to rationalise fertilizer subsidies takes care of the needs of small farmers and proposes to bring fertilizer prices to the level of import parity price in a gradual and phased manner over a period of time as follows:

(i) To protect small farmers and marginal farmers who consume a large part of their output from a loss in their real incomes arising out of increase in farm gate prices of fertilizers two options are suggested: (a) introduction of a dual price scheme under which all cultivator households are given 120 kgs. of fertilizers at Subsidized and Rural Works Programme to provide additional incomes to small farmers.

(ii) Dismantling of the control system in a phased manner, leading to a decontrolled fertiliser industry which can compete with import albeit with a small level of protection and a feedstock cost differential compensation to Naphtha/Liquefied Natural Gas (LNG) based units to ensure self-sufficiency.

(iii) The ERC recommends a 7 per cent increase in the price of urea in real terms every year from 1.4.2001. With this order of increase open market price has been reached Rs. 6,903 per tonne by 1.4.2006, a level at which the industry can be freed from all controls and be required to compete with imports, with variable levy ensuring availability of such imports at the farm gate at Rs. 7,000 per tonne of urea. While no concessions will be necessary from this date onwards for gas-based, fuel oil/light sulphur heavy stock and mixed feed stock plants, existing naphtha plants converting to LNG as also new plants and substantial additions to existing plants will be entitled to a feed stock differential with that for LNG plants serving as a ceiling.

(iv) The farm-gate prices of nitrogenous, phosphatic and potassium fertilizers should be set to promote a desired balance of fertilizer use. In the circumstances, it is suggested that once urea price is re-determined every six months, the prices of potassium and phosphatic fertilizers should be suitably adjusted to ensure the desired NPK balance. It will be useful if government could announce in advance the formula to be adopted for fixing the prices of P and K fertilizers with reference to a given urea price.

STUDY-QUESTIONS

1. Explain the concept of public expenditure.
2. Briefly explain developmental and non-developmental expenditure.
3. Write short notes on:
   (i) Capital account.
   (ii) Revenue account.
   (iii) Fertilizer subsidies.
4. Discuss the trends in receipts of the Indian Government.
5. Describe the role of public expenditure in underdeveloped countries.

Taxable Capacity

9

INTRODUCTION

The obligation of a modern welfare state and its commitment to economic planning for development has led to the growth of public expenditure in recent years. Tax is one of the most important sources of public income. High taxation will lead to increase in revenue of the state. Taxation, however, reduces the purchasing power of the people and adversely affects their ability and willingness to work, save and invest. Consequently, while increasing the rates of some taxes or imposing new taxes, the government or the taxation authority has to keep in view the capacity of the people as a whole to pay taxes.

Thus, if the public has the capacity to bear the burden of additional taxes or high taxation, the government will frame its tax policy accordingly. But the question here is: "What do we mean by saying that the public is capable of bearing additional burden of taxes?" So long as there is money in the pocket of a person, he can pay the tax. Although he may not like to pay it, he may try his best to evade it, he may suffer as a consequence, but he can pay it.

DEFINITIONS OF TAXABLE CAPACITY

Taxable capacity refers to sacrifice the community is able to sustain. Taxation Enquiry Commission of India report defined it as, "Taxable capacity of different sections of the community may be said to refer to the degree of taxation, broadly speaking, beyond which productive effort and efficiency as a whole begin to suffer."

According to Sir Joseph Stamp, "Taxable capacity is the margin of total production over total consumption. It is the maximum amount which the citizens of a country can contribute towards the expenses of the public authorities without having a really unhappy and downtrodden existence and without dislocating the economic organisation too much."

According to Findlay Shirras, "Taxable capacity may be defined as the maximum amount which the citizens of a country can contribute towards the expenses of public authorities without having to undergo an unbearable strain."

According to Hugh Dalton, "My general conclusion is that relative taxable capacity is a reality, which can however, equally be expressed in other terms, while absolute taxable capacity is a myth." He further stated that, "Taxable capacity is a common phrase but a confused conception."

Thus, it means that 'taxable capacity' refers to a limit beyond which an additional tax will create misery in the life of the individuals. It brings feelings of distraught in the minds of the people and they become hearty depressed. Individuals should not be compelled to pay tax by taking loan. It should not be unjust.

FACTORS DETERMINING TAXABLE CAPACITY

The 'taxable capacity' of a country depends on several factors. Following are the important factors which determine the taxable capacity of people:

(i) **Wealth of the country:** The volume of wealth will determine the taxable capacity of a country. Other things being equal, the greater the wealth of a country, the greater will be its taxable capacity and vice versa. In wealth, we include both—the natural as well as produced wealth.

(ii) **Distribution of wealth:** The wealth of a nation may be so distributed that a large proportion of country's total population reaches the taxable income or wealth limit which is taxed. This will be the case when the distribution of national income or wealth in the country is more equal. Therefore, in the case of direct taxes, the taxable capacity will be much lower. On the other hand, if there are only few rich people who are subject to all kinds of taxation, and others remain poor, the taxable capacity of the country will be high. Thus, greater the inequality of income, higher shall be the taxable capacity of the country. The reason for this is that the government under such conditions can get an adequate income by imposing taxation on the richer sections of the community.

(iii) **Size of population:** The taxable capacity of a country also depends on the size of its population. Other things remaining equal, greater the size of population, lower will be the taxable capacity of the country. The reason for saying so is that the expenditure on consumption increases as a result of increase in population. However, if the productive capacity of the country increases in the same proportion in which the population increases, the taxable capacity will remain unaffected.

(iv) **Stage of economic development:** The taxable capacity of a country also depends on its stage of economic development. Ordinarily, the taxable capacity of the developed or advanced countries is greater than that of the less-developed countries.

(v) **Nature of tax system:** If the tax system of a country is wide in its scope, the taxable capacity would be high. If the tax system satisfies the canon of economy and convenience, the taxable capacity would be high. On the contrary, if the tax system produces adverse effects on the productive capacity of the people, then the taxable capacity will be low.

(vi) **Price level:** We know that the surplus of income over expenditure forms the taxable capacity of the country. This surplus will be low if prices are high. On the other hand, the low price level will enhance the taxable capacity of the people in the country.

(vii) **Stability of income:** The stability of income also affects the taxable capacity of a country. The national income in the developed countries such as the United States of America and the United Kingdom is generally stable in the sense that there are no violent fluctuations in the national income of these countries. But in an underdeveloped country like India, there is instability in the national income. A large proportion of country's population gets its livelihood from agriculture which is totally dependent on the monsoon rains. If, unfortunately, the monsoons fail and the country is confronted with drought, the national income of the country suffers a serious decline. Consequently, it becomes difficult to devise the taxation system on any scientific basis on account of this instability in national income. This is the reason why the taxable capacity of India is low as compared to other developed countries of the world.

(viii) **Psychology of tax-payers:** The taxable capacity of a country also depends upon the psychology of the tax-payers. For instance, during war time, people are prepared to make greater sacrifices for the country. The sense of democracy, citizenship and responsibility towards the working of the government are those factors which, if present in tax-payers, increase the taxable capacity of the people and vice versa.

(ix) **Political conditions:** Political conditions of a country are yet another important factor which determine the taxable capacity. When some natural calamities like, epidemics, floods, famines, etc. occur in any part of the country, people generally gladly become willing to pay more taxes.

(x) **Standard of living of people:** Other things being equal, the taxable capacity depends also on the standard of living of the people. When the standard of living of people in the country is low, greater surplus is available for taxation purposes.

MEASUREMENT OF TAXABLE CAPACITY

Majority of the economists agree that the taxable capacity in a country depends upon the national income of the country. Once the national income is increased, it is easy to increase the taxable capacity. Higher the national income higher the taxable capacity. National Income or National Dividend, as defined by Alfred Marshall is, 'The labour and capital of a country, acting on its national resources, produce annually a certain—net aggregate of commodities, material and immaterial including services of all kinds. This is the 'Net Annual Income' or 'Revenue of the Country' or the 'National Dividend'. A.C. Pigou defined 'National Dividend' as, "National dividend is that part of objective income of a community including, of course, income derived from abroad, which can be measured in terms of money." For measuring taxable capacity—the national income free from all the improprieties, either in its calculation or in its aggregation is measured.

According to Prof. Dalton, "Taxable capacity cannot be measured." On the contrary, Prof. Marshal, Prof. Fisher and Prof. Pigou are of the opinion that the easiest device of measuring the taxable capacity of a country is the determination of net national income. The correct determination of taxable capacity depends on the determination of net national income of a country. In case of production of national income, a part or amount of the national resources is destroyed, hence for calculating the net national income this destroyed part or amount should be deducted. In the words of Findlay Shirras, "The measurement of taxable capacity is possible only after calculating net national income."

METHODS FOR INCREASING THE TAXABLE CAPACITY SUGGESTED BY SHIRRAS

Prof. Findlay Shirras suggested the following two methods to increase the taxable capacity of the people in an economy:

(a) The personal income method; and

(b) The production method.

(a) **The Personal Income Method:** In this method, the income of every individual in the country is assessed and added together. This method requires an analysis of the income tax returns of the individual, and also income received from death duties and other property taxes. Thus, income includes the income from the following heads:

(a) Income from employment;

(b) Income from land and building;

(c) Agricultural income;

(d) Income earned as profits from a trade; and

(e) Interests earned.

The individual personal income, thus, calculated is added together and so national income is found *ceteris paribus*. If the national income increases, the taxable capacity increases and vice versa.

Mathematical Formula:

$$E.T. = T - E$$

$$G.T.C. = Y - C$$

$$N.T.C. = G.T.C. - E.T.$$

Here;

Y	:	stands for national income.
C	:	stands for supply of minimum needs.
G.T.C.	:	stands for gross taxable capacity.
N.T.C.	:	stands for net taxable capacity.
E.T.	:	stands for affected taxation.
T	:	stands for government expenditure.
E	:	stands for expenditure incurred by the government in the country.

(b) **Production method:** Under this method, the net produce in terms of money from various sources is estimated and added. It means, the net produce from industry and trade, agriculture, etc. is estimated in terms of money and added to get the national income. If the net production increases, taxable capacity also increases in the same proportion, other things remaining the same, and vice versa.

Mathematical Formula:

$$G.T.C. = O - D$$

$$N.T.C. = G.T.C. - E.T.$$

Here O stands for total production.

D stands for deductions (capital loss + capital for future economic development + essential amount of money for minimum consumption).

The idea of net national income is subject to criticism on the following grounds:

(i) A country may take loan from another country. This loan is to be repaid along with interest and is deducted from the calculation of the national income. In this way, the calculation of national income is not correct.

(ii) In this calculation, that part of the production is ignored which is consumed by the producer himself. It makes the calculation of correct national income impossible.

(iii) In case of new investment, in a particular year, the same should be deducted from the national income of that year. However, the same is not done while calculating national income.

Prof. Findlay Shirras refuted the above criticisms in the following words, "a road leading to an important centre has often many crossings, sign posts, danger signals, but this does not lessen its value to the cautious sojourner."

Note: Here the word 'sojourner' stands for traveller.

CLASSIFICATION OF TAXABLE CAPACITY

The concept of taxable capacity has been interpreted by the economists in the following two senses:

(a) Absolute taxable capacity; and

(b) Relative taxable capacity.

(a) **Absolute taxable capacity:** Absolute taxable capacity refers to the maximum amount of taxation that can be collected from a community without causing any unpleasant effects. If the operation of a tax system causes unpleasant effects, the absolute taxable capacity can be said to have exceeded. According to Joseph Stamp, "The absolute taxable capacity of a country is represented by the difference between total production and total consumption." There are two limits to the taxable capacity of the country:

(i) Check to the total production; and

(ii) Check to total revenue yield as a result of the imposition of the high rates of taxation.

If an increase in taxation results in a lower production and does not bring any additional revenue to the government, it should be presumed that the taxation capacity of the country/community has been reached. In the words of Findlay Shirras, "Taxation capacity is the limit of squeezability." In his view, whatever is produced over and above the minimum level of consumption to maintain the present standard of living, is considered the limit of squeezability. In the words of D. Fraser, "When the tax-payers are compelled to borrow money from the banks we should think, the limit of taxable capacity has reached." In this case, the tax-payers are forced to borrow money from their banks so as to pay tax dues. When the term taxable capacity is used, it always implies absolute taxable capacity.

(b) Relative taxable capacity: The relative taxable capacity refers to the taxable capacity of two or more communities/countries. It is the proportion in which two or more communities/countries can contribute in the form of taxes in order to meet some common expenditure. In other words, "The relative taxable capacity is the capacity of the community to contribute some common expenditure in relation to the capacities of other communities." The rich community shall be called to bear a comparatively larger share of such common expenditure as against the poor community. For example, the total expenditure of the U.N.O. is distributed among the member-nations in accordance with their relative taxable capacity. In the words of Prof. Dalton, "If the common expenditure increases, the proportions paid by rich contributors should increase and those paid by the poor should diminish." Thus, if two separate communities are required to meet some common expenditures, it should be in proportion to their relative taxable capacities. This principle is commonly applied in a federal system of government in which different states are expected to contribute to the common expenditure of the country according to their taxable capacity.

WHICH CONCEPT IS MORE SUITABLE

Of the above two concepts of taxable capacity, the question arises as to which is more suitable? According to Prof. Dalton, "There is no logical relationship between absolute taxable capacity and relative taxable capacity." Absolute taxable capacity is the maximum amount of taxation which can be collected from the tax-payer. On the contrary, relative taxable capacity is the maximum limit of realising tax from the tax-payer which can be utilised for the welfare of the society. According to Prof. Dalton, "Relative taxable capacity is a reality which can, however, be expressed in words while absolute taxable capacity is myth." It is because of this reason that Prof. Dalton went on so far as to condemn absolute capacity as a mere fallacy and attempts to give no place to it in the study of public finance. Nevertheless, he recognised the relative taxable capacity. Findlay Shirras also recognises the importance of relative taxable capacity, but he also says that it is necessary to know absolute taxable capacity before knowing relative taxable capacity. However, Prof. Dalton does not agree with the view of Findlay Shirras and says that relative taxable capacity is ascertained and is helpful of itself without any need of going the fallacious notion of absolute taxable capacity. If we apply the absolute taxable capacity concept to India, the vast masses of Indians will be exempted from paying any tax to the government as they have miserably low incomes. On the contrary, if we apply the relative concept of taxable capacity to India, it is possible that the vast majority of Indians will have to bear the larger tax burdens so as to raise capital formation. Thus, we conclude that the concept of relative taxable capacity, is more suitable and helpful than that of absolute taxable capacity concept.

LIMITATIONS OF TAXABLE CAPACITY

With an increase in tax, levels of consumption as well as production are adversely affected, and the limit of the taxable capacity is reached. It is the limit beyond which if taxes are imposed, they would lead to the heavy reduction in consumption, adversely affecting the level of industrial output. When the final level of taxable capacity is reached, then the increase or decrease in national income does not command a proportionate increase or decrease in the consumption. In other words, the consumption of the people does not correspondingly increase with the increase in national income and does not correspondingly decrease with the decrease in national income, and thus, the small surplus is left for tax-imposition.

TAXABLE CAPACITY IN INDIA

Taxable capacity in India is not satisfactory. The reason of its fluctuating trend, and whimpering nature is that the economy largely depends upon agriculture which is the most uncertain sector of production in our economy. Being largely based on weather, it is the still the 'gamble of monsoon.'

As the national income of India is low the taxable capacity is also low. Only 14 to 15 per cent of the national income is received as tax. Colin Clark had stipulated that the proportion of taxes to the national income of the country should be 25 per cent. Judged from this view too, the taxable capacity of the people in India is quite low.

Many views have emerged on the low level of taxation in India. According to one view, there is ample scope of the agricultural sector of the economy. Another view contradicts the former view on the ground that there is widespread poverty in all the parts of the country. Which nullifies any scope of taxation, and the taxable capacity has already been reached.

REASONS WHY INDIA HAS NOT REACHED THE LIMIT OF TAXABLE CAPACITY

India has not reached the limit of taxable capacity on account of the following reasons:

(i) In India, most of the public expenditure is being incurred on development programmes. Since development programmes increase prosperity, thereby taxable capacity also increases.

(ii) National income is directly related with taxable capacity. Since national income is increasing in India, taxable capacity is also increasing.

(iii) Economic inequality is reducing on account of planned economic development in India. Hence, taxable capacity is increasing in India.

(iv) On account of rapid increase in family planning programmes in India during the last 5 years, the rate of population growth is less as compared to increase in production. The standard of living of the people has risen leading to increase in taxable capacity.

(v) Monetary economy has replaced barter system in India. Further emphasis is being given to rapid industrialisation and thereby the taxable capacity has also increased in India.

(vi) Under the Five-Year Plans the volume of national income is increasing rapidly. It is possible, therefore, to have additional taxation which may fall on the additional income created.

(vii) Increasing resort to deficit financing in India and consequent increase in money supply with the people has also increased money and real income for the community. This too offers great scope for additional taxation, particularly for controlling inflationary pressure on account of deficit financing.

From the above study, we conclude that taxable capacity has not been reached in India and there is vast scope for additional taxation in India. The Taxation Enquiry Commission concluded:

"While there is reason to believe that there has been an increase in taxable capacity, the fact remains that the proportion of tax revenues to national income has not undergone any change, as compared to the pre-war period. Indian taxation on the basis of its existing structure and rates has not fully tapped the taxable resources of the country. When this is taken in conjunction with the vast need for additional resources, it is clear that there is justification for some increase in Indian taxation."

CAUSES OF LOW LEVEL OF TAXATION IN INDIA

(i) **Rising population:** Rising population adversely affects the taxable capacity of the individuals, by bringing their living standard to a still lower level. According to the 1971 census, the total population of India was, 54,81,59,652. As compared to the 1961 census, it showed an increase of 24.8 per cent. The main cause of this increase in population is the fall in death rate brought about by better health conditions, effective control of epidemics, efficient holding of famine conditions and general improvement and economic development. The population has gone up despite a fall in the birth rate.

The population of India now has crossed 100 crores. This rapid increase in population reduced the purchasing power of the individuals in our country. Nowadays, many people fall below the poverty line and they cannot afford to pay even a single penny as tax.

(ii) **Low standard of living:** India's major chunk of population is poor people, especially in the rural areas. Low per capita income, and a large number of dependents further reduce the living standard of the people. The purchasing power of the people is very low, which multiplies the miseries and dismal condition of the people. The people, having higher percentage of income, as well as higher standard of living are small in number. Thus, the taxable capacity in aggregate is low. At least a tax cannot be imposed on those, who cannot even afford to buy two square meals.

(iii) **Presence of barter (non-monetized sector):** It is still a widespread practice in rural India to exchange the commodities without using money. The barter system outsmarts the general flow of money. Farmers keep a substantial part of their produce for their consumption, and thus huge amount of produce does not appear in the markets. This practice of barter is prevalent in many parts of the country. It is estimated that nearly 35% of the consumption is out of the purview of money economy. Such non-cash transactions(non-monetised transactions) are not subject to the taxes of sales tax and is again restricts the taxable capacity of the people to a lower level.

(iv) **Low volume of foreign trade:** Government earns revenue by imposing duties on export and import. Greater the volume of imports and exports, greater is the amount of money received as duties. India's international trade, unfortunately is not outstanding. Therefore, it limits the scope of taxation because this commercial sector is small and revenue from this sector cannot be enhanced much.

Thus, there is predominance of the cottage and small-scale enterprises in the country due to the narrow international trade. So the revenue received in the form of sales tax is very small.

SIGNIFICANCE OF TAXABLE CAPACITY

In a modern welfare state, state activities are no longer confined to the maintenance of peace, law and order, defence and justice. Public expenditure has been increasing enormously due to several new heads of expenditure for the welfare of the people such as social security measures and welfare schemes for the weaker sections of the society, subsidised food, milk and other essential commodities to the poor, weak and backward classes of the society. Many public enterprises producing essential goods for supplying public utilities and essential services at low prices incurred losses. Hence, the government of any country, particularly of a developing one like India has to collect more and more revenue for these purposes. In practice, no government today can impose heavy taxes and squeeze its people limitlessly as was done in the past by the despotic monarchical regimes or by the alien colonial rulers like the British in India. Any tax system which exceeds the aggregate capacity of the people to pay taxes, is sure to reduce their ability and willingness to work, save and invest; thereby it affects the future income in the community, consequently resulting in a decrease in government revenues from taxes. Therefore, the concept of taxable capacity plays a very significant role in public finance. The importance of the notion of the taxable capacity lies in the fact that it sets the limit beyond which the government, without being dethroned in this democratic age, cannot tax the people. It is the limit of the people of different classes taken as a whole to bear the burden of taxation beyond which productive efforts and efficiency of production begin to suffer. To say that taxable capacity of a nation is the maximum ability of its people to pay taxes is not a concrete way to define it. The purpose of estimating taxable capacity may be to know as to how much money can be collected from the people to finance extraordinary expenditure like war. The knowledge of taxable capacity may be useful for the mobilisation of economic resources for the purpose of economic development and planning. The concept may be useful for the purpose of comparison of the burden of taxation as between different states of a federal government. In short, the significance of the taxable concept is as follows:

(i) The knowledge of taxable capacity is a must for the Finance Minister of a country on the basis of which he can do justice in taxation.

(ii) The knowledge of taxable capacity may be useful for mobilisation of economic resources of a country for the purposes of economic development and planning.

(iii) The knowledge of taxable capacity may be useful for knowing as to how much money can be collected from the people to finance extraordinary expenditure like famines, epidemics, wars, floods, earthquakes, etc.

(iv) The knowledge of estimating taxable capacity may be useful in establishing sound taxation system in a country.

(v) It may prevent the government from imposing unnecessary and unwanted taxes which may have adverse effects upon production, consumption, investment and willingness to save.

(vi) The knowledge of taxable capacity may be useful for the purpose of comparison of the burden of taxation as between different states of a federal government.

(vii) The economic capacity of the citizens can be determined on the basis of taxable capacity.

(viii) The knowledge of estimating taxable capacity may be useful for the central government for developing the economy of the country as a whole in a balanced manner.

(ix) Even in normal times the knowledge of the limits of taxable capacity will enable the government to provide satisfaction about the rationality of the taxation system to the citizens of the country.

(x) The knowledge of taxable capacity may be useful for the government in fighting against inflation and deflation.

TAXATION AND CAPITAL FORMATION IN A DEVELOPING ECONOMY

It is generally accepted that "a significant improvement in the economic situation of underdeveloped countries in the long run is attainable only through a substantial increase in the rate of capital formation to a level at which special efforts by the government to sustain capital formation will no longer be necessary." In developing countries, the rate of capital formation is low mainly because of:

(i) The poverty of the vast masses of the people;

(ii) The conspicuous and wasteful consumption of the higher income groups who could save and accumulate; and

(iii) The absence of proper opportunities for investment.

It is essential to push up the rate of capital formation if the economy is to grow rapidly. Since the people by themselves may not be able to raise the rate of capital formation, it becomes the duty and responsibility of the government to do so. It is in this context that taxation is given special significance in an underdeveloped country. Tax policy is an important tool for stimulating private savings and investments and mobilising idle resources.

In accelerating the rate of capital formation, the burden will have to be borne by the vast masses of people. It may be thought that they are already subsisting at the lowest possible standard of living and that it would be difficult for them to lower it any further. But restriction of consumption is essential so that resources may be diverted to the production of capital goods. There has been some difference of opinion on this question. While some argue that capital formation can go also with increase in consumption because of the availability of unemployed men and resources, others contend that resources will have to be used to produce capital goods only in the short period and that consumption goods will have to be delegated. However, a more balanced opinion is the one expressed by John Adler who writes: "With the low levels of consumption which prevail in most underdeveloped countries (more specifically, the low level of consumption prevailing among the large majority of the population) even a temporary curtailment of consumption involves too great a sacrifice to be compensated by the prospects of a greater consumption in the future." Accordingly, Adler is of the opinion that per capita consumption should not be allowed to fall below the initial level and that a rising proportion of the additional output should be devoted to additional capital formation. Now, if it is desired to restrict consumption among the low income groups or to prevent it from rising, commodity taxation comes in handy, as direct taxes cannot bring in the lower income groups under this scope.

Further, taxation can be used effectively to curtail the wasteful consumption of the higher income groups. Here, direct taxes become more useful. The income tax, the expenditure tax, the death duty, the wealth tax, etc. fall not on the essential consumption requirements of the rich but upon the non-essential items. The reduction of such consumption will have double significance. For one thing, the resources employed in these industries can be diverted profitably to those industries which may produce capital goods. For another, transfer of monetary resources to the government can be used to increase the capital formation in the country.

Firstly, the government can use the tax revenues placed at its disposal to increase the production possibilities in the country. On the one side, it can provide the social and economic overhead capital which is a basic necessity for industrialisation. Secondly, the government can participate in direct economic activities by setting up industrial units in those industries or regions where there is great scope for development and expansion. The central idea is that the government should encourage saving for capital formation.

Thus, in a developing country, taxation may be used as a form of community's saving. But there are obvious limitations. The low taxable capacity of people is well-known, because of the very low levels of income. The number of people liable for the payment of direct taxes is a macroscopic minority of the population. For instance, in India, those who are subject to income tax constitute less than 1 per cent of the total population, and even among these people, the majority belongs to the lower middle class and their taxable capacity is not high. Even the commodity taxes which would fall heavily on lower income groups may not be significant because of the poor purchasing power of the masses living on or below subsistence level.

STUDY-QUESTIONS

1. Define the term 'taxable capacity'. Also discuss the factors affecting the taxable capacity.
2. Discuss the classification of taxable capacity. Also explain which is more suitable?
3. Give the various methods of measurement of taxable capacity. Also explain limitations of taxable capacity.
4. Discuss the taxable capacity in India. Do you think that India has reached the limit of taxable capacity? Explain the causes of low level tax in India.
5. Describe the importance and significance of taxable capacity.

❖❖❖

Public Debt in India

10

INTRODUCTION

In modern times, borrowing by the government has become a normal method of government finance along with the other sources of public finance like taxes, fees, etc. In all countries of the world, public debt has shown the tendency of increasing. In fact, the debt burden, particularly the external debt burden, of world's less-developed countries has grown phenomenally and quite disproportionately to the debt servicing capacity of these poor countries. At present, the external debt burden of the Third World countries has crossed the staggering figure of 700 billion-mark and in the case of several individual developing countries, the annual debt servicing burden of payment exceeds or nearly equals their total export earnings.

The medieval system of public borrowing gave rise to the modern system. Moreover, during 17th and 18th centuries, the Dutch methods of commerce and finance were initiated in Britain and this brought into existence the English funded debt which became an example to other states. In the 19th century, under the influence of *laissez-faire* philosophy, economic life was restricted only to unavoidable minimum duties of the state with the result that functions performed by the state were only a few essential functions. But in the modern times, the growth of public debt is the result of changing economic and political institutions. Prof. J.K. Mehta noted, "Public debt is a comparatively modern phenomenon and has come into existence with the development of the democratic form of government in the world." Therefore, the growth of public debt is the result of changed economic and political situation all over the world. Today, borrowing by the government has become a normal feature of government finance along with the other sources of public finance like taxes, fees, etc. In all the countries of the world, public debt tendency has been increasing. Presently, the burden of external debt of the Third World countries has touched 700 billion mark and in the case of several individual developing countries, the annual debt servicing burden of payment exceeds or nearly equals their total export earnings. In fact, the burden of external debt of these countries has been mounting constantly year after year adding to the grave situations of these underdeveloped and poor countries.

MEANING AND DEFINITIONS OF PUBLIC DEBT

The concept of public debt has been defined by various economists. Prof. J.K. Mehta has rightly mentioned, "Public revenue, therefore, consists of the money that the government is not obliged to return to the very individual from whom it is obtained. Public debt, on the other hand, carries with it the obligation on the part of the government to pay money back to the individuals from whom it has been obtained."

According to Prof. Findlay Shirras, "National debt is a debt which a state owes to its subject or to the nationals of other countries." Similarly, Prof. P.E. Taylor states: "The debt is the form of promises by the treasury to pay to the holders of these promises a principal sum and in most instances, interest on that principal. Borrowing is restored in order to provide funds for financing a current deficit."

Prof. Carl S. Shoup defines public debt or government borrowing as: "The receipt from the sale of financial instrument by the government to individuals or firms in the private sector to induce the private sector to release manpower and real resource and to finance the purchase of those resources or to make welfare payments or subsidies."

In a broad sense, public debt may be called 'revenue' of the state. Just as the taxes levied and collected in any given year constitute the income of the government, in the same way, loans raised or debt incurred and received in that year also constitute the income of the government of that year. However, the vital difference between public debt and other traditional sources of public revenue (taxes, fees, etc.) is that, while the former has to be paid back with interest, the latter are not. Taxes are collected from the public without any promise or commitment on the part of the government to provide the tax-payers any service, much less the commitment of paying them back to the tax-payers but public loans or debts are taken by the treasury or government from the banks, institutions and individuals on the explicit understanding given in writing that these shall be repaid on maturity while interest shall be paid regularly, half-yearly or yearly as stipulated in the terms of the loan.

SOURCES OF PUBLIC BORROWING

Every government has two major sources of borrowing– internal and external. Internally, the government can borrow from individuals, financial institutions, commercial banks and the central bank. Externally, the government borrows from individuals and banks, international institutions and foreign governments.

(i) Borrowing from Individuals

When individuals purchase government bonds, they are diverting funds from private use to government use. Individuals may be able to subscribe to government bonds either through curtailment of current consumption needs (this may be very rare) or through diversion of funds from their own business or diverting funds into government bonds from corporate securities. Normally, the sale of government bonds to individuals should not curtail either consumption or business expansion. To a large measure, the bonds will be absorbed out of funds that would have been lying idle or would have been used to buy other securities.

(ii) Borrowing from Non-banking Financial Institutions

Another source of government borrowing is borrowing from the non-banking financial institutions. When non-banking financial institutions such as insurance companies, investment trusts, mutual savings banks, etc. buy government bonds, they reduce their idle cash balances by making investment in government bonds. However, these institutions prefer to invest their funds in government bonds on account of these bonds being perfectly free from credit-risk, and also due to their high negotiability and liquidity. The rate of interest paid on government bonds is, however, relatively low. Consequently, in bank cases financial institutions prefer to invest in the high-risk—high-return giving securities, particularly in the equity shares of companies under the management of familiar and experienced industrialists. When the non-banking financial institutions purchase government bonds, they do so in order to reduce their cash holdings.

(iii) Borrowing from Commercial Banks

While individuals and non-banking finance institutions take up government bonds out of their own funds, commercial banks can do so by creating additional purchasing power—known as credit creation. The banking system, as a whole, can make additional loans up to an amount several times as great as the excess cash reserves. This is possible because the loans that bankers grant, are typically book entries in the names of borrowers who pay in the form of cheques to others who have also maintained bank accounts. The result is that so long as cash is not withdrawn from the banks, it serves as the basis for the expansion of loans.

Commercial banks can subscribe to government loans through creation of credit. They need not contract their other loans and advances. Whenever the banking system has excess cash reserves, it can absorb an amount of government bonds considerably greater than the excess cash reserves. It is important to note that the power to buy bonds is essentially created rather than merely transferred. So, if commercial banks create additional purchasing power and place it at the disposal of the government to finance the latter's expenditures, inflationary pressures will be generated (if previously, the economy has been working at full employment).

(iv) Borrowing from the Central Bank

The central bank of the country can subscribe to government loans. This action is similar to the system of creating purchasing power by the commercial banks. The central banks credit the account of the government by purchasing government bonds. The latter pays to its creditors out of its accounts maintained with the central bank. Those who have received cheques from the government on the central bank, will deposit the amount in their banks. Consequently, these banks find themselves with large cash reserves which become the bases for additional loans and advances. It must be mentioned here that the borrowing from the central bank is the most expansionary of all the sources, for not only the government secures funds for its expenditure but this banking system gets additional cash. This amount can be utilised as the basis for further credit expansion. On the contrary, the borrowings from individuals and financed institutions are merely transfers of funds from private to government use and so, it will not be expansionary in their effect on the economy.

(v) Borrowing from External Sources

Government may borrow from other countries too. These borrowing can be used to finance war expenditure, or to procure defence equipment, or to pay for development projects, or to pay off adverse balance of payments. Formerly, the floating of loans for any specific development projects, like, railway construction, was taken up by individuals and banking and other financial institutions. However, in recent years, apart from this source, two important sources have become prominent. They are:

(a) International financial institutions, *viz.* I.M.F., the I.B.R.D., the I.D.A. and the I.F.C., which give loans for short-term for overcoming temporary balance of payments difficulties and for long-term for development purpose; and

(b) Government assistance generally for development projects. For developing countries like India, external sources of borrowing are becoming considerably important in recent years.

CLASSIFICATION OF PUBLIC DEBTS

Following are the different kinds of public debts:

(i) **Voluntary debt:** Voluntary debt is the debt which is paid without any legal enforcement. The lender is not compelled or encroached by the government to lend money. It is in the option of the lender to lend without any fear or compulsion. It was prevalent in the ancient times.

(ii) **Compulsory debt:** Compulsory debt is legally-forced in nature. In this case there is no option to the people but to pay to the government. They may be compelled to pay even through curtailing their expenditure on necessities. War-time debts are generally compulsory in nature.

According to Hugh Dalton, "A compulsory or a forced loan is a rarity in modern public finance since it combines the disadvantages, while lacking the advantages of both a tax and a voluntary loan."

(iii) **Funded debt:** It is a kind of long-term or 'definite period' debt. A proper agreement and terms and conditions of repayment with the percentage of interest payable is declared and the debt is paid according to the agreed policy. A fund is maintained by the government to secure the money and thereafter to pay it back.

According to Findlay Shirras, "Funded debt is a debt which is repayable at a distant date and for the payment of interest on which regular provision is made."

(iv) **Unfunded debt:** It is a kind of debt which is for a short time, and for an indefinite period. Government does not create any kind of fund for this purpose since it is to be paid within a short period of time. It is paid through the income received from other sources. It has also been named as floating debt. However, in India the pattern is different to define floating debt and unfunded debt.

(v) **Internal debt:** Internal debt is the debt which has been raised by the persons, institutions, or banks, which are in the territory of the government which borrows the money. Hugh Dalton has defined an internal debt, as: "A loan is internal if subscribed by persons or institutions within the area controlled by the public authority which raises the loan." In such a debt, only national capital circulates in the market.

(vi) **External debt:** External debt is the debt which is borrowed from the external sources like foreign governments, International capital supply agencies and foreign individuals, etc. According to Findlay Shirras, "External debt means the transfer of wealth from the lending to the borrowing exists when the loan is made, and a transfer in the reverse direction when interest is periodically paid or when the principal is repaid."

(vii) **Productive debt:** The productive debt is the debt which is backed by the assets of the same or larger amount. The income received from these assets is paid as the interest to all the debt. To quote Findlay Shirras, "Productive or reproductive loans are debts which are fully covered by assets of equal or greater value. The source of the interest is the income from the ownership of these as railways and irrigation works."

(viii) **Unproductive debt:** Dead-weight or unproductive debts are not backed by any productive assets. For example debt taken for war, consumption, etc. It does not increase the productive capacity of the nation. Shirras has defined such a debt in following words, "Dead-weight or unproductive debts are those which have no existing assets."

(ix) **Redeemable debt and irredeemable debt:** Redeemable debts refer to those loans which the government promises to pay off at some future date. As against this, irredeemable debts are those principle amount which are never returned by the government although it pays the interest thereon regularly. Therefore, the difference between the two kinds of debts is that when a loan is reimbursed, the government has to make some arrangements for its repayment. Money has to be arranged for this purpose. If it is decided to pay it off from tax money and fresh taxes have to be imposed, under these circumstances, it is not wise to go on borrowing without paying off little by little. Such a policy would plunge the state into heavy and growing public debt. It would also result in mounting of interest burden and raising heavy taxation on the tax-payers. Hence, redeemable debt seem to be reasonable and preferable to irredeemable debt on the ground of sound finance and convenient method of payment.

(x) **Short-term and long-term debt:** Short-term debts are the ones which may mature within a period of three to nine months. They are like treasury bills and advances from the central banks. Interest on such repayable amount is generally low. On the contrary, long-term debts are repayable in a long period, say roughly after 10 years or more. Usually such type of debts bear a higher rate of interest. Similarly, in between short-term debts and long-term debts, there is medium-term debts also.

DIFFERENCE BETWEEN PRIVATE AND PUBLIC DEBT

There are similarities and dissimilarities between private debt and public debt.

Similarities:

(a) *Diversion of funds:* Both private and public debt involve the diversion of funds from one use to another.

(b) *Requirement:* Government (public) as well as private individuals incur debt to meet their immediate and temporary requirements.

(c) *Interest:* Both have to pay interest on loans (debts) that they have taken.

(d) *Capacity:* The capacity of both to borrow depends more or less upon the capacity to repay loans.

Dissimilarities:

(a) *Resources:* The government has internal as well as external resources for taking loan (debt). But a private individual can borrow from external resources only.

(b) *Compulsion:* The government can force the people to lend to it, but no private individual can compel another individual to provide loan to him.

(c) ***Repudiation of loans:*** The government can repudiate loans taken from the public. On the contrary, the private individual cannot refuse repayment of loans to another private individual.

(d) ***Objects:*** The loans taken by the government are generally spent to promote the welfare of the people, including the creditors. On the contrary, private loans are not spent in the interests of the creditor.

(e) ***Redemption of the debt:*** For the payment of the debt to the public, the government takes fresh debt from the public. On the contrary, the individual has to repay the debt from his own earnings.

(f) ***Productive and unproductive:*** The government usually borrows money for productive purposes. On the contrary, an individual may borrow money for both productive and consumption purposes.

(g) ***Rate of interest:*** The rate of interest on public loans is generally lower than that on private loans on account of the greater credit of the state.

(h) ***Period of loan:*** The government can take loans from the public for a very long period, *e.g.* from 5 to 20 years. On the contrary, a private individual can take loans for a shorter period only, *e.g.* from a week to one year.

(i) ***Insolvency:*** Excessive debt may lead the individual borrower into a state of insolvency. The same may not be true for the government because: (i) it can force the people to pay additional taxes for the repayment of debt; (ii) it can resort to printing of fresh paper currency (money); (iii) it can raise fresh loans from the public, etc.

(j) ***Impact:*** Public debt produces a deep impact on production of wealth in the country. On the contrary, the private debt produces no such impact.

(k) ***Policy:*** The government may resort to borrowings as a matter of policy, even if it does not need funds such as loans taken to meet inflation. On the contrary, the individual may not borrow, when he does not need money.

(l) ***Realisation:*** Under public debt, the creditor can realise his money (loan) by selling the government securities in the open market before the due date. On the contrary, it is not possible in case of a private debt.

(m) ***Secrecy:*** Public debts are taken openly and the question of secrecy does not arise. On the contrary, private loans are usually kept secret.

(n) ***Burden of loan:*** In case of public debt, the burden falls on the public. On the contrary, in case of private loan the burden falls on the person who has taken the loan.

(o) ***Security:*** Public debt is given on the credit of the government simply on a piece of paper. On the contrary, private loan is given on the personal security of the person concerned.

(p) ***Credit:*** Since the government's credit is high, it is able to secure loans at cheaper interest rates than the private borrowers.

ECONOMIC EFFECTS OF PUBLIC DEBTS

The economic effects of public debt depend on the nature, form, conditions, duration, rate of interest, the mode of repayment, etc. of public debt. As a matter of fact all types of loans affect the different sections of the society. Its uniqueness lies in the fact that it has revenue effect as well as expenditure effect. Economic effects of public debt are classified under the following specific heads:

(i) **Effects on consumption:** When people purchase public loan (government securities), it is not always necessary that they do it out of past savings. Sometimes, people buy these public loans out of their present income which they could otherwise spend in purchasing some other commodity. In this way people refrain from consumption and buy public loan. Therefore, the consumption is affected in the same way as it is affected by taxes. In times of war or in period of emergency, substantial pressure may be applied to induce individuals to curtail consumption and to subscribe to government loans.

(ii) **Effects on investment production:** If people buy government bonds/securities by withdrawing money from their industrial concerns or by selling debentures and shares of industrial concerns or financial institutions and even commercial banks subscribe to government loans out of funds meant for investment or for accumulation of stocks, then the investment is adversely affected leading to adverse effects on production. However, if the government utilises this money in commercial public enterprises, the total investments available for production may not be adversely affected.

(iii) **Effect on distribution:** Public debts also affect distribution. If the public loans are subscribed by rich people only and the amount so realised is spent by the government on the economic welfare of poor people or low-income groups, the benefit will be a narrowing down of inequalities and a more equal distribution of income between people. But if the burden of public debt along with interest payment falls on the poorer classes also, the tendency of public debt would be to increase the inequalities of incomes.

(iv) **Level of economic activities or effects on economic activity and employment:** Public debt also affects the economic activities and employment situation in a country. Some economists hold the view that this should be the only object of public debts. The aim of public debt should be not only to get money for the government but also to affect the level of economic activities and employment situation. As a matter of fact, public debts reduce the quantity of money in the hands of the people and their purchasing power is automatically curtailed. This ultimately affects the country's price level and employment situation.

(v) **Effects on foreign loans:** Foreign loans can influence both consumption and investment favourably. Foreign loans are meant to finance the import of goods without paying for them immediately through exports. If foreign imports consist of consumer goods, they tend to reduce the inflationary pressure which may exist due to shortage of goods. On the other hand, if foreign imports consist of high priority goods and services such as machinery, industrial raw materials, technical know-how, etc. it will have favourable effect of speeding up industrialisation as well as rapid growth of the economy.

(vi) **Effects on liquidity:** People who buy government securities, possess highly negotiable and highly liquid form of assets. They can be used for any purpose at any time such as taking loan from the bank or for speculative nature.

(vii) **Effects on resource allocation and national income:** Unlike tax finance, there is little effect of public debt on resources allocation and national income. When investment level is reduced, it causes decrease in the relative output of capital goods against the total output in periods of full employment.

(viii) **Effects on money market:** Existence of public debt also affects the money market. For example, if demand of funds from the private sector is on a higher level, government will have to fix higher interest rates to attract purchases of its securities and vice versa. Thus, it has to conform to the general pattern of demand, supply and prices as any other borrower in the market.

(ix) **Effects on private sector:** Public expenditure increases the demand of goods because it increases the purchasing power of the people and puts more money in circulation. However, when the expenditure is financed through taxation, current consumption is reduced. On the contrary, when it is financed through public borrowings, idle savings are generally utilised and thus, the consumption is not reduced.

(x) **Effects on cost of production:** The cost of production depends upon the prices of raw materials and other factors used in production. If the government utilises the borrowed money to supply raw materials, etc. to producers at cheaper or on subsidised rates, on providing cheaper transport and on providing cheaper technical and non-technical training to the workers, the cost of production is reduced to a great extent.

(xi) **Effects on production:** As Mrs. Urshala Hicks points out, a large public debt cannot be regarded with complete indifference, since it needs a considerable proportion of national income to be devoted to the payment of service charges, such as interest, the principal and cost of debt management. There are expansionary effects of a large internal public debt even after the period of borrowing is over.

(xii) **Effects upon employment:** When the government borrows the savings of the people, it affects adversely the capital formation and the level of production of the country. If the government utilises money in unproductive channels, it does not affect production and unemployment at all. On the contrary, if the government borrows money for productive purposes, it creates additional employment opportunities in the country.

IMPORTANCE OF PUBLIC DEBT

In the words of Prof. J.K. Mehta, "Public debt is a comparatively modern phenomenon and has come into existence with the development of democratic form of government in the world. These days there is probably no nation in the world which does not incur any debt whether internal or external. The growth of public debt is the result of changing economic and political institutions." The importance of public debt may be studied under the following heads:

(i) **Increase in production:** Production can be increased through public debt. Public debt can be used in such plans which involve heavy risk and huge investment of capital and thereby the private investor is not ready to invest his capital.

(ii) **Establishment of basic industries:** Establishment of basic industries like iron and steel, coal and power, etc. requires heavy investment of capital for a comparatively longer period. It is possible through long-term public debt policy only.

(iii) **National calamities:** Every country has to face national calamities from time to time, such as, floods, famines, earthquakes, etc. Under these circumstances, relief work is to be carried out on a wide scale which requires huge expenditure. This expenditure can be met by taking internal and external debt only.

(iv) **Increase in state functions:** In recent years, state functions have increased considerably. Now to perform these functions, greater amount of money is required. It is possible through raising public debt only.

(v) **Meeting war finance:** These days war finance has become very costly. It is evident from rapidly increasing defence budget in every country of the world including India. For example, Indian defence budget in 1939-40 was Rs. 4 crores only which rose to Rs. 89,000 crores in 2006-07, which includes an allocation of 37,458 crore for capital expenditure.

(vi) **Financing development plan:** In an undeveloped country and developing country too, economy always suffers from acute shortage of funds. The governments of these countries cannot resort to heavy taxation because of low taxable capacity and also fear of stiff opposition from the public. Now to remove poverty and to break the vicious circle of poverty, the financing of development plans is of utmost importance.

(vii) **International co-operation:** Nowadays, foreign loans are taken both for economic development and for developing international cooperation. Foreign exchange crisis, which is most common in developing and underdeveloped countries, can also be met by taking foreign loans for a longer duration.

(viii) **Controlling inflation:** Inflation is a condition of raising prices. Hence, the government, by raising public debt, can withdraw a larger volume of purchasing power from the people, and thus, it may check prices from raising and thus inflation can be controlled.

LIMITATIONS OF PUBLIC DEBT

Following are the demerits or shortcomings of public debt:

(i) **Danger to country's freedom:** Sometimes the amount of foreign loan becomes so much so as to threat the very freedom of a country. For example, Egypt and Iran had to lose their freedom due to this factor. At present, Pakistan is facing danger to the freedom of the country on account of excessive foreign loan burden.

(ii) **Political slavery:** Excessive foreign loan is a sign of political slavery. Most of the Asian countries are facing political slavery on account of huge foreign loans taken by them from America and other Western countries.

(iii) **Exploitation of resources:** If certain conditions are imposed on a country when taking loan from a foreign country, as it is done by Western developed countries like America, it is not possible to use the resources in the interest of the country.

(iv) **Burden on figure generation:** Sometimes, huge internal and external loans are taken by the government without making any plan for their judicious use which burdens the future generation.

(v) **Capital formation adversely affected:** If any country borrows money both from internal and external sources, huge amount of money is to be paid every year by way of interest which affects adversely the rate of capital formation in the country.

(vi) **Fear of misuse:** In case the loans both internal and external are easily available to a country, there is always fear of misuse by the government.

(vii) **Danger of insolvency:** It is feared that if the government resorts to heavy borrowings both internal and external, there is always danger of insolvency of the government.

(viii) **Economy is weakened:** Foreign loan, in particular, weakens the economy of the country and makes it dependent on foreign countries for its economic development.

(ix) **Crisis:** Excessive and unwanted loans both internal and foreign cause political and non-political crisis in a country and create war-like situation in a country.

BURDEN OF PUBLIC DEBT

Public borrowings are to be paid along with interests. Government imposes new taxes upon the people to repay the loans and meet the annual interests on such loans. The sacrifice of the people in the form of tax payment is the burden of public debt. The burden of debt may be of two kinds:

(i) Direct Burden; and

(ii) Indirect Burden.

(i) Direct Burden

Direct money burden is measured by the amount of money payment involved and the amount of taxes to be raised to meet the revenue requirements. Direct money burden is equal to the amount of goods and services sacrificed by the people due to rise in taxes.

(a) ***Direct money burden***: In an effort to pay the loan and interest, the debtor nation is deprived of certain goods and services. Every year, a large amount of money has to be paid by the debtor country in lieu of interest on the loan. After maturity of period, the principal amount has to be paid in the form of foreign exchange. This is possible only through making exports without getting any payment from foreign countries. Such type of exports are called as 'unrequired exports'. This is the direct money burden of an external debt.

(b) ***Direct real burden:*** According to Prof. Dalton, "Direct real burden is measured by the loss of economic welfare which these payments involve to members of the debtor community." The debtor government imposes new taxes on the people to pay off the external debt. It is obvious that the burden of these taxes will fall more on the weaker sections of the society. Hence, it is the direct real burden of external public debt. Not only that, in an effort to pay the external debt, debtor community is deprived of certain benefits. In a real sense, it represents the direct real burden.

(ii) Indirect Burden

The taxes are increased to meet the repayments. Such an increase in taxation affects the level of production; it is called as indirect money burden of public debt.

Thus, to define the burden of debt precisely, we have to ask this question: "What difference does it make to us and to future generations that certain past government expenditures were financed by borrowing rather than by taxation, there would not be no debt and there could be no 'burden' of that debt."

Prof. Dalton defines internal debt as: "A loan is internal if subscribed by persons or institutions within the area controlled by the public authority which raises the loan." In the opinion of Prof. Dalton, the burden of internal public debt is not much significant as the payment of principal amount and its interest involves taxation. It is merely transfer of purchasing power from one person to another. In other words, money does not flow out of the national money market.

(a) ***Indirect money burden:*** The debtor nation often pays interest in terms of the goods and services to the creditor country. That means, the debtor has to export goods and services in a huge quantity. As a result of this, the price of these goods and services in the country shoot up and sometimes, it creates scarcity of these goods. This leads to the loss of economic welfare of the nation. From one angle, foreign debt is a blessing in disguise as it pushes the production to manifolds at home. But, it is a fallacious view as domestic resources are exhausted only for the sake of repayment of debt.

(b) *Indirect real burden:* To pay off the external debt, taxes are imposed on the people. If these taxes are heavy, it adversely affects the willingness and ability of the people to work and save. This has unfavourable effect on production. Further, the heavy debt payment also checks the public expenditure on productive channels which is otherwise socially desirable.

Estimation of the Burden of Public Borrowings or Public Debt

There is no single method of unanimity to measure or estimate the burden of public debt upon the different sections of the community. It is suggested that a proper combination of all the methods should be adopted to estimate the burden of debt.

The best suggested methods are the following:

(i) Estimation of burden of public debt by taking into account the ratio of public debt to national income and wealth.

(ii) Estimation of burden by calculating the percentage of expenditure on the debt services to total general expenditure.

In order to find out the burden of public debt more lucidly, a separate study of internal debt and external debt is appreciated.

BURDEN OF INTERNAL DEBT

When government borrows money from its own money market (*i.e.* the domestic money market) it is called internal debt. Hugh Dalton defines internal debt as: "A loan is internal if subscribed by persons or institutions within the area controlled by the public authority which raises the loan." The burden of internal public debt may not be significant because the payment of interest and principal amount taken as loan involves taxation, and this is nothing but the transfer of purchasing power from the tax-payers to the bond-holders, when the tax-payers and the bond-holders are the same people. In such a case there may not be any net burden upon the community. But if the tax-payers and bond-holders belong to different groups, there may occur changes in the distribution of income among the people belonging to different groups within the community. Thus, money does not flow out of the national money market.

An analysis of the purpose of internal debt becomes necessary before saying anything about the burden. In case the debt has been taken and utilised in productive fields, the debt can be paid out of the profit earned therefrom. In case a loan has been taken to finance unproductive heads of expenditure, like war, the repayment has to be made through taxation, because such debts are dead weight debts. In case of productive debts, there is no burden, whereas in the case of non-productive debt, there may not be any burden because the benefit awarded to the tax-payers in the form of interest on bonds will negate the burden of tax upon them.

Dalton maintains that "this may cause direct real burden upon the people belonging to sector other than the wealthier class, and the progressive taxation may not be so sharply progressive as to counter balance, among the wealthier classes, the income derived from public securities." This brings net burden of debt on the community.

The effect of the internal debt is to increase the income of the old, and passive people, and it cuts down the income of the enterprising young individuals. Such a transfer of income to the old and passive people harms both the distribution and production. It is one of the most dangerous drawbacks of the internal debts.

From the above discussion, it is clear that the debt should be taken for the productive purposes since non-productive debt is an unnecessary and harmful burden on the community. It is practically unrealistic to think that internal debts do not impose any burden.

BURDEN OF EXTERNAL DEBT

External debt is the sum of money borrowed from the individuals, associated with or belonging to the foreign countries, or in other words it is a loan taken from outside the domestic money market. This includes the loan acquired from foreign governments. To quote Findlay Shirras, "External debt means the transfer of wealth from the lending to the borrowing country when the loan is made, and a transfer in the reverse direction when interest is periodically paid or when the principal is repaid."

In one way the internal and external debts are similar to each other in the sense that both the debts are repaid out of the revenue received by the government through additional taxation. Dalton appropriately remarks that, "As a general rule, an internal debt is likely to involve an additional and indirect burden on a community, an external debt does the same."

However, the burden of external debt is far greater than the burden of internal debt, since in the case of internal debt the repayment of interest along with the loan are made within the country and it involves merely the transfer of wealth from one sector of the community to another and sometimes, the tax-payers and the bond-holders are the same people or in other words, the tax-payer and the interest receivers are the same. In the case of external debt, repayment is paid to those belonging to the foreign countries; the repayment of the foreign loan and interest earned thereon, reduces the net income of the country borrowing from external sources. In this aspect an external debt imposes more burden than the internal debt.

There is direct as well as indirect real burden of the external debt. Dalton writes, "During any given period the direct money burden is measured by the sum of money payments, for interest and repayment of principal, to external creditors, and the direct real burden by the loss of economic welfare, which these payments involve, to members of the debtor community."

In an effort to pay the loan and interest, the debtor community is deprived of certain goods and services. The extent to which the debtor country is deprived of the goods and services, shows the direct real burden on the community of external debt.

REDEMPTION OF PUBLIC DEBT

Redemption is a way of escape from the burden of a public debt. Redemption means repayment of loan. Redemption is quite distinct from repudiation. Repudiation means 'refusal to pay a debt' by the state. It is an extreme form of clearing public debts which constitutes a breach of contract when the government wilfully flouts its obligations. Repudiation would, thus, cause a loss of public confidence in the government. It would disable the state in floating further loans.

Advantages of Debt Redemption

Debt redemption has the following advantages:

(i) It saves the government from bankruptcy.

(ii) It exercises a sort of check on the recklessness on the part of the government.

(iii) It sustains public confidence, especially of potential lenders, in the government's creditworthiness.

(iv) It thus enables the government to float loans easily in future.

(v) It saves the cost of debt administration and the costs of collecting taxes to service the debt.

(vi) It helps in sustaining a healthy climate for the private sector investments; for when the government loans are repaid, resources may, in turn, be transferred to the private sector's productive efforts.

(vii) It can also serve as a deflationary measure. For, when taxation is raised to meet debt servicing, aggregate consumption expenditure might be curbed to some extent. Moreover, the money received by debt holders in repayment of their debts may generally be reinvested by them rather than being spent on consumption.

(viii) Further, repayment of debt improves public credit and makes possible the lowering of the rate of interest on public loans, so that the burden of debt is lightened, which means reduced taxation.

(ix) It saves posterity from shouldering the burden of debts when it is redeemed at an early stage.

A modern government, thus, always makes increasing efforts to reduce the burden of debt through redemption of loans.

METHODS OF DEBT REDEMPTION

The chief methods usually adopted for the retirement of redemption of public debts are:

(i) Refunding

Refunding of debt implies the issue of new bonds and securities by the government in order to repay the matured loans. In the refunding process, usually short-term securities are replaced by long-term securities. Under this method, the money burden of debt is not relinquished but is accumulated owing to the postponement of debt redemption.

(ii) Funding

Funding is the conversion of a short-term debt into long-term debt. Another principle of debt management is that it should help to convert short-term borrowings into long-term borrowings. But at the same time, it must take proper precaution that economic stability is not disturbed at all. Simultaneously, this operation must not be undertaken to raise the undue rate of interest in the long-run which adversely affects the rate and volume of private investment.

(iii) Conversion

Conversion of public debt implies changing the existing loans, before maturity, into new loans at an advantage in servicing charges. In fact, the process of conversion consists generally of converting or altering a public debt from a higher to a lower rate of interest. The government might have borrowed at a time when the rate of interest was high. Now, when the rate of interest falls, it may convert the old loans into new ones at a lower rate in order to minimise the burden. Thus, the obvious advantage of such conversion is that it reduces the burden of interest on the tax-payers. Furthermore, lower interest rates on public loans would mean a less unequal distribution of income.

The success of conversion, however, depends upon the following factors:

(a) The creditworthiness of the government;

(b) The maintenance of adequate stock of securities; and

(c) The efficiency in managing the public debt.

(iv) Surplus Budgets

Quite often, surplus budgets (*i.e.* by spending less than the public revenue obtained) may be utilised for clearing off public debts. But, in recent years, due to ever-increasing public expenditures, surplus budget is a rare phenomenon. Moreover, heavy taxes have to be imposed for realising a surplus budget, which may have dire consequences. Or, when public expenditure is reduced for creating a surplus budget, a deflationary bias may develop in the economy.

(v) Sinking Fund

This method was first established by Hugh Walpole in England. Soon the practice was adopted by different countries. This method is the most systematic and best method of repaying public debt. It is used by almost all the governments in the world. In this system, the government establishes a separate fund known as 'sinking fund'. A fixed amount of money is credited by the government to this fund. So, by the time the debt matures, the fund accumulates enough amount to pay off not only the principal amount of the debt but also the interest on the loan as well.

Sinking fund is of two types as: (a) certain sinking fund, and (b) uncertain sinking fund. A 'certain sinking fund' is one in which the government credits a fixed sum of money annually. 'Uncertain sinking fund', on the other hand, is one in which the amount is credited, when the government secures a surplus in the budget. There is one danger in this method, *i.e.* a government which is in need of money, may not have the patience to wait till the end of the period of maturity, but may utilise the fund for purposes other than the one for which originally the sinking fund was instituted.

In modern times, sinking funds are not accumulated. But some funds are kept every year for repayment of some part of the debt in the same year. The amount is not put in a fund allowed to be accumulated but is used every year either to pay off the bonds which are maturing or to buy off bonds from the market. In short, sinking fund is a slow method of debt redemption. Thus, Dalton prefers capital levy. He also prefers that sinking fund should be made from current revenue of the government and not out of loans.

(vi) Terminable Annuities

This method of debt redemption is similar to that of the sinking fund. Under this method, the fiscal authorities clear off a part of the public debt every year by issuing terminable annuities to the bondholders which mature annually. Thus, it is the method of redeeming debts in instalments. By this method, the burden of debts goes on diminishing annually and by the time of maturity, it is fully paid off.

(vii) Additional Taxation

The simple measure of debt redemption is to impose new taxes and get the required revenue to repay the loan principal as well as the interest.

This method causes redistribution of income by transferring the resources from tax-payers to the hands of bond-holders. It may also impose a burden on the future generation if new taxes are levied to repay the long-term debts.

(viii) Capital Levy

This method has been the most controversial method of debt repayment. Capital levy provides for imposing 'all at once' tax on all the capital value possessions of the people. All capital goods are taxed above the capital possessions of minimum limit of value. This method has been suggested by economists like Ricardo, Pigou to levy the capital to pay heavy debts taken during the time of war and other emergencies. According to Prof. Ricardo, "A country which has involved itself in the difficulties attending this artificial system would act wisely by ransoming itself from them at the sacrifice of any portion of its property which might be necessary to redeem the debt."

(ix) Surplus Balance of Payments

The redemption of external debt, however, is possible only through an accumulation of foreign exchange reserves. This necessitates creation of a favourable balance of payments by the debtor country by augmenting its exports and curbing its imports, thereby improving the position of its trade balance. Thus, the debtor country has to concentrate on the expansion of its export sector industries. Further, loans raised must be productively utilised, so that they may become self-liquidating, posing no real burden on the country's economy.

In underdeveloped countries like India, where external debt has increased tremendously, it is necessary that its burden is reduced by changing the terms of repayment or by rescheduling the debts.

In fact, the best redemption policy is that a part of the public debt, internal as well as external, is redeemed every year, so that there is no mounting of the total real burden of debt upon the present generation or on the posterity.

BANKRUPT THROUGH PUBLIC DEBT

It is sometimes claimed that with mounting public expenditure, the country would become bankrupt. Before discussing this issue, we should know the meaning of bankruptcy. Bankruptcy means 'inability to repay the money borrowed from the lender'. Thus, when a person fails to repay the money borrowed, he is declared bankrupt. So far as the country is concerned, the public debts are mainly of two types:

(i) Internal Public Debt; and

(ii) External Public Debt.

(i) **Internal public debt and bankruptcy:** Internal public debt means public debt floated within the country. The country can repay its internal public debt by raising money in any of the following ways:

(a) Raising money by issue of fresh internal public debt;

(b) Raising money by imposing additional taxation;

(c) Raising money by issue of fresh currency;

(d) By imposing a heavy capital levy and paying off the public debt at one stroke;

(e) By repudiation of public debt; and

(f) Finally, postponement of payment of public debt and paying the interest thereon. Thus, it is evident that a country cannot be declared bankrupt because of its internal public debt.

(ii) **External public debt and bankruptcy:** External public debt is one which is taken from a foreign country, foreign national and international institutions. The circumstances may arise when a country may not be able to repay its external public debt, such as external public debts taken by underdeveloped and developing countries including India. The amount of foreign public debt including interest is increasing rapidly, whereas the export surplus, if any, is not sufficient to repay them. In most of the cases of undeveloped and developing countries, imports exceed exports. The alternatives available before a debtor country are:

(a) To seek postponement of the foreign public debt; or

(b) To float new foreign public debts in order to repay the old public debts.

Only in extreme cases, it may repudiate foreign public debts. This last measure is an extreme measure and may affect the reputation of the debtor country adversely in the international capital markets and will again not be able to raise external public debts in the future. That is why so far, none of the debtor countries has resorted to this last measure as yet. However, it is evident that in case of external public debt also, a country cannot be declared insolvent.

DEBT BURDEN AND FUTURE GENERATION

There is hot legitimate debate on the question of public debt in economic literature whether the public borrowing shifts the burden on the shoulders of the future generation (leads to posterity). In this regard, it is discussed that the repayment of debt through taxes will compel the future investment and productive activities. In this manner, the real burden of public debt is borne by the future generation. On the other side, the infliction of sacrifice upon present generation is totally unjust and undesirable.

Adam Smith felt that once the sovereign started to borrow, his political power was increased because he was no longer dependent on tax exactions from his fellow beings. He aptly remarked, "The ability to engage in loan finance makes for irresponsibility in sovereign." David Hume opposed public debt saying, "Nations, once they began to borrow, would be able to resist until they reached the point of bankruptcy."

In this context, Prof. Dalton said, "The burden of a public debt is not something which can be thrown backward and forward through time and made to fall at will, wholly on one generation or wholly on another." However, subsequent thinkers like Mill, Malthus, Sidgwick, Cairnes and others had some liberal views about the impact of public debt. In the words of Prof. Malthus, "The material debt is not the evil which it is generally supposed to be. Those who live on the interest from the national debt, like statesman, soldiers and sailors contribute powerfully to distribution and demand... the debt, once created, is not a great evil."

MODERN VIEWS ON BURDEN OF PUBLIC DEBT

Modern economists including J.M. Keynes, Harris, Hansen, Buchanan, Bowen, Davis, Musgrave, Kopt, Modigliani and others have challenged the version of classical economists and hold opinion on the subject of burden of public debt. They submit that there is no shift of the basic burden to the future generation (posterity) because the same posterity which pays the additional taxes will be benefited from the repayment of the debt. The Great World Depression of thirties gave way to the development of the new theory of public debt. Moreover, the classical theory of public debt also assumed full employment and unproductiveness of public expenditure as the basic pillars. Modern theory, on the other hand, is based on the assumption that public expenditure is never wasteful but it can be productive and an essential means of increasing employment in the economy. Prof. Harris has rightly stated, "Once the economists, in a mere realistic mood, they allowed for unemployment, assumed elasticity in monetary supplies and agreed that government expenditures could be productive and need not necessarily be wasteful."

Prof. James Buchanan in his book *Public Principles of Public Debt* holds that a burden implies a compulsory sacrifice. In his opinion, the present generation of bond-holders subscribes to the public debt voluntarily which results no burden upon them. However, it is a burden on the future generations which will have to pay taxes compulsorily for its retirement and interest payments. He, thus, argues in favour of individual attitude which for him, is a burden while subscribing to debt is not a burden. It must be remembered here that such an approach does not hold good for an economy because the debt burden consists in terms of the loss of resources either on the basis of voluntary or compulsory. In short, the burden of public debt can be shifted to the future posterity.

Recently, some eminent economists have openly referred to the no burden thesis and tried to establish the fact that public debt creation poses a burden and also be shifted to future generations. This type of reasoning has also been severely attacked. They pointed out their arguments in favour of no burden thesis. In this regard, Lerner held the opinion that "A statement that public debt does not matter, must be understood in the same sense as when a man, who finds the rumour has converted a twisted ankle into a broken neck, tells his friends that he is perfectly alright."

PUBLIC DEBT MANAGEMENT

The term 'debt management' refers to the debt policy designed to achieve certain objectives and actual implementation of this policy. The public debt management is concerned with the decisions regarding the forms of public debt issued, terms on which new bonds are sold, maturing debts are redeemed or refunded, the proportion in which different forms of public debt should be issued, the pattern of maturities of the debt, its ownership, etc. In short, it is concerned with the determination of the structural characteristics of the public debt. Hence, the management of public debt is concerned with refunding, floating or retirement of public debt, etc. The management of public debt is very significant because there can be important economic effects of the changes in the size of the public debt on the operation of an economy. These changes must be faster or offset monetary and fiscal policies.

Public debt management refers to the various authoritative decisions, policy formations and their implementation concerned with the receipt, assessment and utilisation of public debt collected from external as well internal sources. Public debt management is to manage the collection and repayment of public debt with the following:

(i) The form of issue of public securities.

(ii) The form in which the public debt is refunded.

(iii) The proportion of different types of debt to be issued.

(iv) The pattern in which the public bonds will be considered mature.

(v) The decision relating to the ownership of the bonds.

It means that public debt management is concerned with the manner of floating, refunding and investment of public debt.

NEED OF PUBLIC DEBT MANAGEMENT

There is a no denying the fact that the management of public debt is highly essential for the proper utilisation and augmentation of its effects on various economic activities in the country. Besides several factors, public debt management is necessary due to following reasons:

(i) There is sizeable effect of the increase or decrease of public debt on the working of the economy.

(ii) The changes which are brought due to the utilisation of public borrowings, may foster or hamper the economic development.

(iii) Public debt policy plays a significant role in the formation of economic policy of the country.

(iv) Public debt management is necessary to know the exact amount of requirements, outstanding amount of debt, and other related things, the knowledge which is necessary to implement planning policies in the economy.

OBJECTIVES OF PUBLIC DEBT MANAGEMENT

Public debt management is chalked out to fulfil the following aims:

(i) Neither the mode of borrowing from the public nor repayment should have any adverse effect on the economic condition of the country.

(ii) The methods adopted for collecting and repaying should help in building the economy.

(iii) Public debt should help in fighting inflationary and deflationary tendencies in the economy and must ensure smooth flow of money.

(iv) Public debt should help in creating more job opportunities, building up of basic industries and breaking up the vicious circle of poverty.

PRINCIPLES OF PUBLIC DEBT MANAGEMENT

(i) Satisfaction of the Objects of Investors

Public debt should be managed in such a way that the objectives for which the investors invest money is fulfilled. Such needs of the investors are concerned with the types of the securities issued by the government and terms on which such securities are issued.

Without fulfilling the aspirations of the investors, the government may find it difficult to issue securities. If the government wants to issue long-term securities, it must offer attractive terms and conditions so that the investors may become ready to invest money in such securities. In such cases government may offer a scheme to convert the securities into cash after a period of time. It will safeguard the investors, interests against any damage or loss.

(ii) Minimum Interest Cost of Servicing Public Debts

It is argued that the interest cost of servicing public debts should be kept at the lowest possible level. The government has to repay the loan along with the interests and thus the tax-payers have to bear the burden of debt, so higher interest cost of servicing public debts would mean more taxation and this would affect the economic condition more adversely.

If the interest cost is minimum, government will impose smaller amount of tax to raise the revenue requirement for the repayment of such debts. It will have mild effects on the incentives to the willingness to work and save.

It is suggested that in order to keep the low rate of interest, the bank rate policy of the Central Bank of the country should be employed.

(iii) Funding of Short-term Borrowings into Long-term Borrowings

Public debt should be managed in such a way that to the maximum possible extent, short-term borrowings are concerted into long-term borrowings. The most fantastic example of this type of debt is the 'British controls', which never reaches its time of maturity.

However, it should be taken care of that this type of funding does not affect the economic stability of the country.

(iv) Public Debt Policy must be in Co-ordination with Fiscal and Monetary Policy

For the implementation of the developmental plans, the coordination of the public debt policy with the fiscal and monetary policy is highly essential. If the government advises the Central Bank to adopt low bank rate policy in order to reduce the cost of serving the public loans, it may bring inflation in the economy because money then becomes easily available and its circulation speeds up in the economy. This condition can only be avoided if the public debt policy and monetary policy are properly coordinated with each other.

(v) Proper Adjustment of Maturity

Periods of maturity should be so kept as it may be able to bring high degree of liquidity in the markets. Because in such a situation, it will be quite difficult to control inflation.

PUBLIC DEBT IN INDIA

Public debt in India can be studied under the following heads:

1. Public Debt before Independence

In the early British days in this country, government borrowings were mainly for war purposes. India was saddled with the expenses of all the foreign wars and expeditions in Afghanistan, Burma, China, Persia, Abyssinia, and Egypt. During the First World War, India made a gift of pounds 100 million to the British Government which added to the unproductive debt of this country.

(i) **Unproductive public debt:** Public debt in India originated with the establishment of East India Company which borrowed mostly for waging wars with the French and Dutch who were their trade rivals. The company also fought with the native rulers, and after defeating them began to acquire their territory. When they first became the Masters of Bengal in 1765, they were already in debt. In 1860, when the East India Company rule came to an end, the total public debt amounted to Rs. 10 crores. Till now the public debt was unproductive as it was due to wars and home charges.

(ii) **Productive public debt:** From the year 1860, the government of India started spending money on productive purposes such as railway construction, irrigation works, etc. By the end of 19th century, the total public debt stood at Rs. 231 crores. During the World War II, the total internal debt of the government of India increased from Rs. 736 crores in 1939 to Rs. 1,946 cores in 1946, an increase of Rs. 1,210 crores. This increase in the internal debt was largely on account of war expenditure.

(iii) **Composition of public debt before independence:** The total public debt of India before independence was either in rupees known as 'Rupee Debt' or in Sterling Pounds known as 'Sterling Loan'. The Sterling Loan was more important than the Rupee Loan till the end of First World War. The reason for this was that the Indian capital was shy at that time and people liked to hoard money rather than to invest in government loans. Further, there was no organised money market in the country and even banks were not much advanced. Therefore, the government of India used to float loans in England where the response of the public was better.

2. Public Debt Since Independence

Public debt has increased in the post-independence period largely because of the rising needs of planned economic development. Foreign assistance has also to be resorted to because of foreign exchange requirement of the Five-Year Plans. Foreign assistance has been available to India in various forms but a large part of it has been in the form of interest bearing loans. In December 1947, an agreement was concluded between India and Pakistan. According to it, India assumed the whole public debt of undivided India. Pakistan was allowed only 300 crores which was to be paid by it in 50 instalments starting from 1952.

NEW CLASSIFICATION OF PUBLIC DEBT OF GOVERNMENT OF INDIA

The public debt of the government of India has now been classified into the following three major groups:

(i) **Internal debt:** Internal debt comprises market borrowings or market loans raised in the open market through sale of securities or otherwise. These loans were formerly known as funded debt or permanent debt. They also include compensation and other bonds, 15 years annuity certificate. Besides, it also includes borrowing of temporary nature. Such borrowing includes treasury bills issued by government of India, state governments, commercial banks, etc.

Table 10.1: Public Debts of Government of India

(Rs. in Crores)

Year	Internal Debt	External Debt	Other Liabilities
1950-51	2,022.00	32.00	811.07
2001-02	9,13,061.12	71,545.79	3,81,801.51
2002-03	10,20,689.79	59,612.06	4,78,900.51
2003-04	11,41,705.58	46,124.49	5,48,848.33
2004-05	12,75,971.30	60,877.45	6,57,572.82
2005-06	13,55,943.00	68,391.77	7,71,051.56
2006-07	15,22,030.70	76,715.69	8,74,815.83

(ii) **External debt:** External debt comprises loans taken by the government of India against the non-negotiable, non-interest bearing securities insured to international financial institutions, such as, IMF, IBRD, IDA, International Fund for Agricultural Development, Asian Development Bank, etc. Besides, the government of India has also raised loans from friendly countries outside India.

(iii) **Other outstanding liabilities:** Other outstanding liabilities comprise loans taken against the various small savings schemes, public provident fund, state provident fund contribution and non-government provident fund contributions, income-tax annuity deposit schemes, reserve funds of central government departments (such as railways, post and telegraph, etc.) and certain other deposits like deposits of income tax, super tax, etc. All these are outstanding liabilities which the government of India is liable to repay on maturity. They were formerly known as unfunded debt.

The table given above indicates the rising trend of all the above loans as taken by the government of India. The rising trend is mainly due to loans taken by the government of India for financing the development plans during Five-year Plans.

STUDY-QUESTIONS

1. What is public debt? Why is public debt incurred? What are the objectives and aims of public debts?
2. What are the different types of public debts? Distinguish between productive and unproductive debt, and redeemable and irredeemable debts.
3. Differentiate between public and private debts.
4. Make a distinction between internal and external debt. External debt is more burdensome than the internal debt— Why?
5. Describe the sources of public borrowings.
6. What are the floatations of public debts?

7. Explain the methods of raising public debts.
8. Explain the redemption of public debt. Also describe the advantages and methods of public debt.
9. Can a country become bankrupt through public debt?
10. Explain the economic effects of public debts.
11. What is the burden of public debt? Discuss the burden of internal as well as external debt.
12. Explain the importance or advantages and disadvantages of public debt.
13. What are the various limitations of public debts?
14. Which is better—tax or the public borrowings?
15. Distinguish between loans and taxes.
16. Discuss the comparative merits and demerits of loans and taxes in financing development plans of an economy.
17. Discuss the role of public debt in underdeveloped and developing countries.
18. What is public debt management? What are the principles underlying public debt management?
19. Discuss the object of public debt management? What principles do you suggest for a proper management?
20. Explain the economic effects of public borrowing.

Fiscal Policy

11

INTRODUCTION

The deliberate use of fiscal policy as a possible means to achieve and maintain full employment and price stability in the economy is a characteristic feature of the past four decades. The significance of fiscal policy as an instrument of economic control was first emphasised, in the mid-nineteen thirties, by Keynes in the *General Theory of Employment, Interest and Money*. According to Mrs. Urshala Hicks, "Fiscal policy is concerned with the manner in which all the different elements of public finance, while still primarily concerned with carrying out their own duties (as the first duty of a tax is to raise revenue), may collectively be geared to forward the aims of economic policy."

In the views of American Economic Association, "Fiscal policy should mean the policy which concerns itself with aggregate effects of government expenditure and taxation on income, production and employment." Otto Eckstein also defines fiscal policy as "Changes in taxes and expenditure which aim at short run goals of full employment, price level and stability."

Harvey and Johnson M. defines fiscal policy as: "Changes in government expenditure and taxation designed to influence the pattern and level of activity."

Prof. Gardener Ackley is of the opinion that, "Fiscal policy involves alterations in government expenditures for goods and services of the level of tax rates." Unlike monetary policy, these measures involve direct government entrance into the market for goods and services (in case of expenditure) and a direct impact on private demand (in the case of taxes).

According to G.K. Shaw, "We define fiscal policy to include any design to change the price level, composition or timing of government expenditure or to vary the burden, structure of frequency of the tax payment."

UN Report on Taxes and Fiscal Policy says, "Fiscal policy is assigned the central task of wrestling with the pitifully low output of underdeveloped countries, sufficient savings to finance economic development programmes and to set the stage for more vigorous public investment activity."

Aurther Smith defines fiscal policy as, "A policy under which the government uses its expenditure and revenue programme to produce desirable effects and avoid undesirable effects on the national income, production and employment." This definition tells about the objectives and tools of fiscal policy.

Keynes used the term fiscal policy when referring to the influence of taxation on savings and of government investment expenditure financed by loans from the public. He looked at fiscal policy as one form of state action as a balancing factor. Thus, for the purpose of interpretation of Keynes' thought we can define fiscal policy "as a policy that uses public finance as a balancing factor in the development of the economy." Government activities as regards spending, taxing, borrowing, deficit financing and budgeting are known as fiscal activities and the purposeful manipulation of these activities to attain desired objectives, say, economic stability, rapid economic growth and full employment—is known as fiscal policy. Fiscal policy is fundamentally concerned with the aggregate effects of public expenditure and taxation on income, output and employment.

OBJECTIVES OF FISCAL POLICY

Different economists have given different objectives of fiscal policy. According to Musgrave, "The objective of fiscal policy is higher employment, stability in prices, balance in trade and increase in economic development." The main objectives of fiscal policy are as follows:

(i) The first and the foremost objective of fiscal policy is to eliminate cyclical fluctuations in economic activity and to maintain it at a stable level. The up-and-down swings in business are checked by compensatory fiscal action to counteract fluctuations. Strict steps are taken to control both inflation and deflation, and efforts are made to make the budget more or less balanced over the period of the cycle.

(ii) Another objective of fiscal policy is to break the vicious circle of poverty and to use in a rapid development of both agriculture and industry.

(iii) To restrict monopolies and check the concentration of economic power in a few hands only.

(iv) Fiscal policy is considered as an effective instrument for reducing unemployment and securing full employment. Full employment occurs where there is job available for everyone who is fit to work and wants a job at the prevailing wage rates.

(v) To accelerate the rates of saving, investment and capital formation.

(vi) To bring stability in prices.

(vii) The second important objective of fiscal policy is to maintain a continuous upward trend in economic activity. Total outlay is increased in depression but is not allowed to decrease correspondingly in boom. Stability continues to be an important aim of fiscal policy.

(viii) To establish balance in foreign trade.

(ix) To have rapid economic development of the country.

(x) In case of developed countries, the main objective of fiscal policy is to have long-term stability.

(xi) In case of underdeveloped and developing countries, the main objectives of fiscal policy are:

(a) Promoting the growth of savings and investments; and

(b) Reducing income and wealth inequalities.

FEATURES OF FISCAL POLICY

The main features of fiscal policy are as follows:

(i) **Public debt:** Public debt can also be employed by the government as an instrument to fight depression and unemployment. The deficits in government's budgets shall have to be met partly, if not wholly, through public borrowings. But while adopting the fiscal policy of public borrowing (public debt), the government shall have to keep the following two considerations in mind. Firstly, in order to keep the burden of public debt low, the government should aim at a policy of low interest rates during depression. Secondly, the government should try, as far as possible to borrow from those sections of the community with whom the funds are lying idle. The idea is to utilise those idle funds through borrowing for productive purposes.

(ii) **Taxation policy:** In order to fight depression and unemployment, taxation policy of the government, according to Keynesians, should be so designed as to stimulate both consumption and investment simultaneously. The only way to do it successfully is to reduce the general burden of taxation on the community. The commodity taxes should be cut down to the minimum so as to stimulate consumption on the part of the public. Further, to promote increased investments, it may also be essential to cut down business and corporate taxes.

(iii) **Budgetary policy:** The old classical economists advocated a policy of balanced and small budgets. However, this policy will not help to tide over depression and unemployment according to Prof. J.M. Keynes. The need at such a time is to increase the flow of income-stream into the economy and it could be made possible, according to Prof. J.M. Keynes, only through deficit budgeting. Hence, it is essential that the government should incur large deficits in the budget and then meet these deficits either by borrowing from the banks, etc.

or through printing fresh currency notes. It will inject fresh purchasing power in the economy, helping it to fight depression and employment effectively.

(iv) **Public expenditure:** An increase in public expenditure can also be employed by the government as an instrument to fight against depression and unemployment. Increase in pubic expenditure at such a time may take the following two forms:

(a) Pump Priming, and

(b) Compensatory Spending.

Pump Priming refers to that public expenditure which helps initiate and revive economic activity in an economy where stagnation reigns supreme consequent upon depression. The object is to increase private investment through an injection of purchasing power in the form of an increase in public expenditure.

On the other hand, Compensatory Spending refers to the government expenditure which is undertaken with a view to compensating the decline in private investment. Usually private investment suddenly declines at the time of depression. Under these circumstances, there is no alternative before the government except to resort to public investment. However, public investment should be undertaken on a large scale so as to have an effective impact on the employment situation.

FISCAL POLICY AND INFLATION

Fiscal policy is the key-instrument in the hands of the government to achieve all-round stability and prosperity. It is a tool through which the economic resources could be allocated in the best possible way.

Inflation is a result of the aggregate demand for goods and services being in excess of the aggregate supply. Therefore, the obvious fiscal remedy for it is to reduce total demand. This, as we have seen, is possible by the government budgeting for a surplus. Inflation causes continuous fluctuations by creating disequilibrium in the economy. It becomes highly essential to check inflation and the fast depletion and misuse of vital economic resources. When inflation of the type which occurs due to excessive public spending in war or for the economic development of an underdeveloped country has to be dealt with, a surplus budget is not a feasible proposition. The huge government expenditure during war-time cannot be reduced. Nor can the government in an underdeveloped country scale down its expenditure which it incurs as a part of a long-term plan for economic development. Large government expenditure is inevitable in such conditions and is the primary cause of inflation. Inflation as a long-term evil, therefore, cannot be effectively attacked from the expenditure side and most of the fiscal action taken by the authorities is confined to the revenue side alone.

Furthermore, inflation is caused by one more of two groups of factors. It is either due to an increase in demand or a result of changes in costs. The changes in costs often stem from rises in wages. A rise in prices gives rise to demand for higher wages on the part of organised labour, and if these demands are met, the rise in wages causes costs and prices to rise further. This kind of wage-induced inflation cannot be controlled by reducing demand alone by increasing taxation. In fact, indirect taxation raises prices and costs of living and results in demands for higher wages, thus worsening the inflationary situation. Subsidies on consumption to bring down the prices of essential commodities help in some measure to provide a solution to the problem in this case.

Moreover, when increased taxation adversely affects production, the inflationary pressure is increased as is likely to happen in an underdeveloped country. Private investment in such countries must increase in order to increase the national income in the long-run. Thus, how far is an increase in taxation and an appropriate anti-inflationary device is often difficult to decide.

In the following four ways fiscal policy helps in fighting against inflation and bring home the economic stability:

(i) Public Borrowing;

(ii) Government Spending;

(iii) Taxes; and

(iv) Private Savings.

(i) Public Borrowing

When the government is unable to meet the expenditure, through the revenue received, it tries to meet it through public borrowings. This technique can be adopted to check extra purchasing power and unwarranted possession of money by the people. So far as the public borrowing reduces the purchasing power of the people, it may be called as an anti-inflationary measure. A high degree of programme for public borrowings should be introduced by the government if it wants to check the inflationary process.

This may be done in many ways, as by providing higher rates of interest on savings; introducing the compulsory savings scheme, 'deferred plan' helps in making the consumers to purchase some saving certificates, and redeem it when the economy is passing through depression phase.

(ii) Government Spending

It is suggested that the spending by the government on different heads should be curtailed to the extent that it may be able to contract the increased spending of the private sector. This reduction in spending should go parallel to the raising of taxes so that it might be able to reduce the disposable income of the people. If the government reduces its spending, the pressure on the aggregate demand is reduced to that extent and this helps in maintaining economic stability.

Now it is for the government to see, the amount which it can reduce and the heads of expenditure, whose allocation can be curtailed. Various non-economic factors like, political situation, wars and international conditions affect the policy of the government. In the immediate post-war period, the expenditure of the government is most likely to increase due to various reasons like the reconstruction of destructed houses, farms, factories, etc.

(iii) Taxes

Inflation occurs at the point of full employment or a level very close to it. It becomes highly essential to curtail the extra-purchasing power of the people at this stage. It is essential also because, there are no 'left out' or idle resources which could be absorbed by extra investment outlays. Government can check the investment of speculative nature and also the extra-consumption. For this, old taxes should be widened and new taxes should be imposed in order to check the inflationary trend prevailing in the economy. Government should chalk out the 'strategic points', at which the aggregate demand should be checked. Taxes should be imposed at these 'strategic points' for controlling the increasing aggregate demand. The burden of tax should fall on those, who possess a comparatively higher marginal propensity to consume. So, the government should impose high taxes on necessities and must raise sales tax and should adopt regressive personal income taxes.

Inflation can be controlled if the fiscal policy is implemented efficiently. It is well said that, "fiscal, monetary and debt policies are appropriate means for attacking the problem of instability in a fine society." The problem of instability is essentially a problem of broad forces affecting the overall magnitude of the economy. The problem increases when millions of workers are simultaneously unemployed, or when there is a general although probably uneven, rise of most prices. The advantage of fiscal, monetary, and debt policies is that they allow the government to influence the overall forces—especially the level of aggregate demand—that determine the stability of the economy without necessarily involving the government in detail control of the particulars of the economy. These overall measures will, of course, affect different individuals and business differently. But the differences are determined by the market process, not by the government decisions.

(iv) Private Saving

Private savings have a strong disinflationary effect on the economy, and an increase in these is an important measure for controlling inflation. Government policy, therefore, must include devices for increasing savings. The strongest inducement to people to save more is a rise in the rate of interest. But this conflicts with the government policy of cheap money. Therefore, a savings drive in times of large government spending often comprises only publicity devices and provision of facilities in respect of contribution and withdrawal of money and receipt of interest without any appreciable rise in the interest rates.

Furthermore, private voluntary saving is discouraged by high taxation, which is paid partly out of consumption and partly from savings. When tax levies are high, people's desire for cutting their expenditure on consumption is not very strong. In fact, a certain minimum level of consumption is thought to be necessary by every society, and when taxation threatens to lower standards below that level, saving suffers. Inflationary forces, therefore, cannot be controlled in this way.

FISCAL POLICY AND FULL EMPLOYMENT

The term 'full employment' is purely a formal concept. It does not imply that in the country every individual, who is fit and free to work, is employed productively on every day of his working life. On the contrary, full employment may be quite consistent with frictional, seasonal, structural and technological unemployment. Even though a society is fully employed, it may not be wholly free from frictional, seasonal, structural and technological unemployment.

Fiscal policy is considered as an effective instrument for securing full employment. Prof. J.M. Keynes, in his book *Theory of Employment* gave an important place to fiscal policy as a weapon to fight deflation and mass unemployment. Economists have defined a situation of full employment as one where all people who are fit and wish to work at the existing wage rate in the labour market, will in fact, be able to find a job. In other words, full employment occurs where there is job available for everyone who is fit and wants a job at the prevailing wage rates.

FISCAL POLICY AND ECONOMIC GROWTH

In a long period, the aims of economic policy are both—elimination of cyclical fluctuations and maintenance of a high rate of growth. The rise in the long-run rate of growth depends partly on the long period aggregate demand not falling short of the long period supply at full capacity of manpower and capital equipment and partly on the rise in full capacity output itself. So far as the first factor is concerned, the appropriate fiscal policy is the same as that for controlling a cycle. But for raising full capacity output, a continuous increase in total outlay is required. This means an increasing deficit—financed expenditure must be an essential element in the long period fiscal policy of the government.

The problem of long-run growth needs further elaboration. Economic growth has a number of dimensions. It involves increase in physical capacity, resources in technical skill, and volume of employment. An increase in one need not necessarily be accompanied by increases in others, and full employment of one does not essentially mean full employment of others. For example, capacity in capital equipment may be more or less than what could provide full employment to the labour force, *i.e.* labour and equipment have different points of full employment. Usually, the point of full employment of physical capacity is higher in developed countries but lower in underdeveloped ones. In an economically developed country, full employment of labour is achieved leaving unutilised capacity while in an undeveloped country, an increase in the employment of labour beyond a point is strictly dependent on new capital formation. Thus, fiscal policy, though basically the same, is bound to differ in details in different conditions. In an advanced country, fiscal policy is likely to aim at increasing the volume of employment of labour. In an underdeveloped country, fiscal measures will be more for increasing capital formation in both the public and private sectors.

Deficit spending for long period expansion is different in character to that done as an anti-slump measure. The question of timing is not important in this case, for deficits of some years are not covered by surpluses of other years. An increasing public debt need not be a problem. Deficits of this type can be financed by credit creation. Even when debts are incurred, the interest charges on growing debts can be financed by credit creation. When the volume of public debt becomes too large, the servicing of the debt may require increased taxation. But increased taxation will not be to burdensome in a growing economy. The growing taxation need not be restrictive in its effects, provided the composition of the tax structure is so altered as to let the incidence of a major part of it fall on higher income groups while most of the expenditure benefits the poorer classes. When fiscal policy causes a redistribution of the national income from the richer to the poorer classes, consumption is stimulated and the multiplier is raised. People in the lower income groups have a higher propensity to consume and since they receive their income at short intervals (usually daily or weekly), a rise in their incomes raises the income-velocity of money.

For raising the level of economic activity over the long period, the composition of public expenditure is very important. It could be both on investment and consumption, but expenditure on various heads has different effects on the economy. For example, outlay on housing which is classed as investment may not have such a marked effect on an expenditure on technical education which is consumption expenditure. When a large part of expenditure is for relief to the poorer classes, the secondary consumption expenditure resulting from that has a high multiplier effect. Thus, careful regulation of government spending policy is essential to achieve the maximum effect.

The effectiveness of public spending for long-term growth depends on a few other conditions. Public expenditure on investment must not adversely affect private investment. As we have already seen, if government's new investment is concentrated on industries which normally form part of the private sector, private investment will be discouraged. Moreover, the adverse effects on interest rates are harmful, psychological reactions of government deficit-financed investment are likely to cause a shrinkage in private investment. Such conditions must be avoided if public investment is to be really effective. Furthermore, public expenditure must not be allowed to reduce private resources for consumption. The 'multiplier' effect of government spending must be kept high by maintaining private consumption at a high level. The increase in total investment and the consequent increase in employment in investment goods industries might be at the expense of employment in consumption goods industries, and there might, thus, be no multiplier effect of increased consumption. This, however, need not necessarily be so, and proper safeguards against this can be adopted to have the maximum effect of an expansionary policy. The 'multiplier' plays a very important role in any policy to raise national income, particularly in the long period. Government deficit expenditure need not be unduly high if the 'multiplier' could be maintained at a high level. Thus, the success of fiscal policy will, in a large measure, depend upon the size the multiplier has acquired as a result of the policy.

FISCAL POLICY AND ECONOMIC STABILISATION

The automatic stabilisation effects of government revenue and expenditure cannot be fully relied upon to maintain stability in the economy. They have a certain degree of steady effect on activity, but the effects are restricted to only small changes. Therefore, deliberate action on the part of authorities is needed. A flexible budget, in which public spending and taxation are varied to counteract the effects of fluctuations in private spending, is required. Anti-cyclic fiscal policy could take various forms.

(i) Public Works

The most important is a policy of public works carried out in a planned way. A long-term programme of public investment is formulated in which all state-controlled bodies, local bodies, public utilities, and socialised industries participate. The resources required and their sources of availability are all planned. The degree in which different parts of the programme could be altered according to the needs of the situation are carefully calculated in advance. The rate of investment is altered from time to time according to the condition of economic activity. When business activity shows signs of slump, public investment is raised, and vice versa. Monetary policy is coordinated with the working of this programme, and interest rates are altered to create conditions for private investment to change in harmony with government investment. A programme of this nature will help to steady national income, and large ups and downs in the government budget will be avoided.

But such a policy has its difficulties. The inconveniences of a long-period programme worked at different times according to the needs of the moment are all too patent. Public works are wanted at a time and cannot be put off or hurried. The technical difficulties of altering outlay may be a great obstacle, and work on some projects once started cannot be interrupted without loss of capital. Public works are required independently of the state of business activity, and relating the two may not be a feasible proposition. A large public investment programme may also have adverse effects on private investment. As has already been considered, public investment may compete with private investment, and adverse changes in interest rates may discourage private investment or sometimes psychological reaction to government investment may not be entirely healthy. The depressing effects of such changes have to be taken into account when long-period plans are formulated. With careful planning, such adverse effects would be avoided, but taking all aspects of the matter into consideration, a long-period plan is more suitable as a device for lifting the economy to higher levels rather than as an anti-cyclical measure.

(ii) Purchases and Sales of Goods by the Government

Another form of anti-cyclical policy is purchases and sales of goods by public authorities. The government purchases commodities in bad times, thus adding to the total demand, and sells them in good times. Price-support programmes, particularly for agricultural products, are adopted by governments in same countries. When prices of agricultural commodities have a tendency to fall, the government tries to keep them up by purchasing the goods in the market, and helps to eliminate the depressing effects. When markets have recovered and prices show signs of rising, the goods are sold. Thus, prices are maintained at a steady level and activity is stabilised. This kind of action, however, cannot be taken in respect of all commodities. Commodities, the demand for which is subject to changes in fashions and tastes, cannot be purchased or sold by the government except at great risk. The financial implications of large government purchases are also an argument against such a policy. The government expenditure in the form of loss of interest on funds tied up for long periods is so large as to make the policy impracticable. Moreover, the undesirability of the government entering into commercial speculation makes such programmes unpopular. Therefore, government purchases and sales, on a scale large enough to be effective, keeping the level of activity steady over long periods are not feasible under all conditions.

(iii) Adjustments in Taxes and Public Outlays

Adjustment in taxes and public outlay is the most practicable device for stabilisation. Reduction in taxation and increase in public expenditure are the chief correcting measures in bad times. Tax reductions increase the disposable income of firms and individuals, and the reaction of firms to such variations are very favourable and private investment is encouraged. Reductions in social insurance contributions, without any change in benefits, have a very healthy effect on activity, for they not only increase the amount of purchasing power at the disposal of workers who remain employed, but also act as a kind of subsidy to employers to employ more workers. Increase in public outlay is possible in respect of minor public works. A subsidy on wages to employees has also been suggested as a suitable anti-depression device. But such a subsidy has practical difficulties. When given in respect of additional workers only, it offers temptation to employers to dismiss workers and then re-employ them to receive the subsidy, thus having no net effect on total employment. When paid in respect of all workers employed by employers, it involves a heavy burden on the exchequer. In times of boom, a reverse policy could be adopted. An increase in taxation and reduction of public expenditure are done to keep down the total spending of the community.

ROLE OF FISCAL POLICY IN AN UNDERDEVELOPED ECONOMY

Fiscal policy as a means of promoting economic development of under-developed countries may have to play the following roles:

1. Fiscal Policy and Employment

Unemployment is the burning problem of under-developed countries. Fiscal policy is an important tool for removing unemployment in a country. Hence, the government should adopt such a policy which can solve the problem of unemployment in underdeveloped countries. The fiscal policy should include the following:

(i) Increase in public and private investments.

(ii) Emphasis on the development of cottage and small-scale industries by giving them:

(a) Financial assistance;

(b) Protection;

(c) Exemption for taxation;

(d) Export incentives;

(e) Technical assistance; and

(f) Supply of machinery and other tools at concessional rates, etc.

(iii) Free technical education.

(iv) Development of employment opportunities.

(v) Unemployment allowance.

(vi) Establishment of training centres on the district level.

(vii) Concession in railway and bus fares to unemployed persons for attending interviews.

2. Fiscal Policy and Price Stability

Apart from the above considerations, fiscal policy must also seek to attain price stability. Attempts to force the pace of development tend to push up prices. This is also because the limited resources of an underdeveloped economy are deliberately diverted into large-scale investment, so that the availability of consumer goods is reduced, specially if the investment is in projects with long gestation periods. Since the foreign exchange resources of underdeveloped countries are also generally limited, the shortage of goods produced within the country cannot be made up by imported goods. While a mild rise in prices may help the process of development, inflation not only causes hardships to large sections of the population but also upsets calculations about costs of plan programmes and it encourages savings. Hence, all measures, including fiscal measures have to be taken to avoid inflationary situations. If deficit financing is adopted and it may often be unavoidable, or may even be desirable, for reasons mentioned earlier, the pressure on prices may become still greater and care has to be taken to see that its extent and timings are such as not to give rise to inflationary situation and that it is accompanied by measures to check inflationary tendencies. Apart from steps to increase production, the fiscal measures that can be adopted are taxation and borrowing to remove purchasing power from circulation.

A situation of falling prices is not so characteristic of developing economies as that of rising prices, but if such a situation develops, fiscal policy along with other instruments of policy will have to play its part.

Apart from influencing the general prices level, fiscal policy may also be used to influence the prices of particular commodities. If the use of certain commodities is sought to be discouraged, they can be heavily taxed. This raises their price and reduces the demand for them. On the other hand, the giving of subsidies has the effect of lowering prices. Essential commodities like foodgrains for example, may be subsidised. Similarly, subsidies may be given if the use of particular commodities is sought to be encouraged.

3. Fiscal Policy and Production

In underdeveloped countries, the production and productivity both are low and fiscal policy is an important tool for increasing both production and productivity. In this connection, the following steps may be taken:

(i) The government can increase production by giving economic assistance.

(ii) Domestic industries can be encouraged by giving them protection, export industries by economic assistance and new industrials can be established by giving tax exemptions.

(iii) New producers can be encouraged by giving them loans at low rate of interest.

(iv) Implementation of productivity-based wage payment method.

4. Accelerating the Rate of Economic Growth

Fiscal policy can also contribute to the acceleration of the rate of growth in underdeveloped countries by increasing the rate of investment through public expenditure and taxation policies. The role of fiscal policy can be positive and dynamic in accelerating the rates of growth by increasing the rates of saving and investment. The government can start various development projects for rapid economic progress of underdeveloped countries. The government should provide opportunities and incentives to save and invest. Equal importance should be given to the development of agriculture and industry. The development of agriculture depends on industrial development as the demand of most of the agricultural products comes from the industrial sector. Similarly, the development for industrial sector depends upon the development of agricultural sector, such as, supply of raw jute, raw cotton, sugarcane, etc. According to Raja J. Chelliah, "The most fruitful line of advance lies along the path of a balanced development of agriculture and industry."

5. Fiscal Policy and Redistribution of Income

The distribution of income and wealth is becoming more and more unequal due to the constantly increasing inflationary pressures on the economy. These inequalities in the distribution of income and wealth adversely affect the pace of economic progress of these underdeveloped countries, create social and political unrest in the country and instability in the economy. Fiscal policy of a country aims to reduce the inequality of income and wealth of an underdeveloped country in the following ways:

(i) ***To change the structure of resource ownership:*** Resource ownership can be changed by death tax and gift tax. Such taxes do not affect the *will* to work and the *will* to save.

(ii) ***To change price structure:*** The government can fix the price of certain commodities and services. It can fix the minimum price of agricultural produce and minimum wages of labourers.

(iii) ***To change the size of income:*** The major part of public expenditure may be in the interest of the poor. Apart from this, direct cash benefits can be given to the poor sections of the society such as unemployment allowance, maternity benefits, old-age pension, etc. The rich section of the society should be steeply taxed by the government.

(iv) ***Planned development:*** The programme of planned development which removes regional imbalances, also helps in equitable distribution of income and wealth.

(v) ***Change in the tax structure:*** A redistribution policy should be aimed at imposing heavy taxation on the rich and exempting poorer section of the community.

6. Mobilisation of Resources

The national income and per capita income of underdeveloped countries is very low, hence the volume of voluntary savings is also low. When the volume of voluntary savings is low, the capital formation too shall be quite low. Hence, financing of development plans poses a very difficult problem for the government of an under-developed country. It is of utmost importance to increase the rate of savings, investments and capital formation so as to raise the rate of economic growth in underdeveloped countries. The government can help mobilisation of resources and accumulation of capital by means of adopting the following methods:

(i) ***Inducement to save:*** Inducement to invest in private enterprise may be effective if: (a) private enterprise is secured and profitable, and (b) there are suitable institutions through which investment can be made. The profitability of private enterprise may be helped by the government in many ways. For example, protection may help certain industries to develop. There may be provision for technical advice and guidance and for the supply of commercial information. The tax burden on desired types of enterprise may be lightened. Profits which are reinvested, may be exempted from taxation or may be taxed lightly. Apart from such measures for helping specific types of enterprise, such other activities of the government as the development of transport and power, etc. are also important.

There must also be suitable institutions through which investment may be canalised. Most underdeveloped countries do not have well developed banking structure. In the absence of facilities for depositing money, the people either do not save at all, or if they do save something, they do so in the shape of hoards of jewellery, etc. Thus, banking facilities have to be made available to as large a proportion of the people as possible. Commercial banks, generally do not provide long-term loans for development projects. State banks or co-operative banks may, therefore, have to be resorted to.

(ii) ***Government borrowing of a non-inflationary nature:*** Government borrowing of a non-inflationary nature is also an important instrument for mobilising private savings and government securities provide a safe outlet for the people's savings. Its aim is to see that different types of securities are offered to the people so that persons of different means, or with different types of requirements may purchase them. Small savings schemes are of special significance in underdeveloped countries. For this purpose, savings banks or other similar institutions have to be set up in large numbers all over the country, specially in small towns and villages. Other steps that can be taken are: attractive rates of interest, different dates of maturity in the case of savings certificates and lotteries. Another possibility is that savings and government borrowing in any particular area may be linked with a specific project so that people may be more willing to subscribe money for it.

(iii) ***Compulsory savings:*** It may happen, however, that in spite of every effort, the volume of voluntary savings may not be very large. This, as we have seen, may be due to several causes. The incomes of the people in underdeveloped countries are generally so low that they cannot save much. Even a rise in income levels due to economic development generally leads not to more savings but to increased consumption. In many underdeveloped countries, whatever little savings are done, in the form of purchases of land or hoarding of cash, all these factors may make it necessary for the government to resort to compelling the people to save and for this some compulsory savings schemes may have to be started.

(iv) ***Taxation:*** Taxation can play an important part in diverting resources from consumption or non-productive uses, into investment. This happens in two ways. In the first place, taxation takes away purchasing power from individuals and firms, and transfers it to the government. Thus, on the one hand, private uses of resources are curtailed, on the other, the government obtains funds with the help of which it can acquire control over these resources and can direct them into investment. Both—direct and indirect taxation have the effect of curtailing consumption. Direct taxes do so by reducing income and indirect taxes by making consumption goods costly. Indirect taxation involves the taxation not only of luxuries and semi-luxuries but even of commodities which are usually considered essential so that the propensity to consume, which is naturally high in poor countries, may be held in check.

(v) ***Surpluses from public enterprises:*** The resources of underdeveloped countries can be increased by mobilising the surpluses from public enterprises. According to Indian Taxation Enquiry Commission, "The making of profit is not necessarily inconsistent with public enterprises; indeed, the generation of surpluses in public enterprises may be considered to be a public purpose for the development of economy." However, nowadays most of the public enterprises are running in loss and hence they are not considered as an adequate source of revenue in underdeveloped countries.

(vi) ***Deficit financing:*** Deficit financing also constitutes an important source for financing development plans in underdeveloped countries. It makes possible capital formation into two ways:

(a) Utilising hidden and idle resources; and

(b) Directing resources from current consumption into investment.

Deficit financing, by placing additional resources in the hands of the government, enables it to acquire resources which were so far unutilised and to use them for productive purposes.

Deficit financing can also bring about a diversion of resources from non-productive uses. As a result of deficit financing, the government acquires control over additional purchasing power and can buy goods and services needed for its investment programmes. Thus, these goods and services are diverted from private uses to government uses. This process of diversion from private to government uses is aided by the tendency of deficit financing to raise prices. Because of the rise in prices, private demand for goods and services tends to decline and, as a result of government purchases (with the help of the additional purchasing power acquired by the government), these goods and services move into uses determined by the government. To what extent this diversion can be considered an increase in the total savings in the economy, depends both on the use to which these resources were being put by private persons and the use to which government puts them. It is clear that deficit financing can have justification only if it adds to the productive capacity of the economy.

7. Fiscal Policy and Economic Stability

Fluctuations in business activities create uncertainties in the underdeveloped economy. The following compensatory fiscal measures may be adopted so as to avoid or restrict cyclical fluctuations:

(i) *Fiscal policy during inflation:* Obviously, inflation is the result of excessive private expenditure, and therefore, fiscal tools must be used to check the inflationary tendencies. The supply of money being more than its demand and on the other hand, the demand for commodities and services being more than its supply become the key factors of inflation. Fiscal measures can be used in various ways:

(a) By spending less.

(b) By imposing new taxes and raising the rate of existing taxes; this will transfer resources from private use to government use.

(c) The government may borrow money to prevent expenditure from increasing.

(d) The government can increase the interest rates by increasing bank rate and may induce people to save more and consume less.

(e) The government may sell goods and services to public in greater amount than before.

(ii) *Fiscal policy during depression:* Deflation or unemployment is the result of deficiency in the private expenditure. This deficiency in private expenditure can be overcome in several ways:

(a) The tax rates may be reduced.

(b) The government may increase its expenditure on old age pension and unemployment benefits.

(c) The government may reduce the rate of interest and may lend liberally to private businessmen to encourage investment expenditure.

(d) The total consumption expenditure should increase. For this, the government should undertake public works programmes during depression period to employ the unemployed persons.

(e) The government can sanction subsidies and grants to the backward and underdeveloped sectors of the economy as agriculture.

(f) It may repay its debt so that consumption and investment expenditure both may increase.

LONG-TERM FISCAL POLICY PREPARED BY THE GOVERNMENT OF INDIA

In India, the Finance Minister presented to the Parliament a long-term fiscal policy on 19th December, 1985. He committed a long-term fiscal policy co-terminous with the Seventh Five-Year Plan 1885-90. It aims at growth, modernisation, self-reliance and social justice. For the achievement of central objectives, long-term-fiscal policy can be spelled out with following:

(i) to make the incidence of the indirect tax system progressive;

(ii) to increase the share of direct taxes in total revenue;

(iii) to mobilise additional resources to finance alleviation programmes.

The long-term fiscal policy formulated in the context of Eleventh Five-Year Plan lays emphasis on strengthening the growth momentum of the economy and harnessing the rapid advances in technology so as to effectively tackle the problems of deep-seated poverty and unemployment. It states that the major contribution of fiscal policy to poverty alleviation has to come through effective programmes for mobilisation of additional resources for financing the anti-poverty programmes, improving the economic and social services on which the poor mainly rely and for funding heavy investments in infrastructural facilities which are necessary for growth of agriculture and industry. The fiscal policy has also to play its crucial role in keeping inflation under firm control by reducing the monetary impact of government's financial operations and financing the plan through non-inflationary sources by placing greater reliance on surpluses generated by the budget and public sector undertakings.

Formulated against this background, the long-term fiscal policy perspective is expected to be beneficial in a number of ways such as:

(i) It will impart a definite direction and coherence to the sequence of annual budgets;

(ii) Achieve a greater role for rule-based fiscal and financial policies, thereby diminishing reliance on discretionary case-by-case administration of physical controls in management of the country;

(iii) Facilitate effective coordination of different dimensions of economic policy—fiscal policy, monetary policy and trade policy; and

(iv) Serve as an effective vehicle for strengthening the operational linkage between the fiscal and financial objectives of the Eleventh Plan and the annual budgeting exercises to be conducted during the plan period.

The task of the fiscal policy in the area of taxation is to bring about a structural reform in the present system. The reforms should ensure that revenues go up automatically and prices rise. It should also aim at securing better compliance and improving the efficiency of the tax structure. The process of reform has to be phased over a number of years and will have to go beyond the Eleventh Five-Year Plan.

(i) Custom Duties

The basic thrust of custom tariff reforms is to shift in a phased manner from quantitative restrictions to qualitative restrictions by increasing reliance on tariff to regulate imports. The main changes proposed in the custom duties would be to have a basic rate on components and progressively reduce the duties on universal intermediates to even lower than the duties on raw materials. Project imports would continue to be a separate category subjected to lower rates of duty. Tariffs for essential consumer goods such as food, edible oils and life-saving drugs would continue to be low or nil with the volume of imports regulated through canalisation procedure.

(ii) Central Excise Duties

A major reform in Central excise duty structure in the implementation of modified value added tax (MODVAT) to relieve input and intermediate products from excise and counterveiling duties. The shifting of excise burden away from inputs and on to the final products will help in tailoring excise duties in such a manner that the well-off bear a higher proportional burden than the poor. The government also proposes to merge various excise duties into a single basic rate (except for additional excise duties in lieu of sales tax) and retain only the cesses as separate levies earmarked for specific purposes. The number of cesses will also be reduced to a minimum.

(iii) Gift Tax

The long-term fiscal policy states that it would be preferable to retain the gift tax on the grounds of both equity and as a check against attempts to reduce tax liability on income and wealth through splitting income and wealth via medium of gifts. Now the gift tax has been abolished by the Government.

(iv) Capital Gains Tax

The government would review capital gains taxation in order to make it more effective and to promote investment in desired channels. Meanwhile, measures will be taken to rationalise capital gains taxation. Investment in bonds issued by the IDBI and HUDCO will also be made eligible for exemption of capital gains tax.

(v) Corporate Tax

The policy makes it clear that the rate of corporate tax will be retained and not reduced further. However, companies will be allowed to deduct 30 per cent of their profits from their taxable income provided the amount is deposited with the Industrial Development Bank of India and other institutions the government may notify.

(vi) Income Tax

The policy states that in order to dispel any uncertainty arising out of the frequent changes in tax structure, the government will keep the preset rate schedule for taxes on personal income and wealth—unchanged for a minimum period of five years. Under certain compelling circumstances, the government will take resources to the basic rate structure. The impact of inflation on effect rates of taxation will be reviewed once every two or three years and adjustments made accordingly in the tax brackets.

(vii) Measures Against Tax Evasion

To effectively tackle the problem of tax evasion, the income tax department will implement a strategy consisting of the following elements:

(a) Acceptance, in general, of returns in all cases (other than Companies and Trusts) showing returned income of not more than Rs. 1 lakh, and in case of the returned income of not more than Rs. 25,000 (except for new assesses). However, a thorough scrutiny of a specified random sample of the accepted returns will be undertaken.

(b) Removing weaknesses in the law which hinder effective prosecution of the evaders.

(c) Ensuring effective follow up of search and seizure operations.

(d) Ensuring speedy trials of economic offences, including tax evasion, by establishing special courts.

(e) Evolving a system of rewards and punishments to promote integrity among senior officials, and modernising the administration of direct taxes with the aid of computers.

(viii) Anti-Smuggling Measures

The government will persist with an anti-smuggling strategy which combines stronger enforcement with economic measure to curb smuggling. With the setting up of Economic Intelligence Bureau, there will be co-ordinated approach to deal with smuggling and tax evasion. Excise administration is being restructured to deal with excise evasion as well as smuggling of goods.

FISCAL REFORMS UNDER ELEVENTH FINANCE COMMISSION

Under the guidelines of the Eleventh Finance Commission, Government of India had drawn up a scheme called the State Fiscal Policy Reform Facility (2000-2001 to 2004-2005). To this end an incentive fund of Rs. 10,607 crore had been sanctioned over a period of five years to encourage states to implement monitorable reforms. There was a provision of additional amounts by way of open market borrowings, etc.

The process of fiscal consolidation has shown results over the last few years resulting in reduction in revenue and fiscal deficit from a high 4.4 per cent and 5.9 per cent, respectively in 2002-03 to 2.6 per cent and 4.1 per cent, respectively in RE 2005-06. The task ahead in order to achieve the end-year FRBM targets is admittedly more challenging, especially the elimination of revenue deficit. The endeavour in this regard is expected to be facilitated by continued buoyancy in revenues on the back of higher growth trajectory and consolidating efforts in further containment of non-developmental revenue expenditure. Under this facility the state governments are invited to draw up a Medium Term Fiscal Reforms Programme (MTFRP).

Table 11.1: Gross Fiscal Deficit of State Governments

Years	In Crore Rs.	As per cent of GDP
1990-91	18,797	3.3
2000-01	89,532	4.2
2001-02	95,994	4.2
2002-03	1,02,123	4.5
2003-04	1,23,070	4.5
2004-05	1,23,635	4.0
2005-06	1,10,070	3.1

Source: Reserve Bank of India.

MEDIUM TERM FISCAL POLICY STATEMENT

On the recommendations of the Eleventh Finance Commission (EFC) Government of India implemented a scheme called the "State Fiscal Reforms Facility (2000-2001 to 2004-05), to incentivise the States to undertake fiscal reforms. As on March 31, 2005, an amount of Rs. 7,217 crore was released to states from incentive fund (Total fund Rs. 10,608 crore) on the basis of improvement in revenue deficits as a proportion of revenue receipts. The following arrangements are made in 'State Fiscal Reforms Facility':

1. The medium term fiscal projections are in line with the commitment made in the Budget 2005-06 to resume the process of fiscal correction with effect from 2006-07 and achieve the FRBM goals by 2008-09. The deficit indicators in BE 2006-07 are consistent with the FRBM roadmap, which envisages an annual reduction of at least 0.3 percentage points in fiscal deficit and 0.5 percentage points in revenue deficit.

2. The Twelfth Finance Commission award and other relevant factors brought out in Medium Term Fiscal Policy Statement were presented along with Budget 2005-06. Government had projected Revenue Deficit during 2005-06 to be at 2.7 per cent, *i.e.* at the same level as RE 2004-05. Fiscal Deficit was budgeted to decline from 4.5 per cent in RE 2004-05 to 4.3 per cent in BE 2005-06. It is a matter of satisfaction that the Revenue Deficit and Fiscal Deficit at RE 2005-06 are estimated to be lower at 2.6 per cent and 4.1 per cent respectively. This improvement in fiscal position is being achieved largely on account of revenue receipts being on target and compression of non-plan expenditure. Demands for additional plan expenditure during the year, including the routing of EAP loans to states through the Consolidated Fund of India, have been met from saving within the BE 2005-06.

Table 11.2: Fiscal Indicators—Rolling Targets (As per cent of GDP)

Indicator	Revised Estimates	Budget Estimates	Targets for	
	2005-06	2006-07	07-08	08-09
1. Revenue Deficit	2.6	2.1	1.1	0.0
2. Fiscal Deficit	41	3.8	3.4	3.0
3. Gross Tax Revenue	10.5	11.2	11.5	11.8
4. Total Outstanding Liabilities at the end of the year	65.7	65.7	64.4	63.1

3. The central government has constituted to follow prudent fiscal policy comprising: (i) a balanced tax structure based on reasonable rates with the minimal exemptions covering a wider class of tax-payers; and (ii) an expenditure policy that aims to moderate growth in non-developmental expenditure and adequately provide for pressing social and infrastructure needs of a developing economy. The Central Government Tax: GDP ratio is estimated to increase from 8.3 per cent in

1998-99 to 10.5 per cent in 2005-06. The Non-plan expenditure, as percentage of GDP has decreased from 12.2 per cent to 10.3 per cent during the same period, even as the Plan expenditure has increased from 3.8 per cent to 4.1 per cent even after discontinuation of Central loan assistance to State Plans with effect from 2005-06. The government convinced of the externality arising from pursuing a sound fiscal policy in terms of a high and sustainable rate of economic growth.

STUDY-QUESTIONS

1. What is fiscal policy? Discuss the components and objectives of fiscal policy.
2. How does fiscal policy help in fighting against inflation?
3. What is the budget policy? What are the essentials of sound finance or balanced budget approach?
4. Discuss the role of fiscal policy in developed countries.
5. Discuss the long-term fiscal policy prepared by the government of India.
6. Explain the role of fiscal policy in underdeveloped countries.
7. What do you mean by fiscal policy? Discuss the objectives of fiscal policy in a developed economy.
8. Outline the essentials of a fiscal policy to promote full employment in a developed country.
9. Write down a detailed note on anti-inflationary fiscal policy.
10. Write a detailed note on fiscal policy and economic stabilisation.